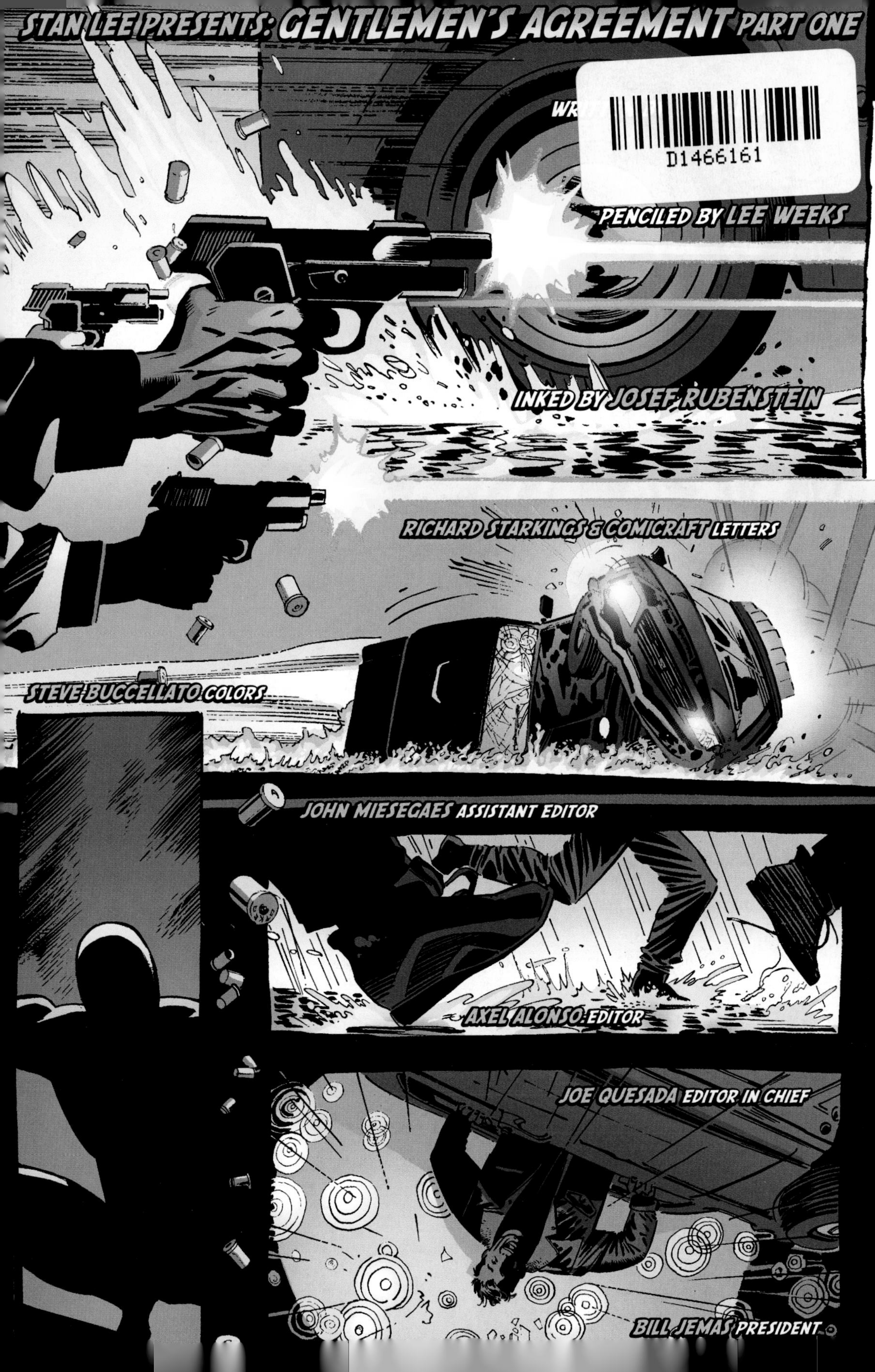
STAN LEE PRESENTS: GENTLEMEN'S AGREEMENT PART ONE
WRIT
PENCILED BY LEE WEEKS
INKED BY JOSEF RUBENSTEIN
RICHARD STARKINGS & COMICRAFT LETTERS
STEVE BUCCELLATO COLORS
JOHN MIESEGAES ASSISTANT EDITOR
AXEL ALONSO EDITOR
JOE QUESADA EDITOR IN CHIEF
BILL JEMAS PRESIDENT

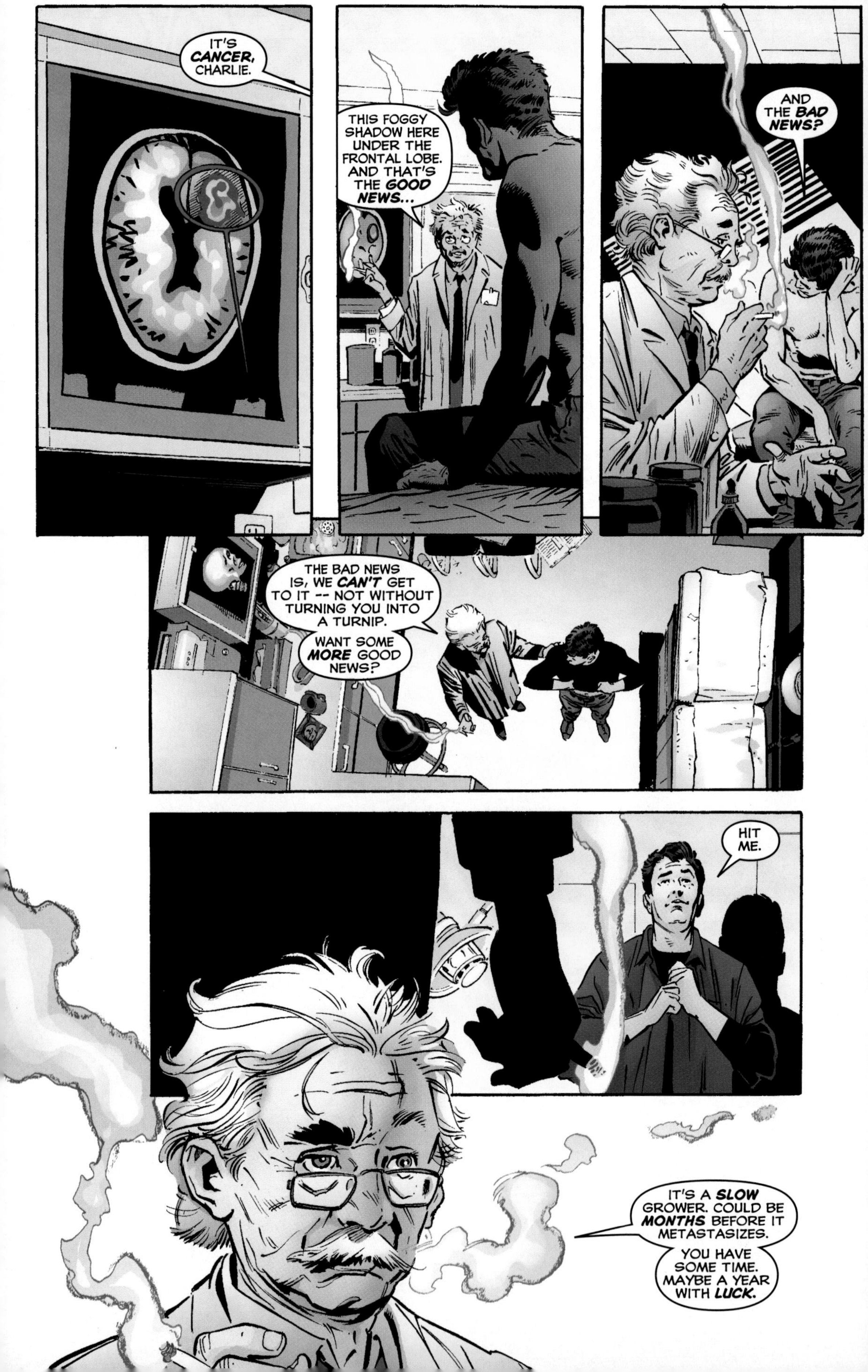
IT'S CANCER, CHARLIE.
THIS FOGGY SHADOW HERE UNDER THE FRONTAL LOBE. AND THAT'S THE GOOD NEWS...
AND THE BAD NEWS?
THE BAD NEWS IS, WE CAN'T GET TO IT -- NOT WITHOUT TURNING YOU INTO A TURNIP.
WANT SOME MORE GOOD NEWS?
HIT ME.
IT'S A SLOW GROWER. COULD BE MONTHS BEFORE IT METASTASIZES.
YOU HAVE SOME TIME. MAYBE A YEAR WITH LUCK.

GEE, THAT IS LUCKY. WHY DO I THINK THERE'S **MORE** BAD NEWS?

∻COUGH. COUGH! HACK COUGH.∻

YOU'LL BE -- ∻COUGH∻ -- LEGALLY **BLIND** INSIDE FOUR WEEKS.

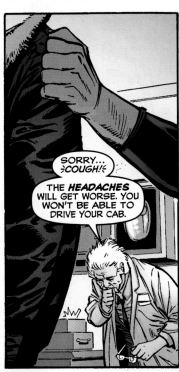

SORRY... ∻COUGH!∻

THE **HEADACHES** WILL GET WORSE. YOU WON'T BE ABLE TO DRIVE YOUR CAB.

I **CAN** GIVE YOU SOMETHING FOR THE PAIN...

GIVE ME SOME MORE GOOD NEWS, INSTEAD.

WELL... YOU CAN **ALWAYS** GET A -- ∻COUGH-COUGH∻ -- **SECOND OPINION!**

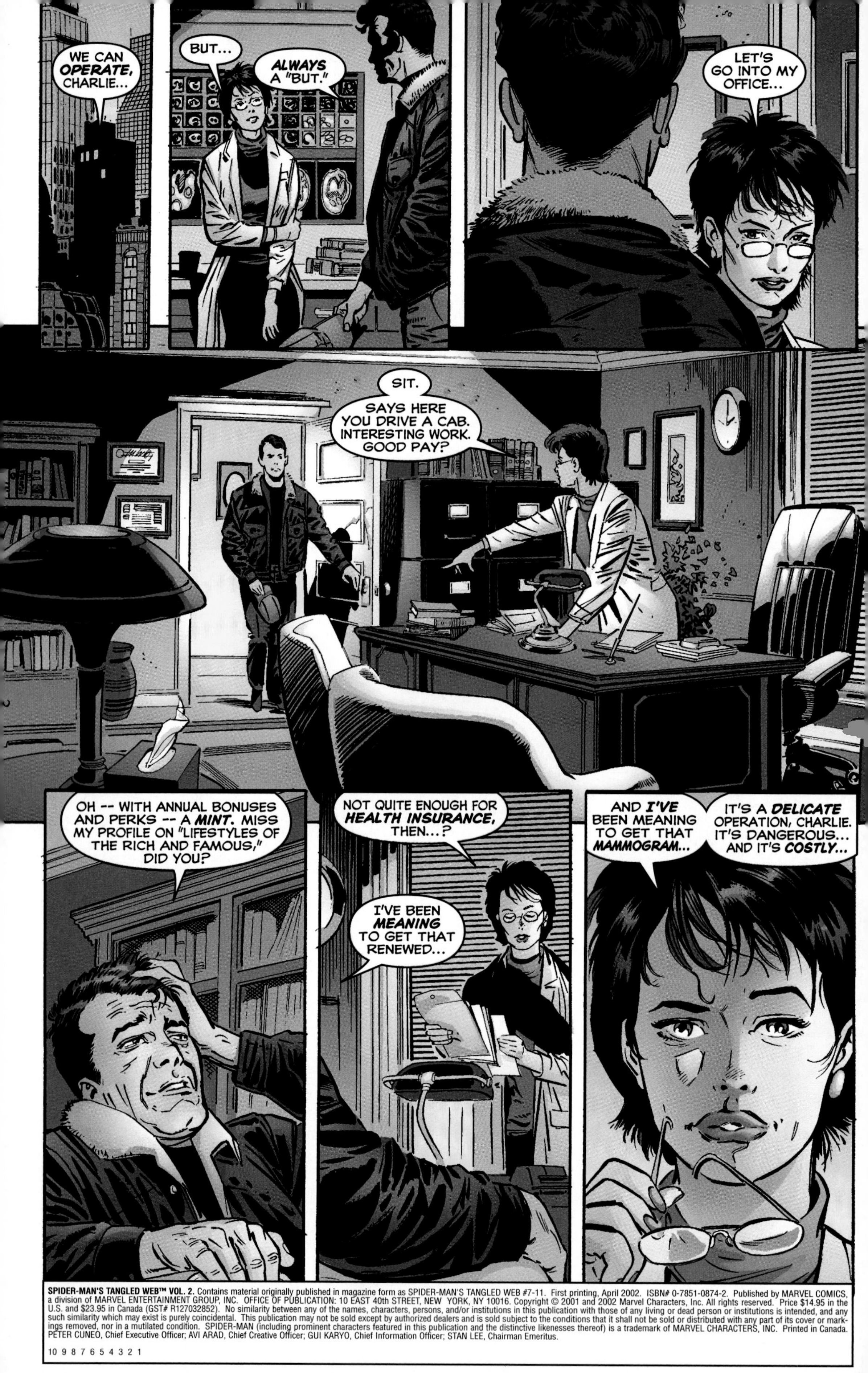
WE CAN OPERATE, CHARLIE...
BUT...
ALWAYS A "BUT."
LET'S GO INTO MY OFFICE...
SIT.
SAYS HERE YOU DRIVE A CAB. INTERESTING WORK. GOOD PAY?
OH -- WITH ANNUAL BONUSES AND PERKS -- A MINT. MISS MY PROFILE ON "LIFESTYLES OF THE RICH AND FAMOUS," DID YOU?
NOT QUITE ENOUGH FOR HEALTH INSURANCE, THEN...?
I'VE BEEN MEANING TO GET THAT RENEWED...
AND I'VE BEEN MEANING TO GET THAT MAMMOGRAM...
IT'S A DELICATE OPERATION, CHARLIE. IT'S DANGEROUS... AND IT'S COSTLY...

SPIDER-MAN'S TANGLED WEB™ VOL. 2. Contains material originally published in magazine form as SPIDER-MAN'S TANGLED WEB #7-11. First printing, April 2002. ISBN# 0-7851-0874-2. Published by MARVEL COMICS, a division of MARVEL ENTERTAINMENT GROUP, INC. OFFICE OF PUBLICATION: 10 EAST 40th STREET, NEW YORK, NY 10016. Price $14.95 in the U.S. and $23.95 in Canada (GST# R127032852). Printed in Canada. PETER CUNEO, Chief Executive Officer; AVI ARAD, Chief Creative Officer; GUI KARYO, Chief Information Officer; STAN LEE, Chairman Emeritus.

10 9 8 7 6 5 4 3 2 1

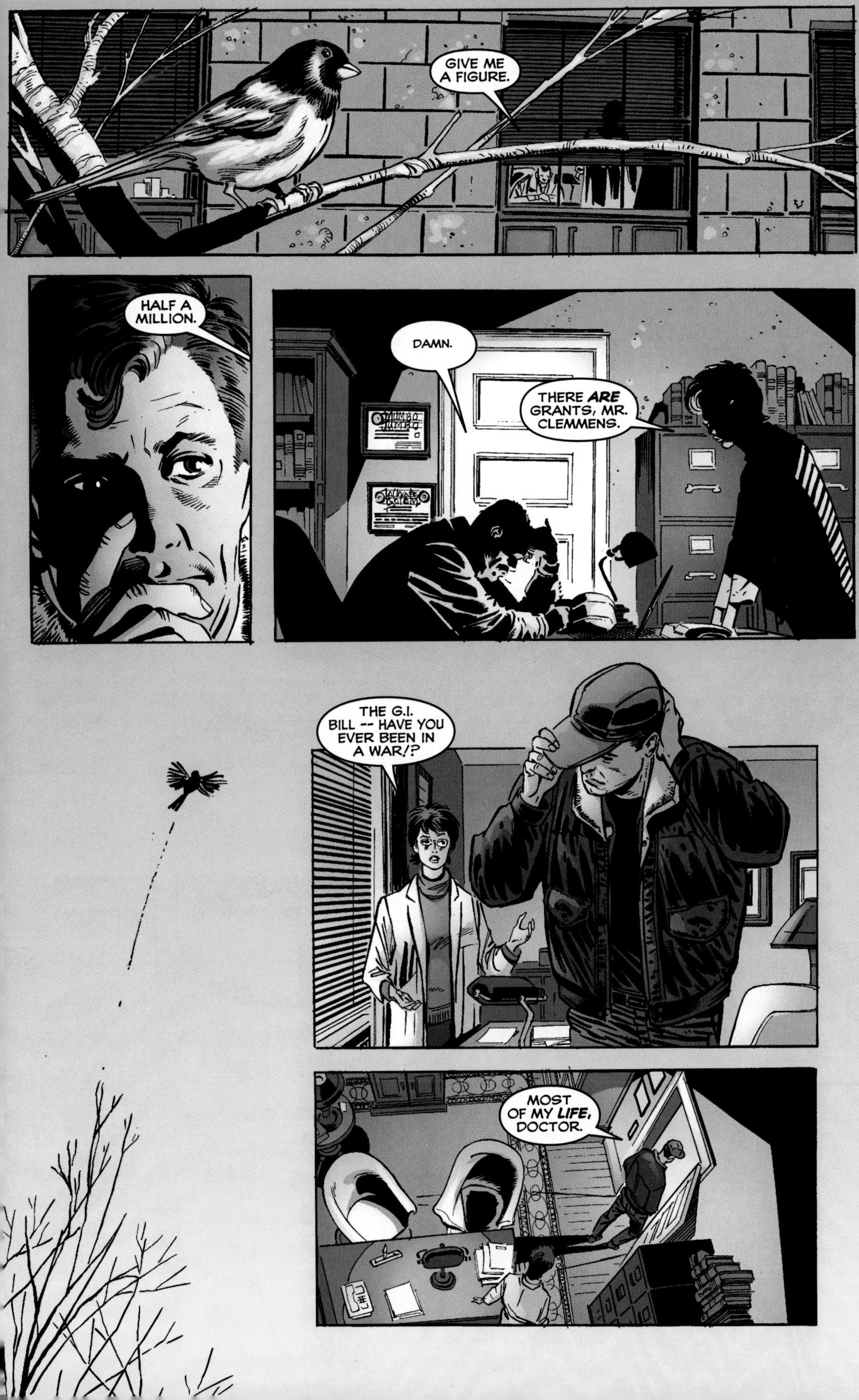
GIVE ME A FIGURE.
HALF A MILLION.
DAMN.
THERE ARE GRANTS, MR. CLEMMENS.
THE G.I. BILL -- HAVE YOU EVER BEEN IN A WAR!?
MOST OF MY LIFE, DOCTOR.

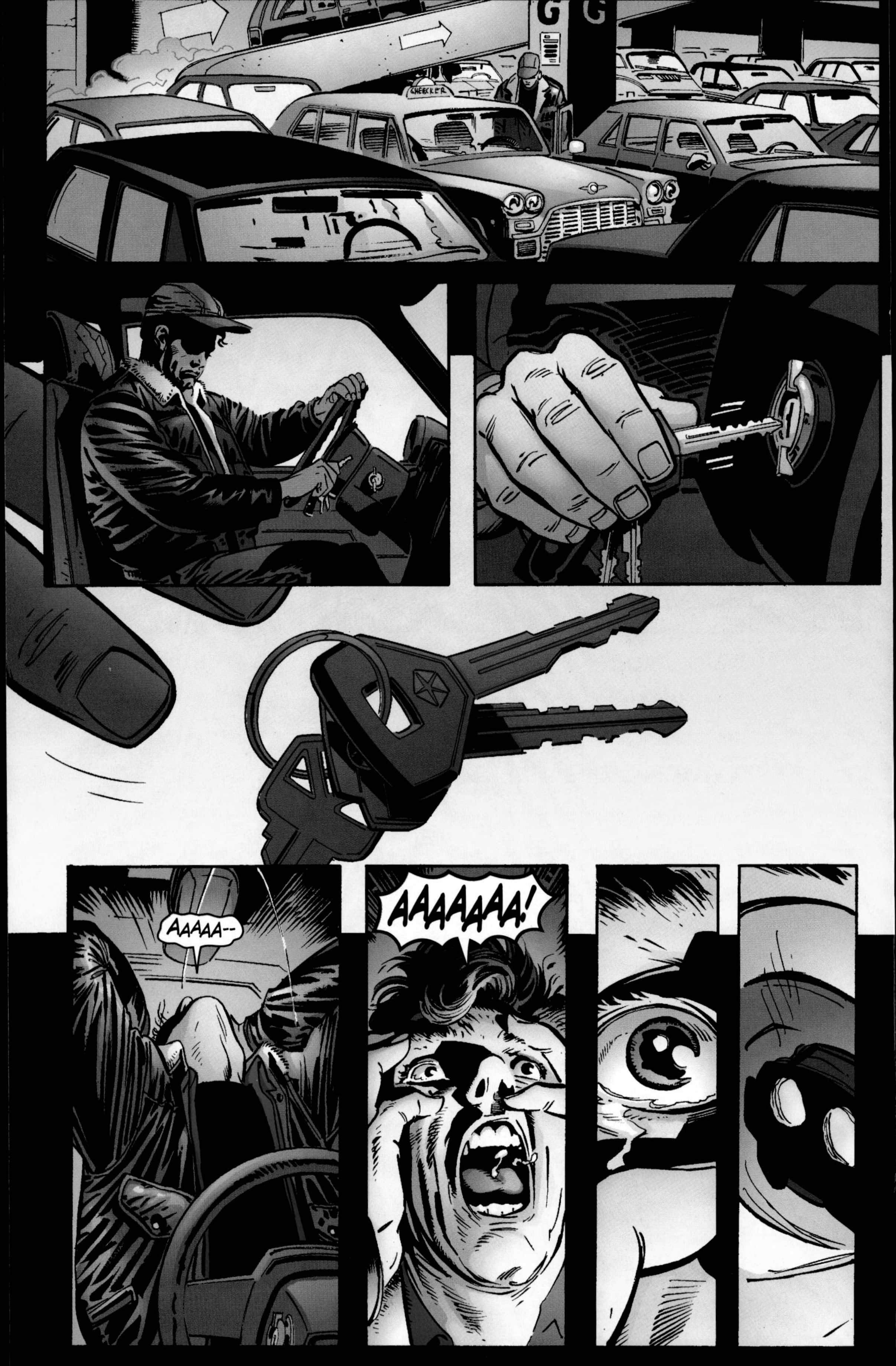

CHECKER
AAAAA--
AAAAAAA!

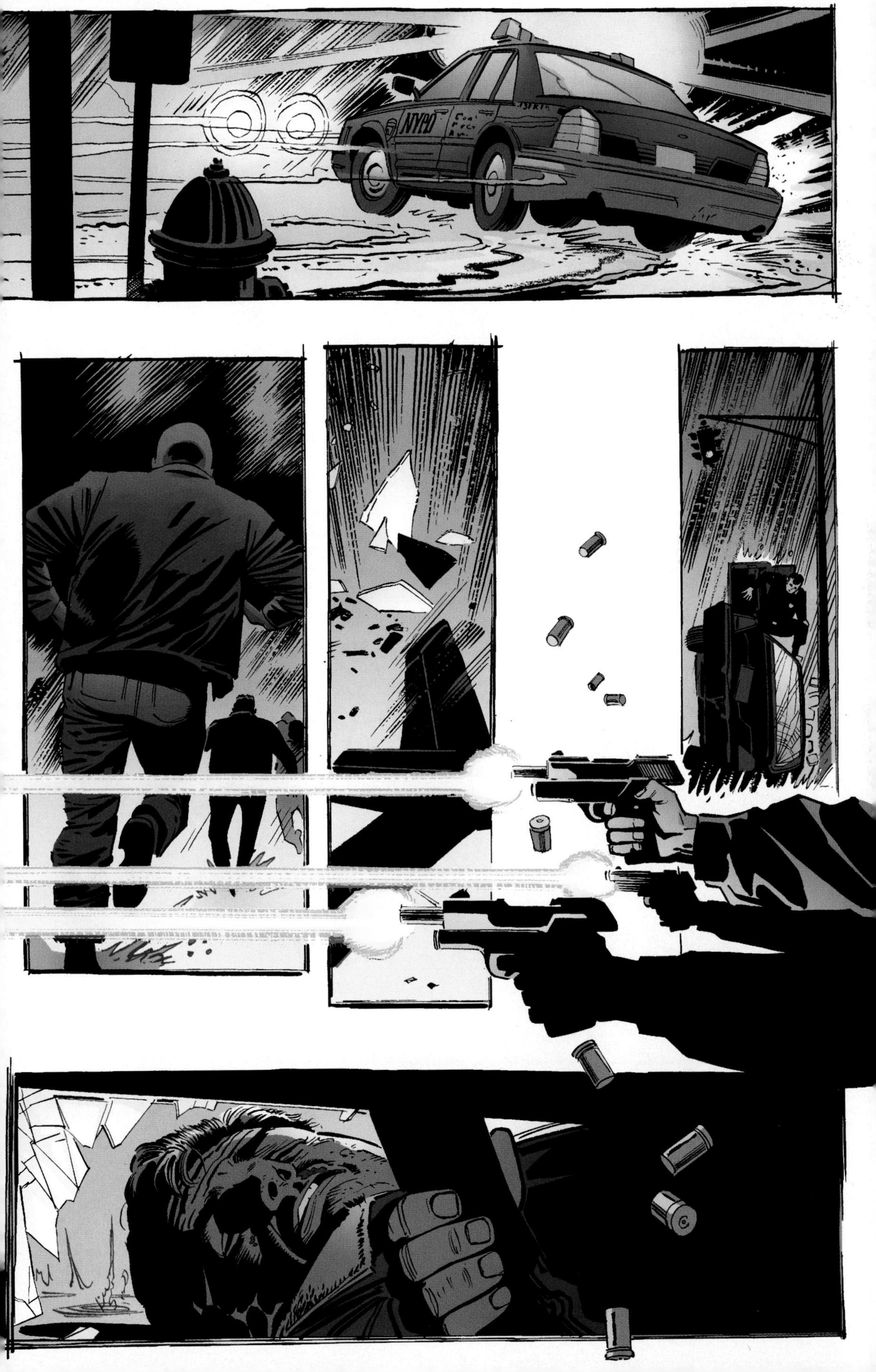
NYPD

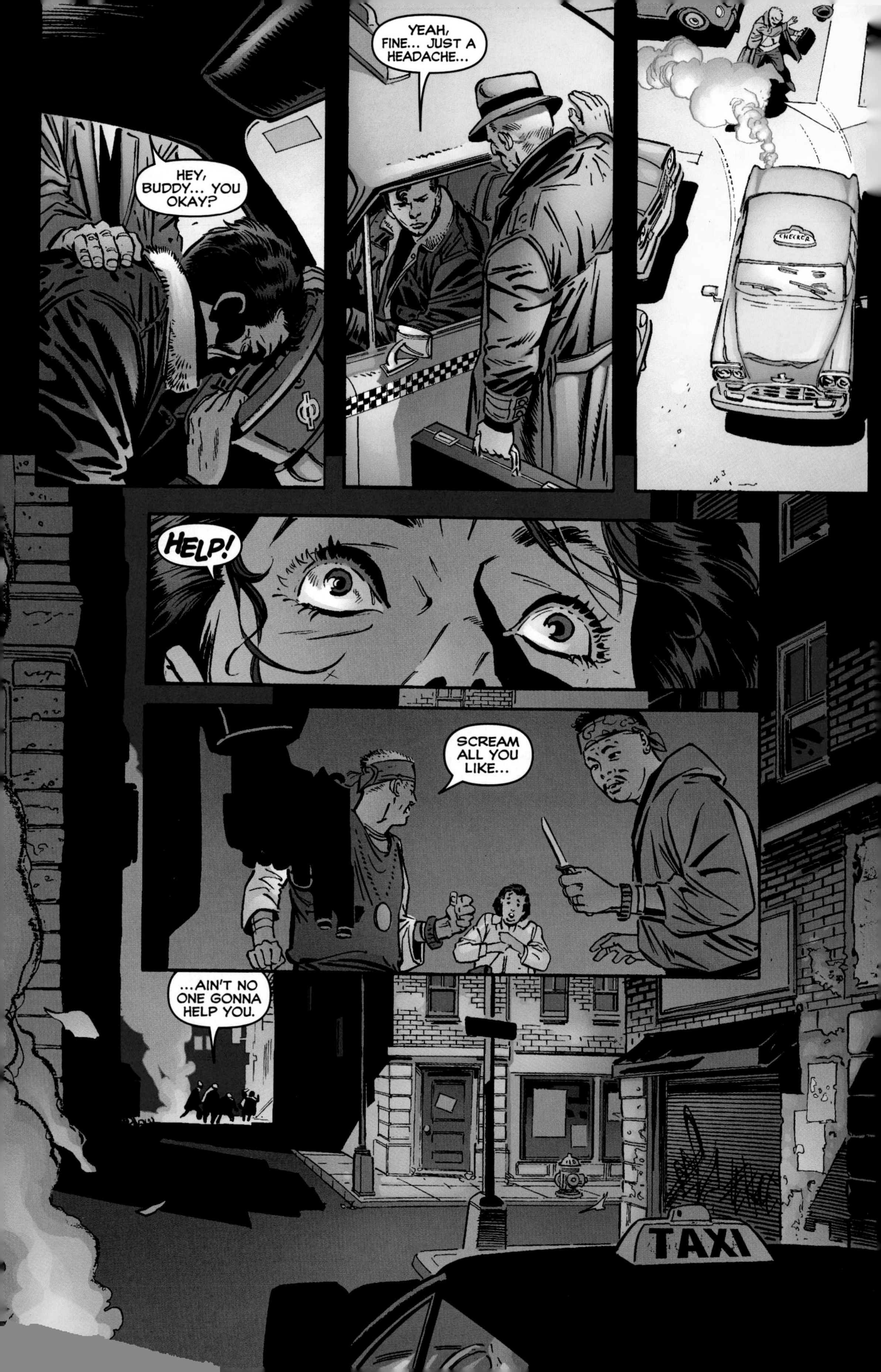
YEAH, FINE... JUST A HEADACHE...
HEY, BUDDY... YOU OKAY?
CHECKER
HELP!
SCREAM ALL YOU LIKE...
...AIN'T NO ONE GONNA HELP YOU.
TAXI

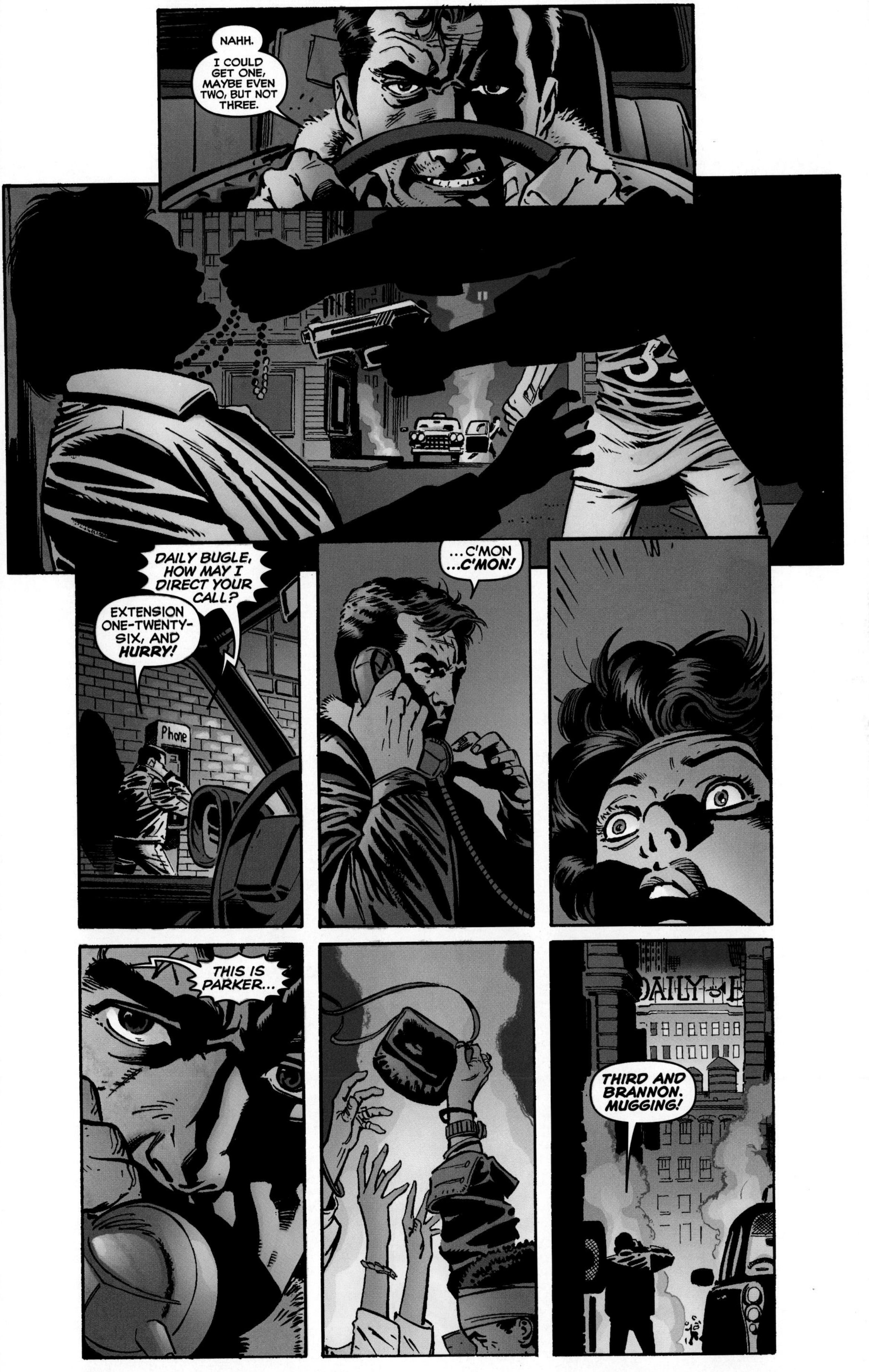
NAHH.
I COULD GET ONE, MAYBE EVEN TWO, BUT NOT THREE.
DAILY BUGLE, HOW MAY I DIRECT YOUR CALL?
EXTENSION ONE-TWENTY-SIX, AND HURRY!
Phone
...C'MON ...C'MON!
THIS IS PARKER...
DAILY
THIRD AND BRANNON. MUGGING!

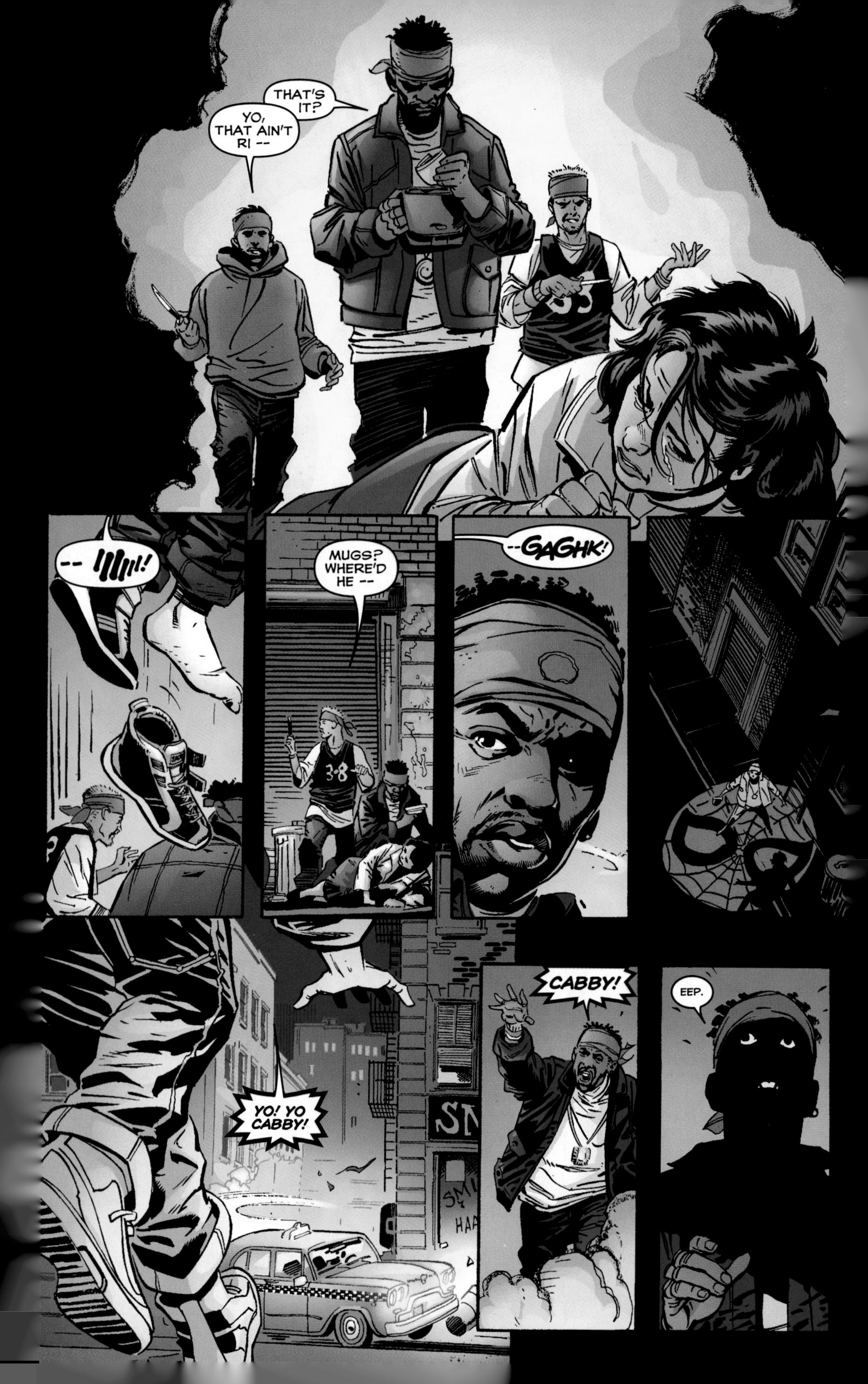
YO, THAT AIN'T RI --
THAT'S IT?
-- !!!!!!
MUGS? WHERE'D HE --
--GAGHK!
YO! YO CABBY!
CABBY!
EEP.

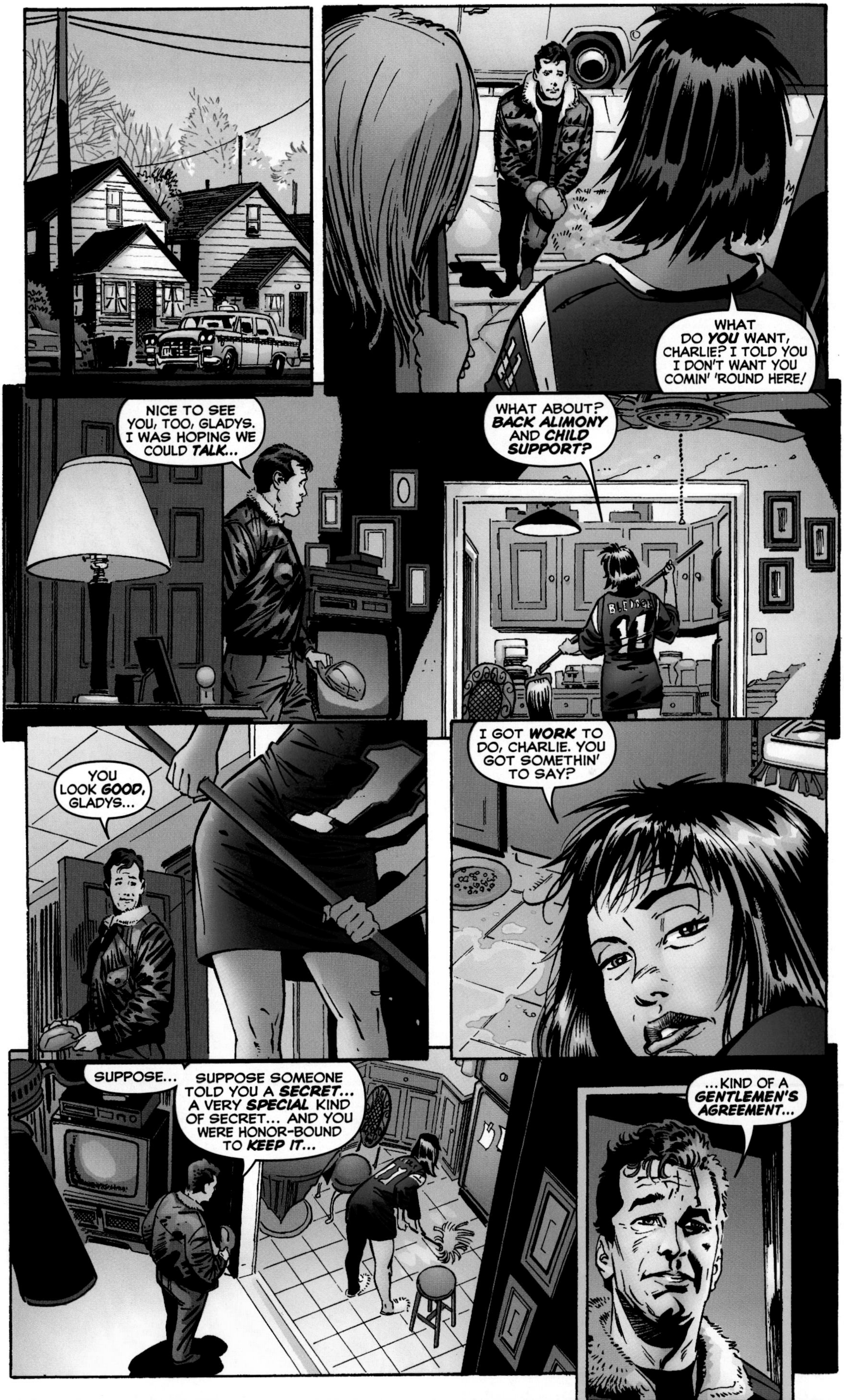
WHAT DO YOU WANT, CHARLIE? I TOLD YOU I DON'T WANT YOU COMIN' 'ROUND HERE!
NICE TO SEE YOU, TOO, GLADYS. I WAS HOPING WE COULD TALK...
WHAT ABOUT? BACK ALIMONY AND CHILD SUPPORT?
YOU LOOK GOOD, GLADYS...
I GOT WORK TO DO, CHARLIE. YOU GOT SOMETHIN' TO SAY?
SUPPOSE...
SUPPOSE SOMEONE TOLD YOU A SECRET... A VERY SPECIAL KIND OF SECRET... AND YOU WERE HONOR-BOUND TO KEEP IT...
...KIND OF A GENTLEMEN'S AGREEMENT...

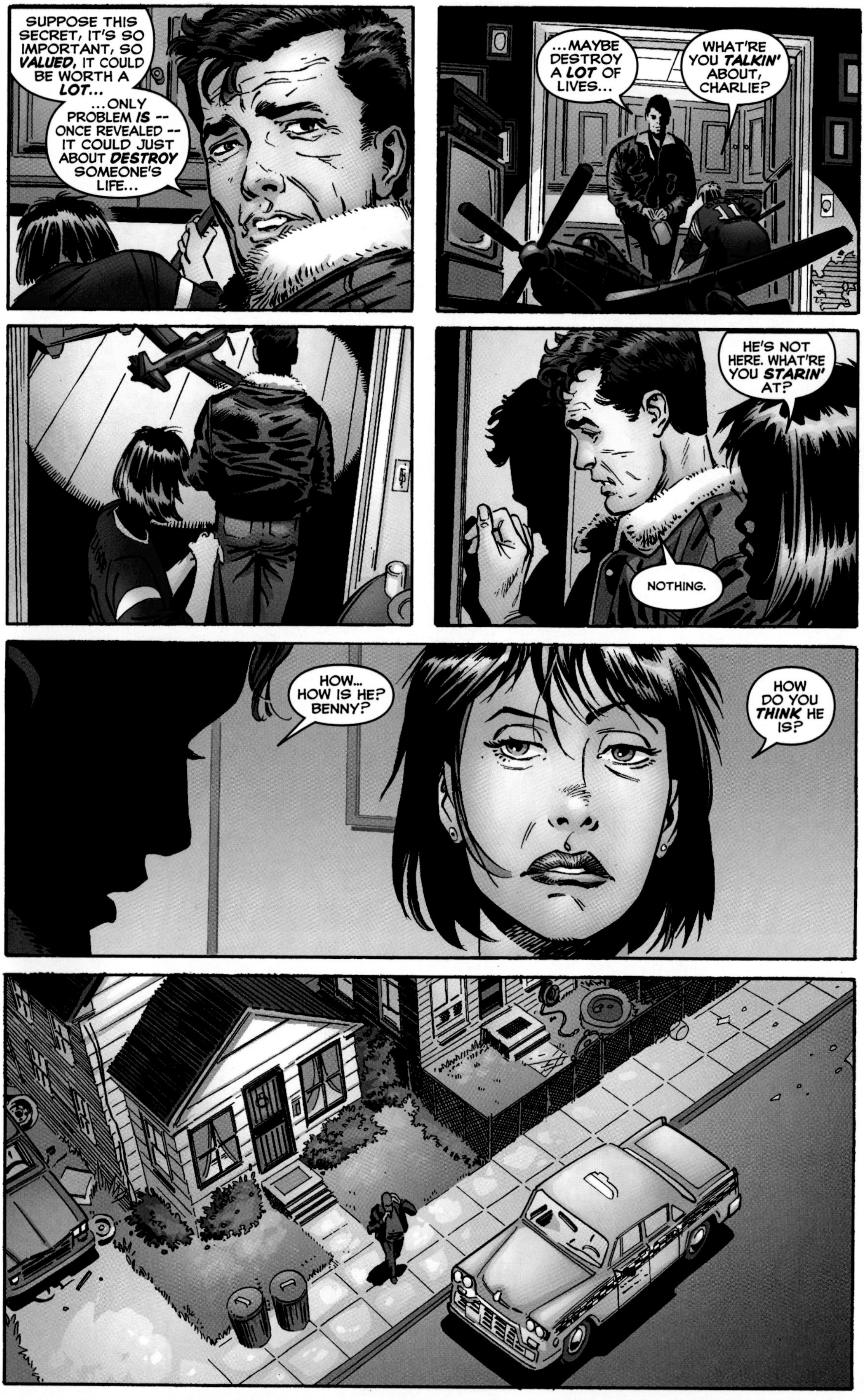
SUPPOSE THIS SECRET, IT'S SO IMPORTANT, SO VALUED, IT COULD BE WORTH A LOT...
...ONLY PROBLEM IS -- ONCE REVEALED -- IT COULD JUST ABOUT DESTROY SOMEONE'S LIFE...
...MAYBE DESTROY A LOT OF LIVES...
WHAT'RE YOU TALKIN' ABOUT, CHARLIE?
HE'S NOT HERE. WHAT'RE YOU STARIN' AT?
NOTHING.
HOW... HOW IS HE? BENNY?
HOW DO YOU THINK HE IS?

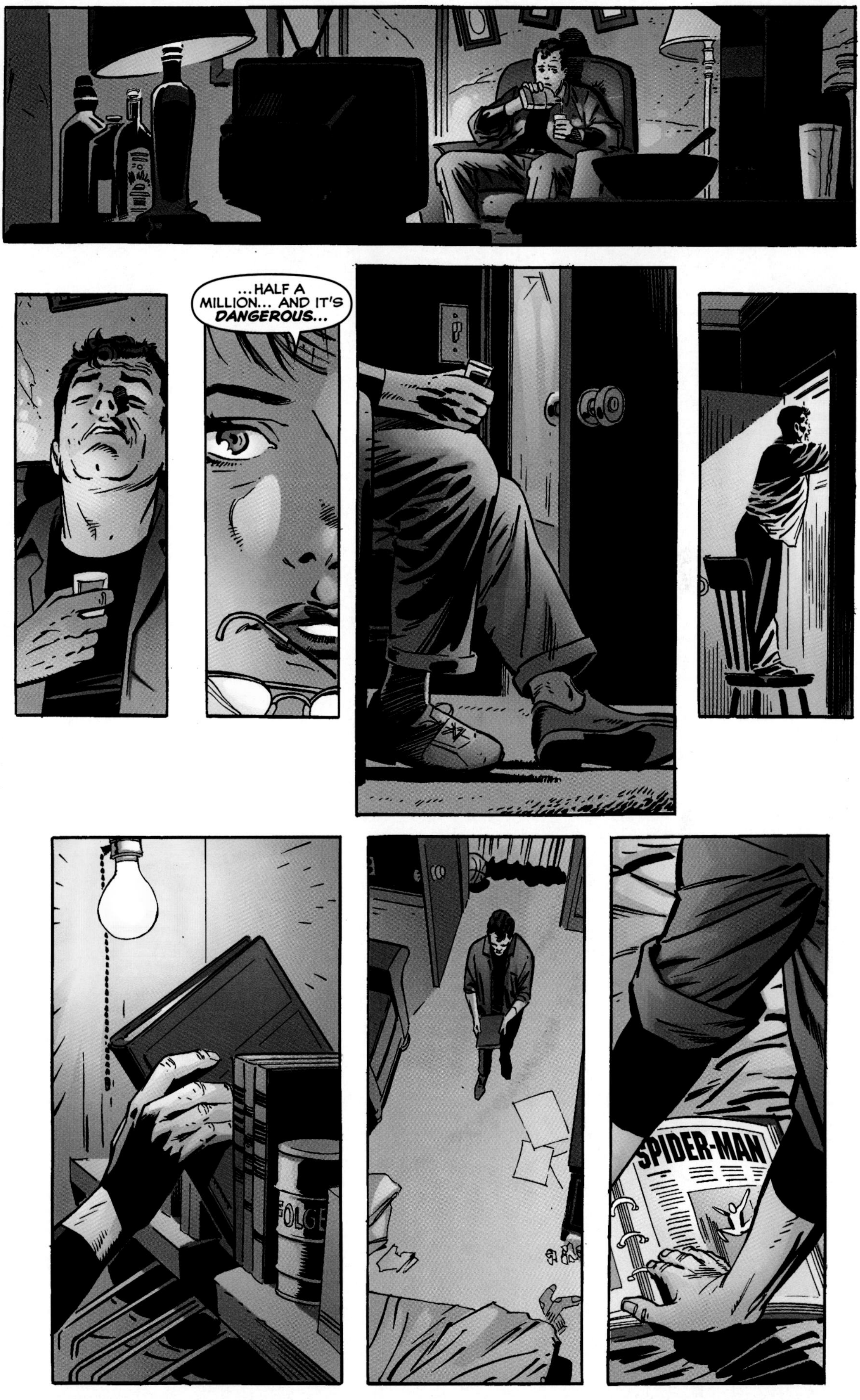
...HALF A MILLION... AND IT'S DANGEROUS...
FOLGE
SPIDER-MAN

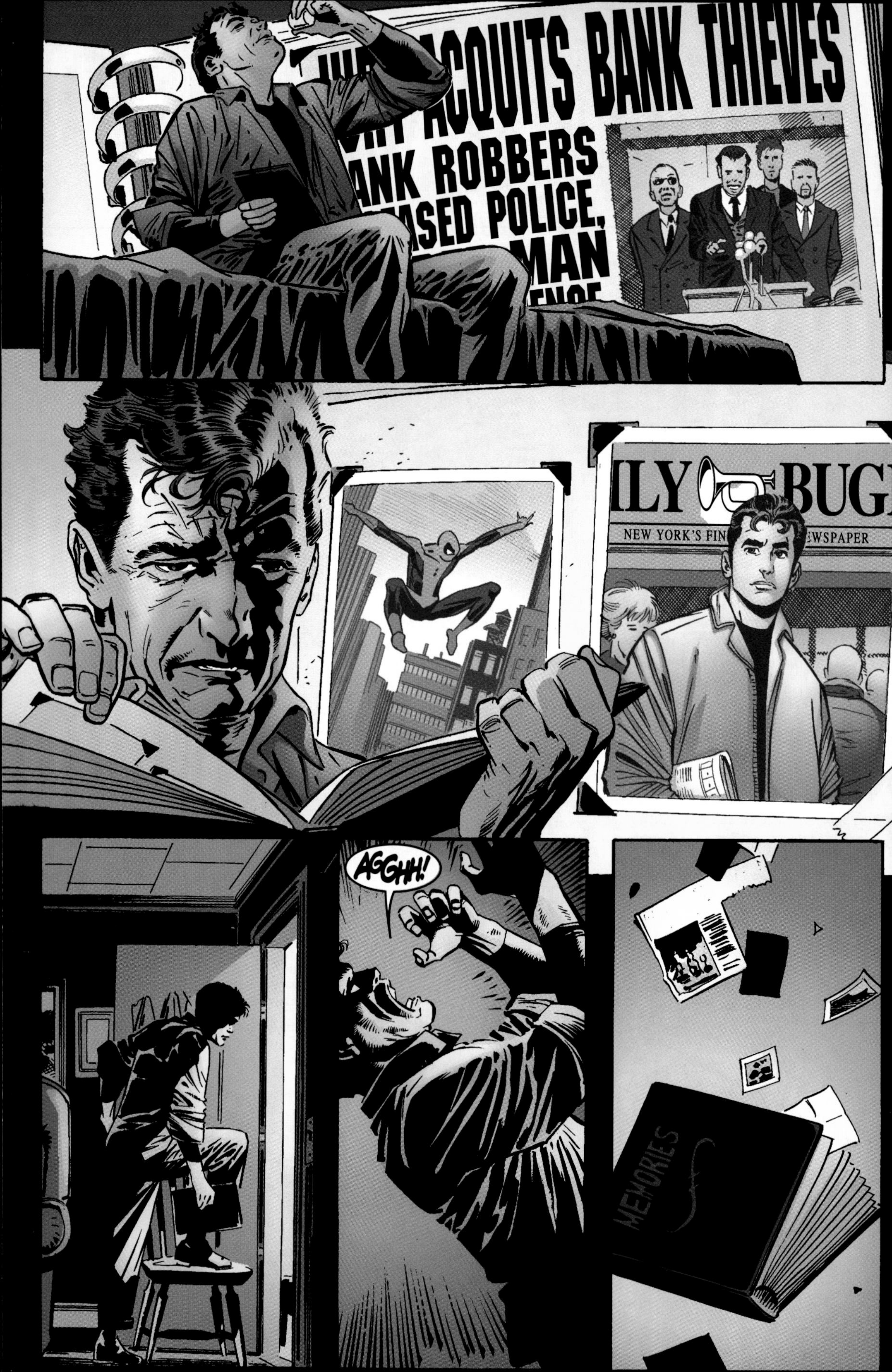
ACQUITS BANK THIEVES
ANK ROBBERS
ASED POLICE,
MAN
ILY
BUG
NEW YORK'S FIN
EWSPAPER
AGGHH!
MEMORIES

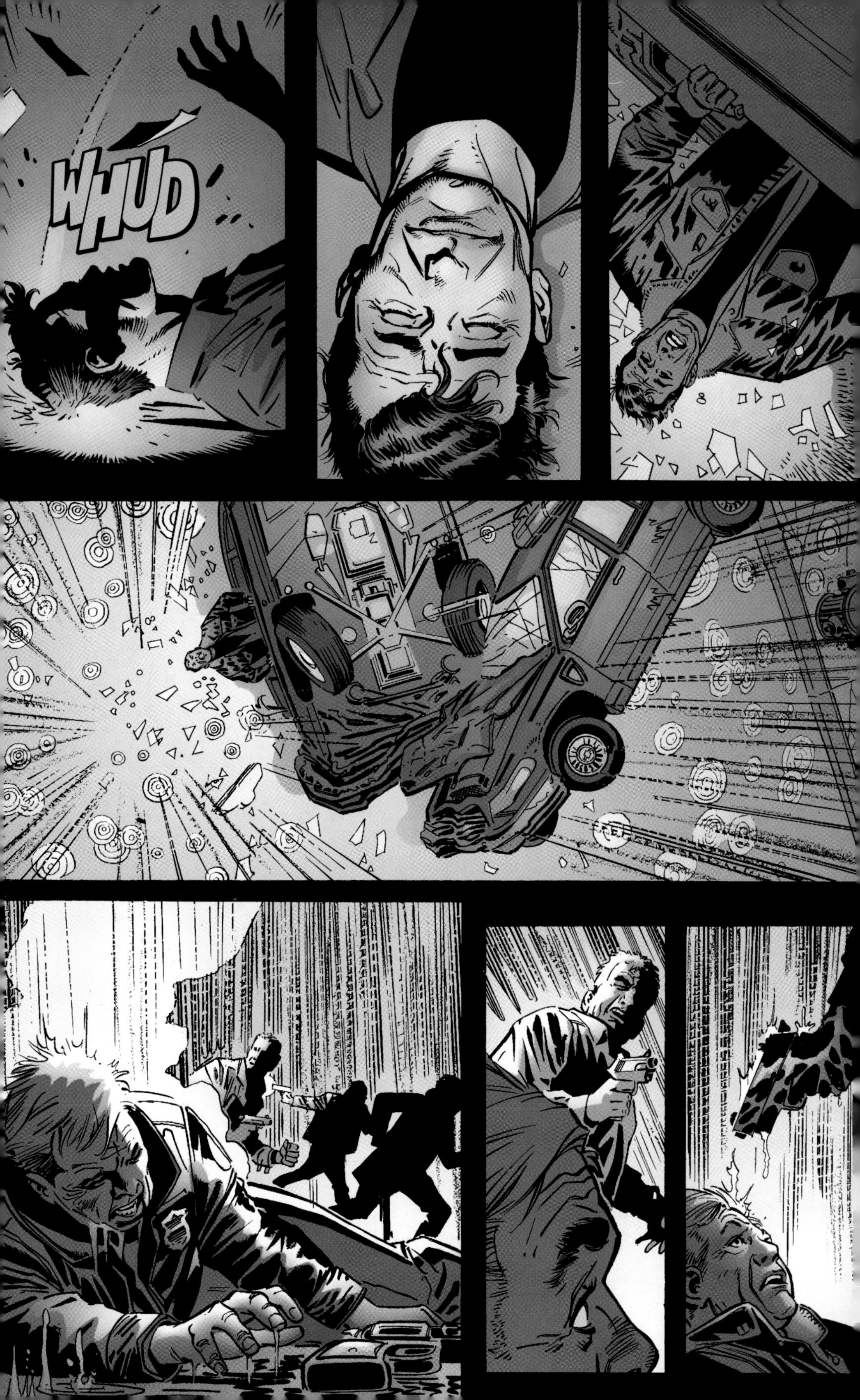
WHUD

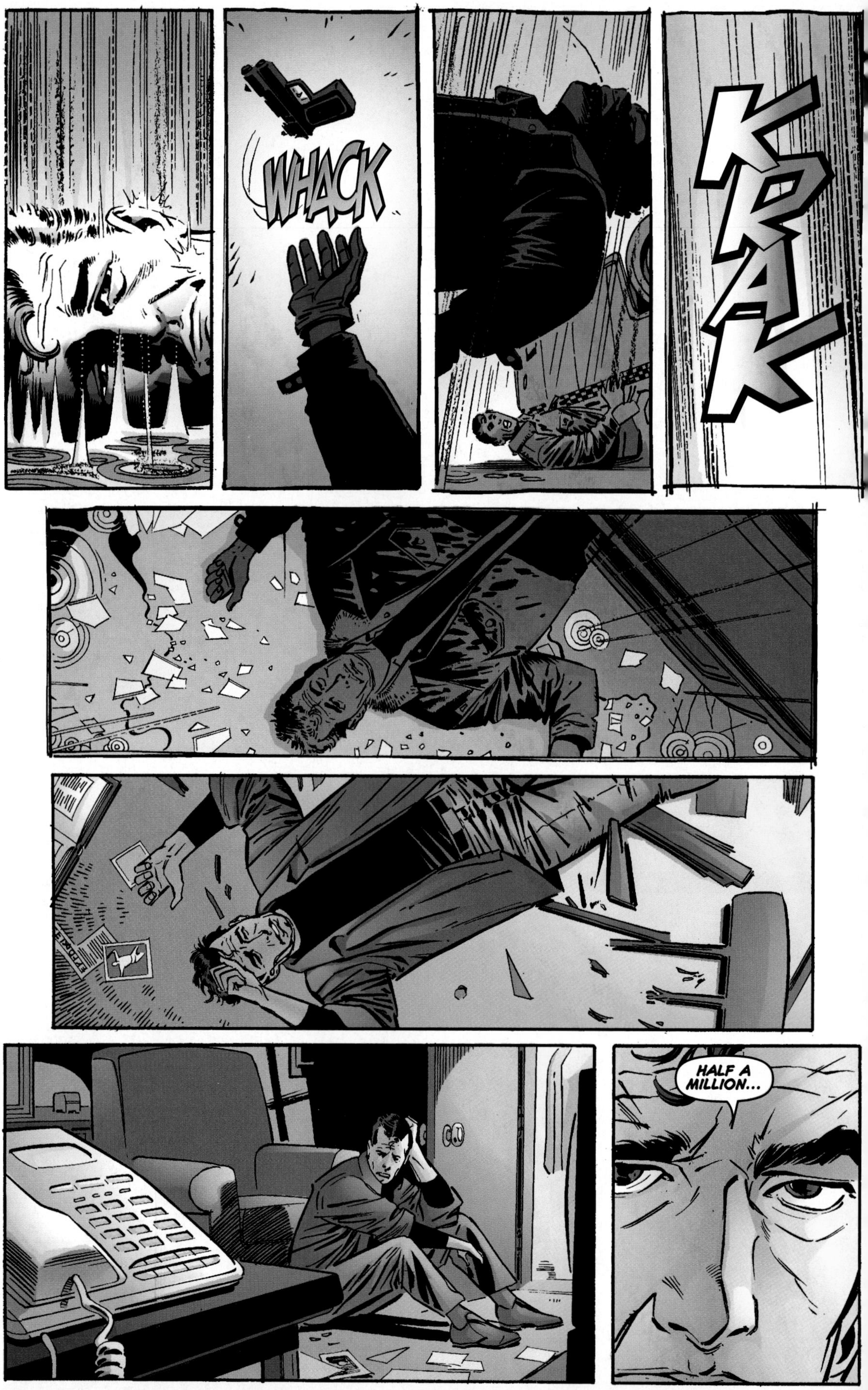
WHACK
KRAK
HALF A MILLION...

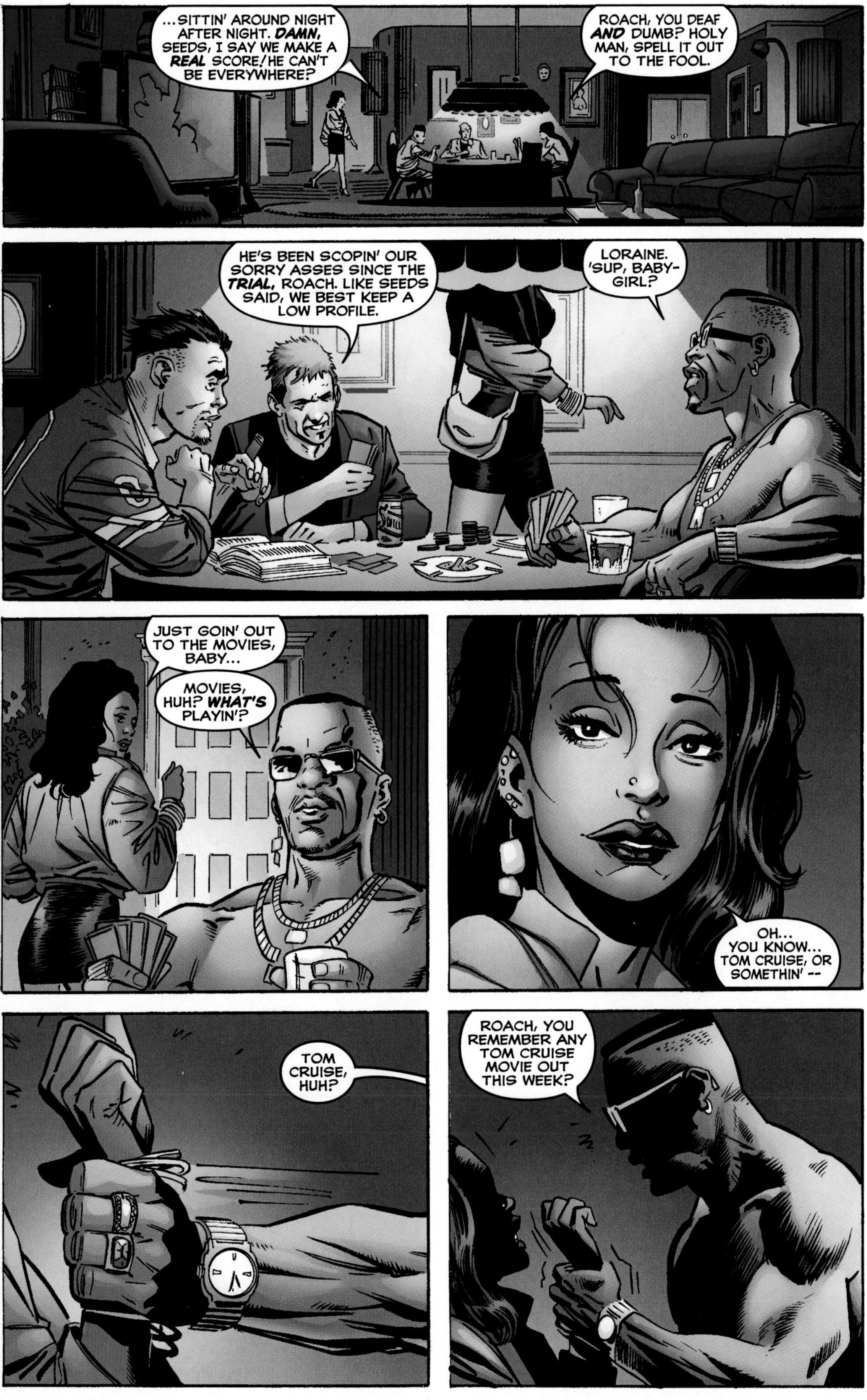
...SITTIN' AROUND NIGHT AFTER NIGHT. DAMN, SEEDS, I SAY WE MAKE A REAL SCORE! HE CAN'T BE EVERYWHERE?
ROACH, YOU DEAF AND DUMB? HOLY MAN, SPELL IT OUT TO THE FOOL.
HE'S BEEN SCOPIN' OUR SORRY ASSES SINCE THE TRIAL, ROACH. LIKE SEEDS SAID, WE BEST KEEP A LOW PROFILE.
LORAINE. 'SUP, BABY-GIRL?
JUST GOIN' OUT TO THE MOVIES, BABY...
MOVIES, HUH? WHAT'S PLAYIN'?
OH... YOU KNOW... TOM CRUISE, OR SOMETHIN' --
TOM CRUISE, HUH?
ROACH, YOU REMEMBER ANY TOM CRUISE MOVIE OUT THIS WEEK?

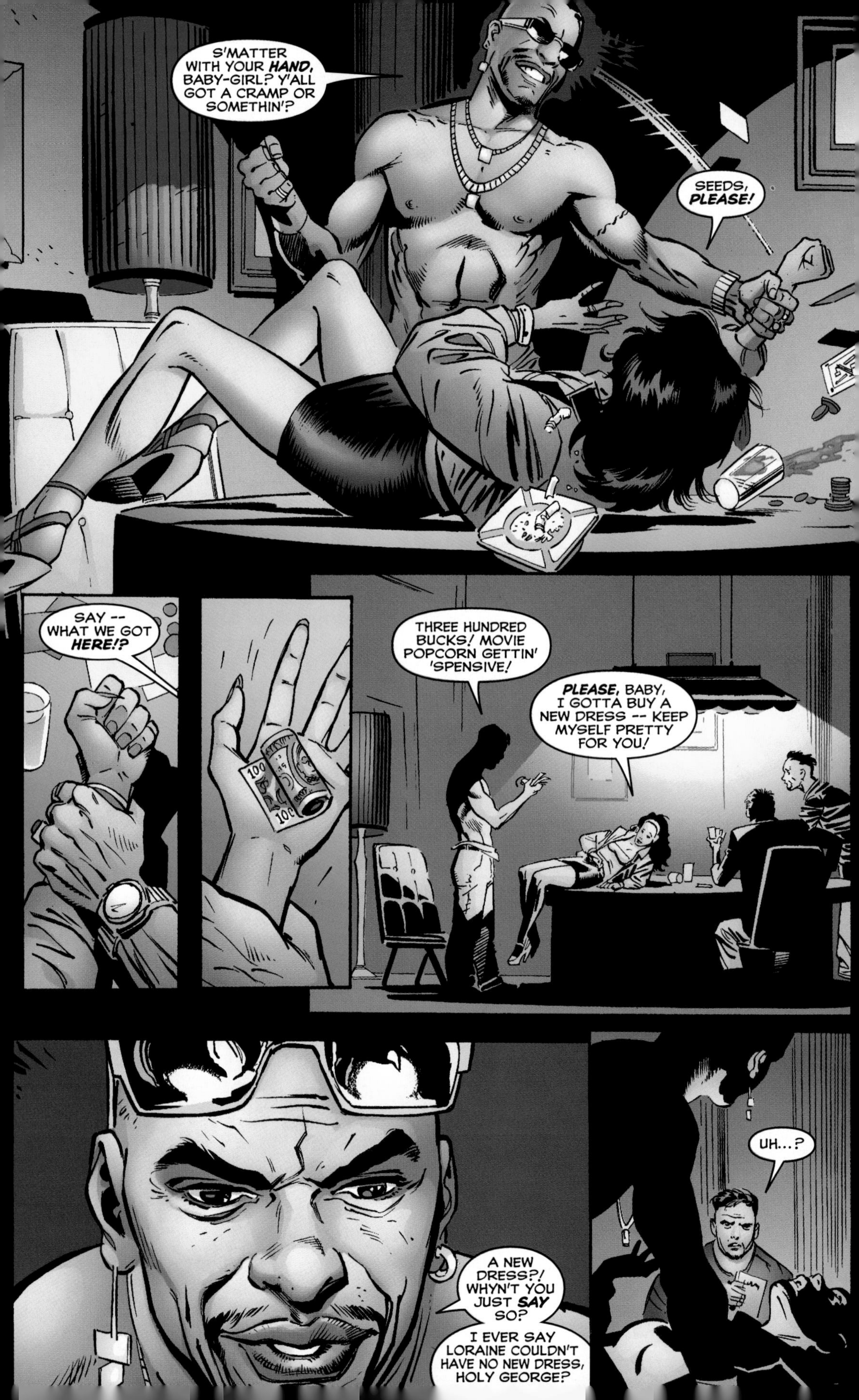
S'MATTER WITH YOUR HAND, BABY-GIRL? Y'ALL GOT A CRAMP OR SOMETHIN'?
SEEDS, PLEASE!
SAY -- WHAT WE GOT HERE!?
THREE HUNDRED BUCKS! MOVIE POPCORN GETTIN' 'SPENSIVE!
PLEASE, BABY, I GOTTA BUY A NEW DRESS -- KEEP MYSELF PRETTY FOR YOU!
A NEW DRESS?! WHYN'T YOU JUST SAY SO?
I EVER SAY LORAINE COULDN'T HAVE NO NEW DRESS, HOLY GEORGE?
UH...?

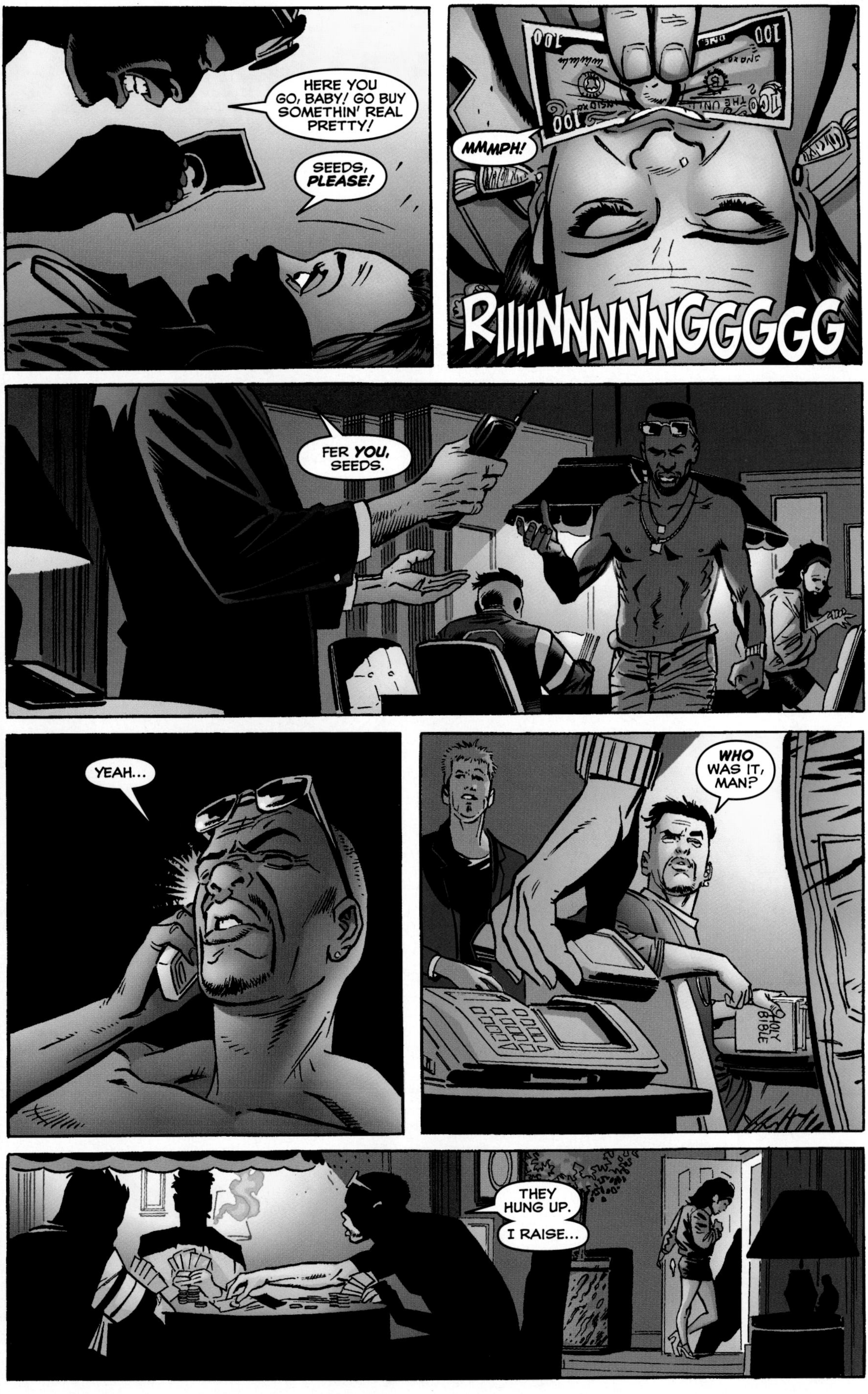
HERE YOU GO, BABY! GO BUY SOMETHIN' REAL PRETTY!
SEEDS, **PLEASE!**
MMMPH!
RIIIINNNNNGGGGG
FER **YOU,** SEEDS.
YEAH...
WHO WAS IT, MAN?
THEY HUNG UP.
I RAISE...

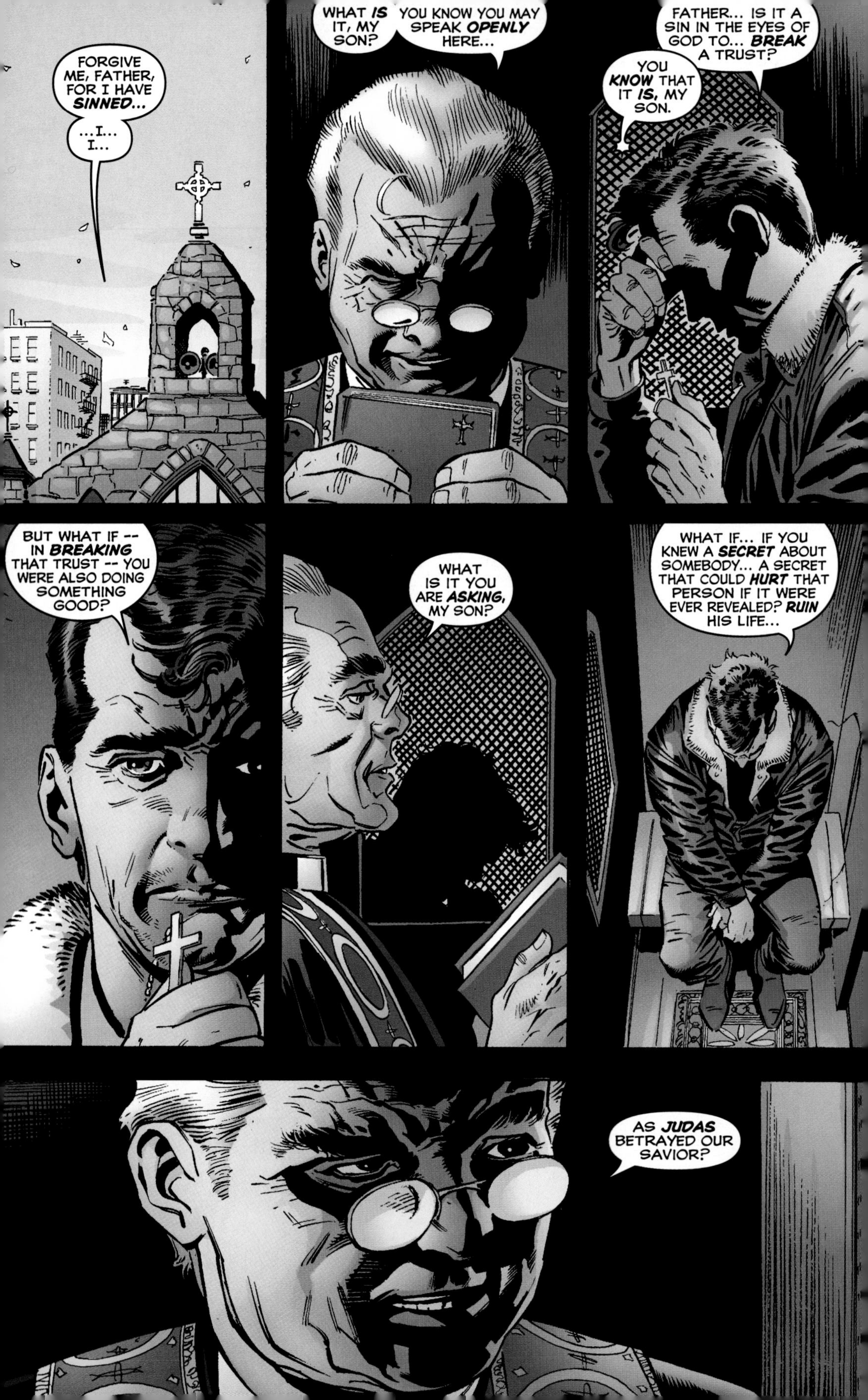
FORGIVE ME, FATHER, FOR I HAVE SINNED...
...I... I...
WHAT IS IT, MY SON?
YOU KNOW YOU MAY SPEAK OPENLY HERE...
FATHER... IS IT A SIN IN THE EYES OF GOD TO... BREAK A TRUST?
YOU KNOW THAT IT IS, MY SON.
BUT WHAT IF -- IN BREAKING THAT TRUST -- YOU WERE ALSO DOING SOMETHING GOOD?
WHAT IS IT YOU ARE ASKING, MY SON?
WHAT IF... IF YOU KNEW A SECRET ABOUT SOMEBODY... A SECRET THAT COULD HURT THAT PERSON IF IT WERE EVER REVEALED? RUIN HIS LIFE...
AS JUDAS BETRAYED OUR SAVIOR?

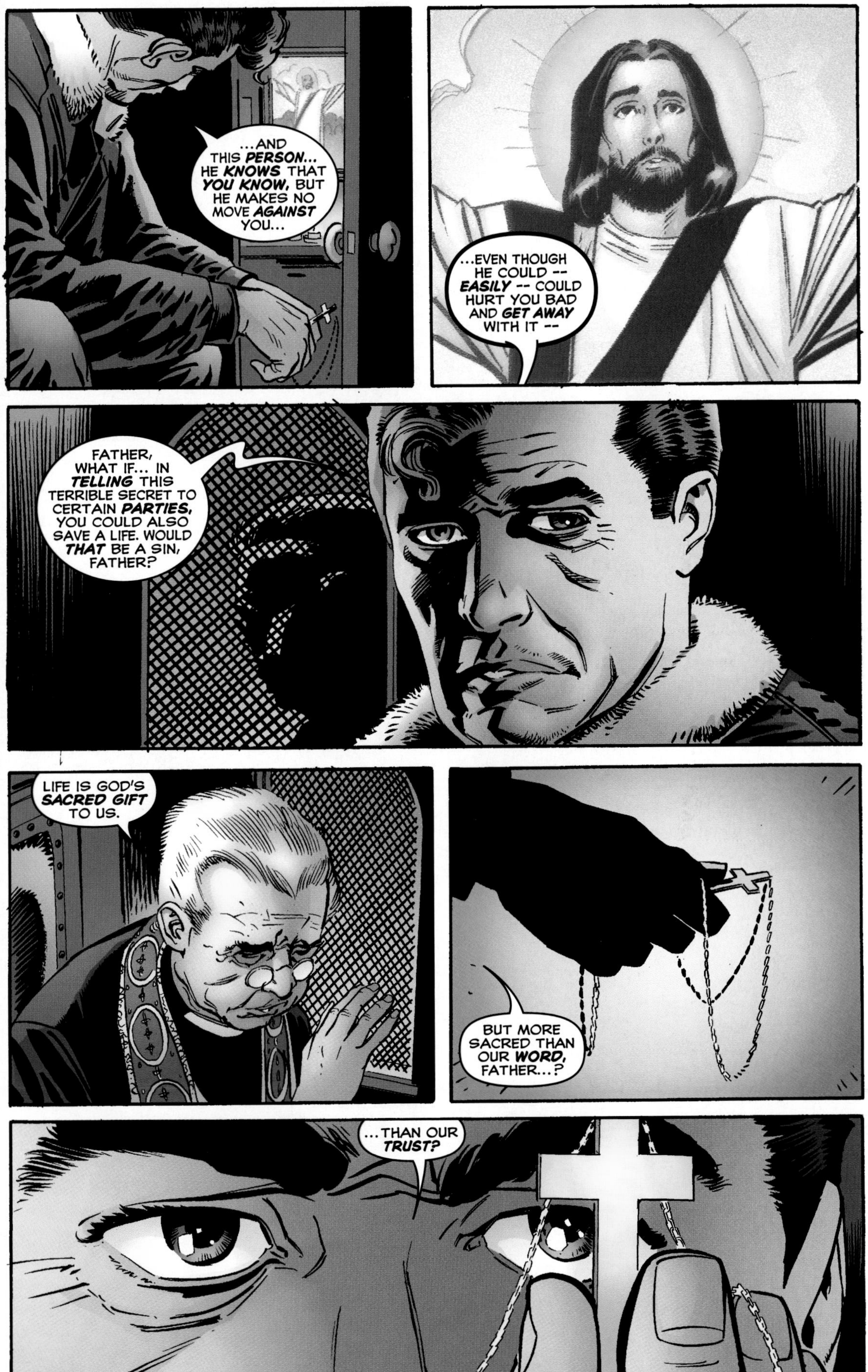
...AND THIS PERSON... HE KNOWS THAT YOU KNOW, BUT HE MAKES NO MOVE AGAINST YOU...
...EVEN THOUGH HE COULD -- EASILY -- COULD HURT YOU BAD AND GET AWAY WITH IT --
FATHER, WHAT IF... IN TELLING THIS TERRIBLE SECRET TO CERTAIN PARTIES, YOU COULD ALSO SAVE A LIFE. WOULD THAT BE A SIN, FATHER?
LIFE IS GOD'S SACRED GIFT TO US.
BUT MORE SACRED THAN OUR WORD, FATHER...?
...THAN OUR TRUST?

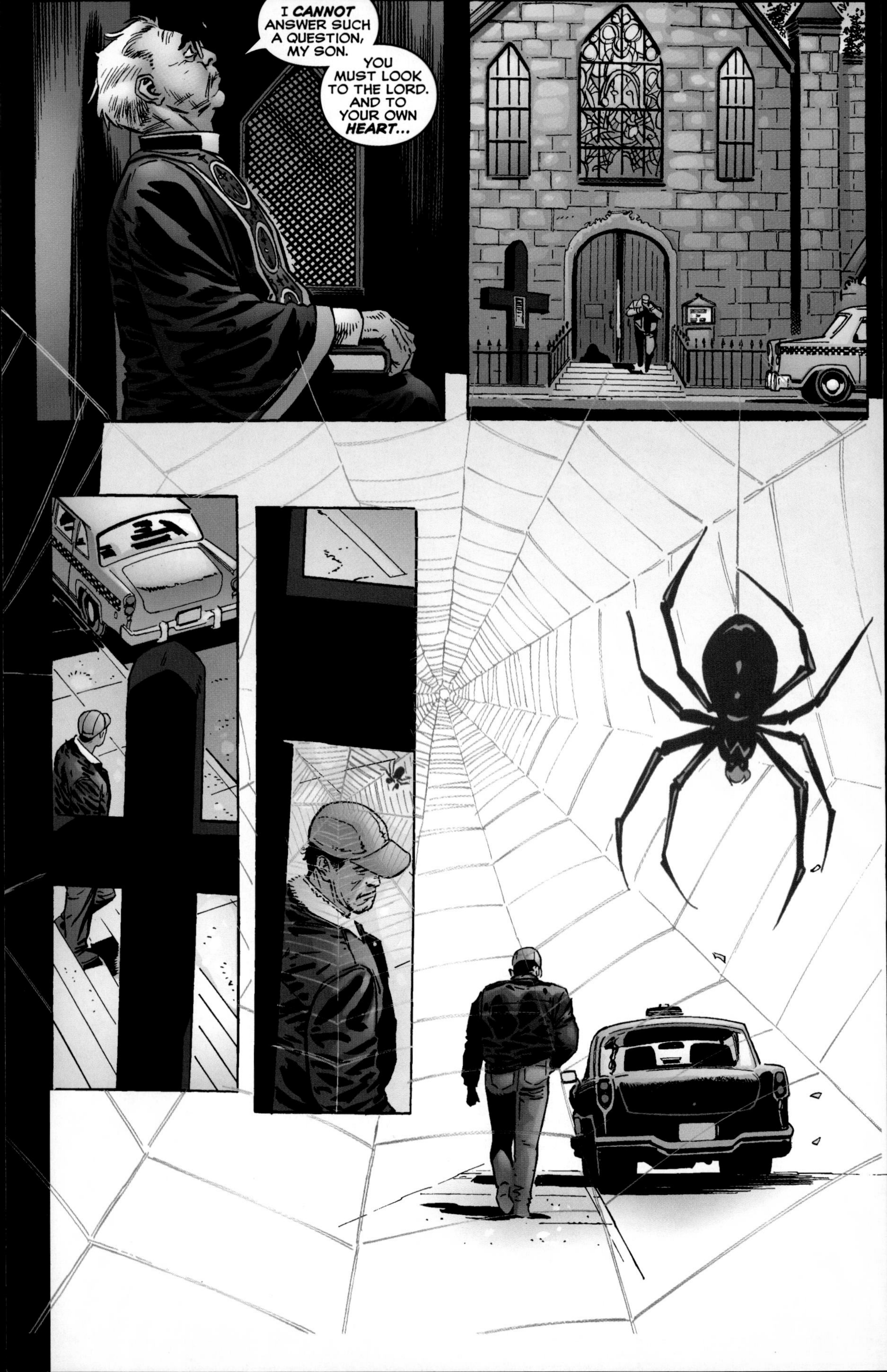
I CANNOT ANSWER SUCH A QUESTION, MY SON.
YOU MUST LOOK TO THE LORD. AND TO YOUR OWN HEART...

WRITTEN BY BRUCE JONES

PENCILED BY LEE WEEKS

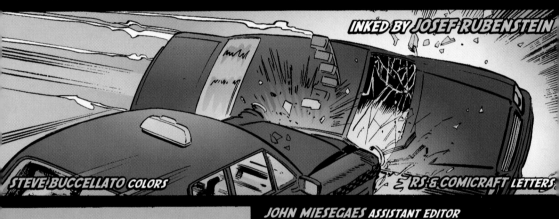

INKED BY JOSEF RUBENSTEIN

STEVE BUCCELLATO COLORS

RS & COMICRAFT LETTERS

JOHN MIESEGAES ASSISTANT EDITOR

AXEL ALONSO EDITOR

JOE QUESADA CHIEF

BILL JEMAS PRESIDENT

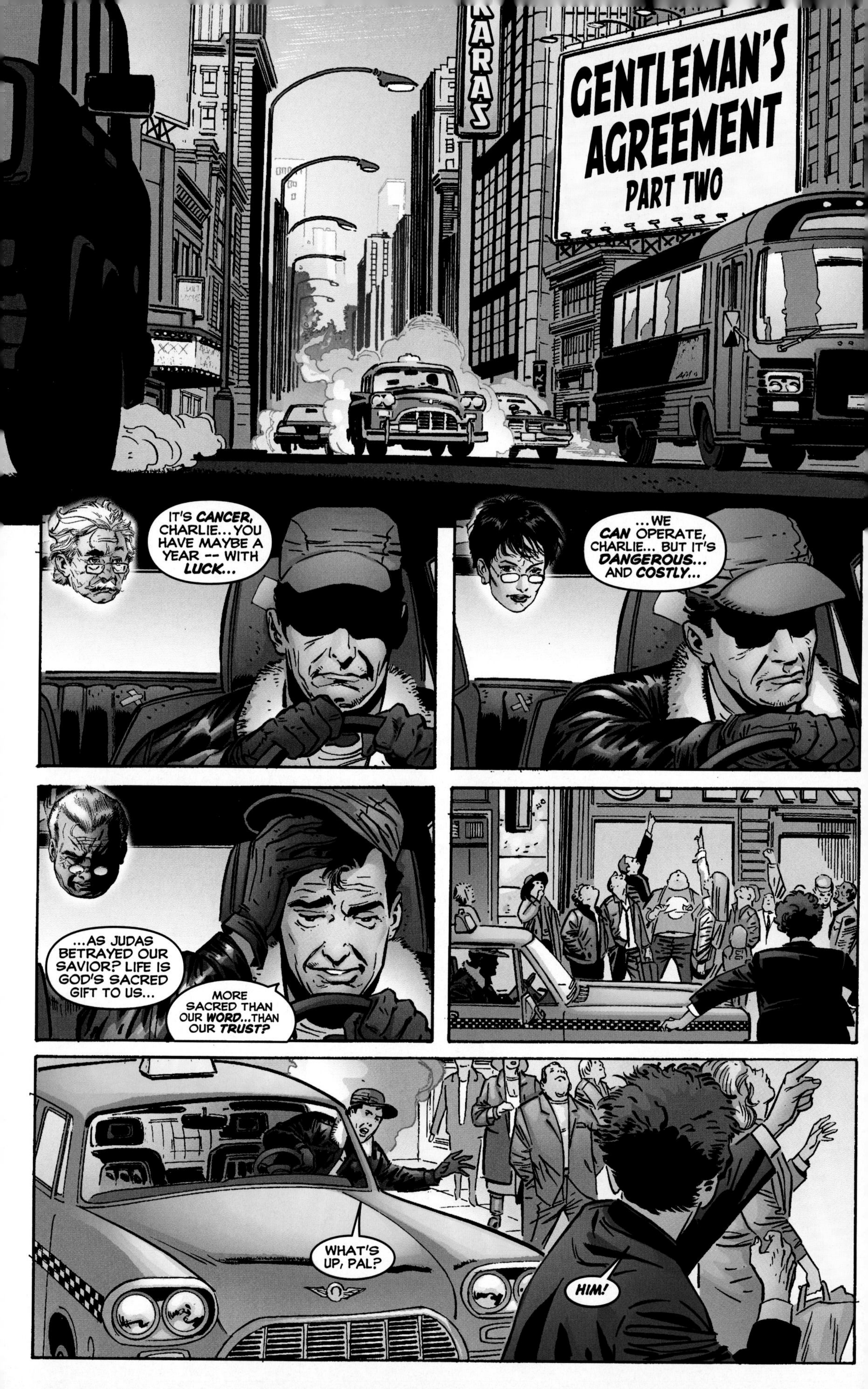
GENTLEMAN'S AGREEMENT
PART TWO
KARAS
IT'S CANCER, CHARLIE... YOU HAVE MAYBE A YEAR -- WITH LUCK...
...WE CAN OPERATE, CHARLIE... BUT IT'S DANGEROUS... AND COSTLY...
...AS JUDAS BETRAYED OUR SAVIOR? LIFE IS GOD'S SACRED GIFT TO US...
MORE SACRED THAN OUR WORD...THAN OUR TRUST?
WHAT'S UP, PAL?
HIM!

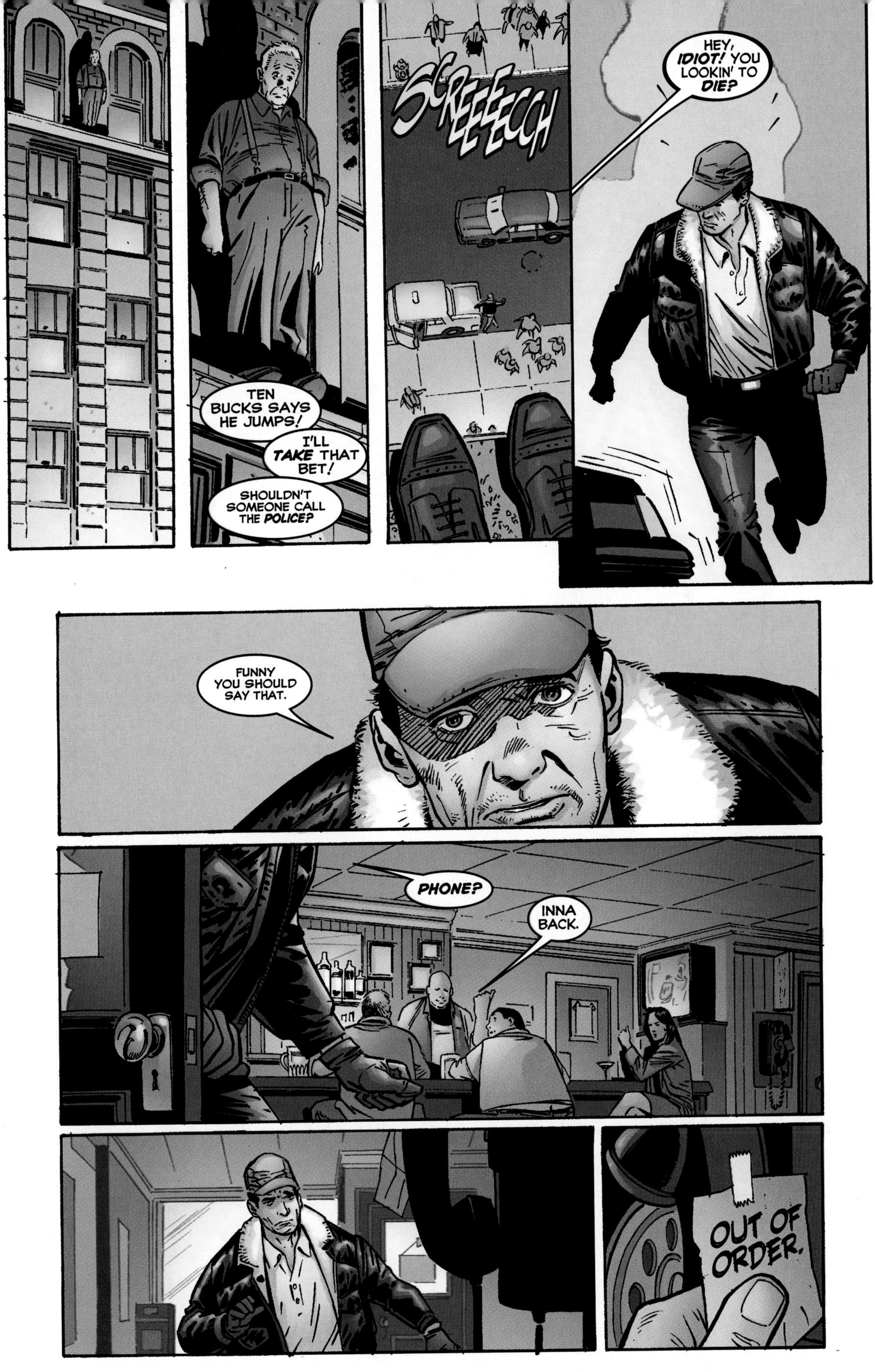
TEN BUCKS SAYS HE JUMPS!
I'LL TAKE THAT BET!
SHOULDN'T SOMEONE CALL THE POLICE?
SCREEEECCH
HEY, IDIOT! YOU LOOKIN' TO DIE?
FUNNY YOU SHOULD SAY THAT.
PHONE?
INNA BACK.
OUT OF ORDER.

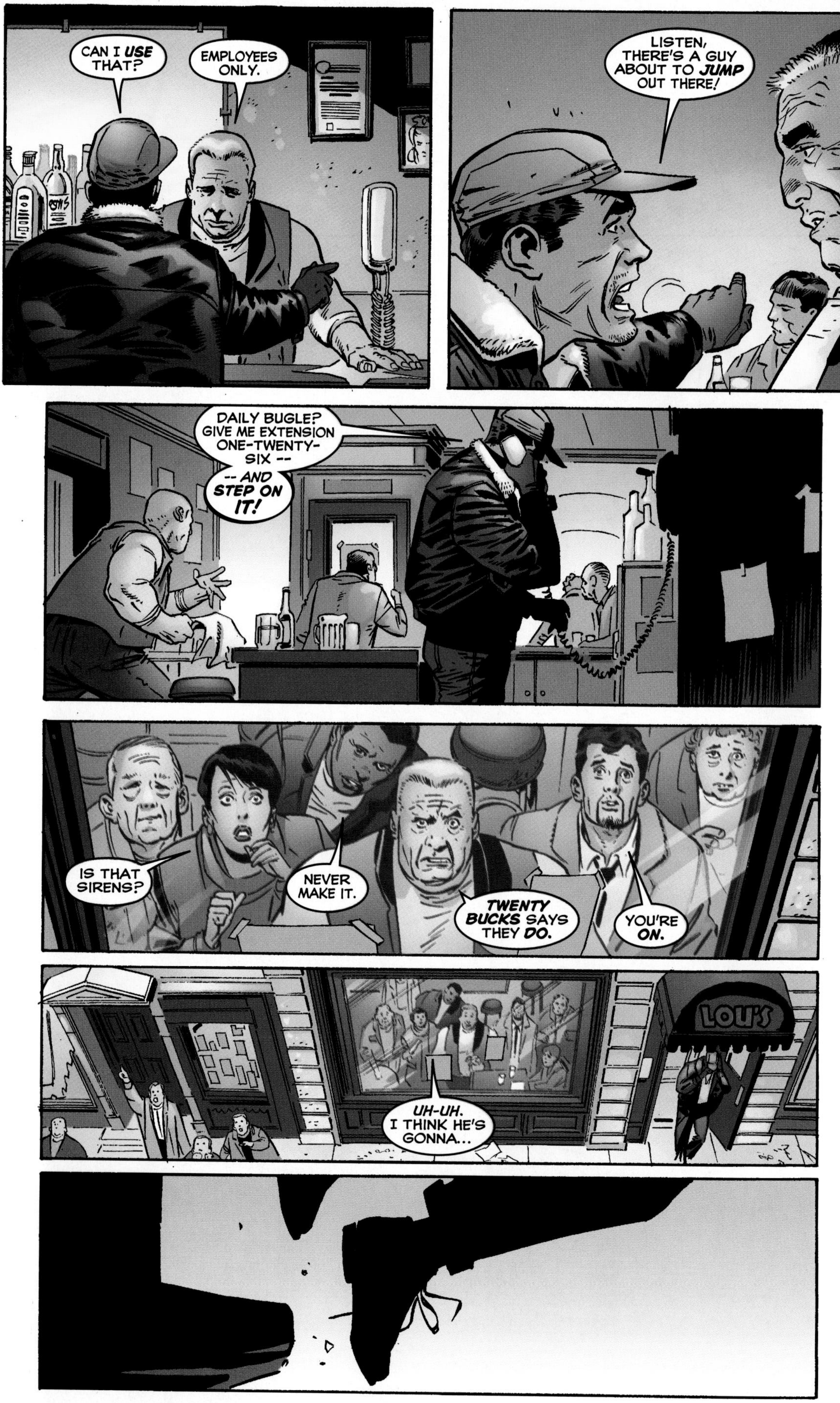
CAN I USE THAT?
EMPLOYEES ONLY.
LISTEN, THERE'S A GUY ABOUT TO JUMP OUT THERE!
DAILY BUGLE? GIVE ME EXTENSION ONE-TWENTY-SIX --
-- AND STEP ON IT!
IS THAT SIRENS?
NEVER MAKE IT.
TWENTY BUCKS SAYS THEY DO.
YOU'RE ON.
LOU'S
UH-UH. I THINK HE'S GONNA...

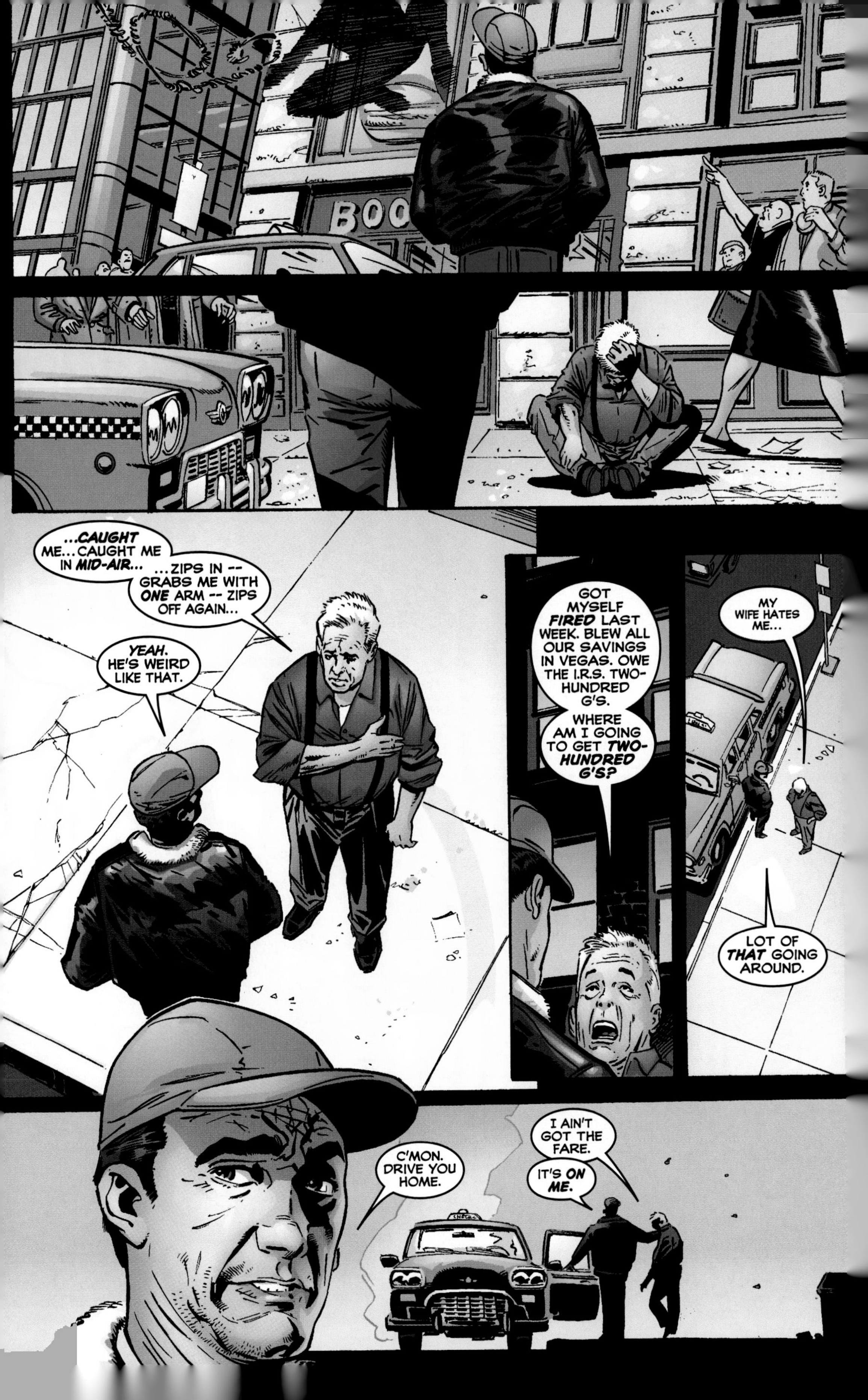
BOO
...CAUGHT ME...CAUGHT ME IN MID-AIR...
...ZIPS IN -- GRABS ME WITH ONE ARM -- ZIPS OFF AGAIN...
YEAH. HE'S WEIRD LIKE THAT.
GOT MYSELF FIRED LAST WEEK. BLEW ALL OUR SAVINGS IN VEGAS. OWE THE I.R.S. TWO-HUNDRED G'S.
WHERE AM I GOING TO GET TWO-HUNDRED G'S?
MY WIFE HATES ME...
LOT OF THAT GOING AROUND.
C'MON. DRIVE YOU HOME.
I AIN'T GOT THE FARE.
IT'S ON ME.

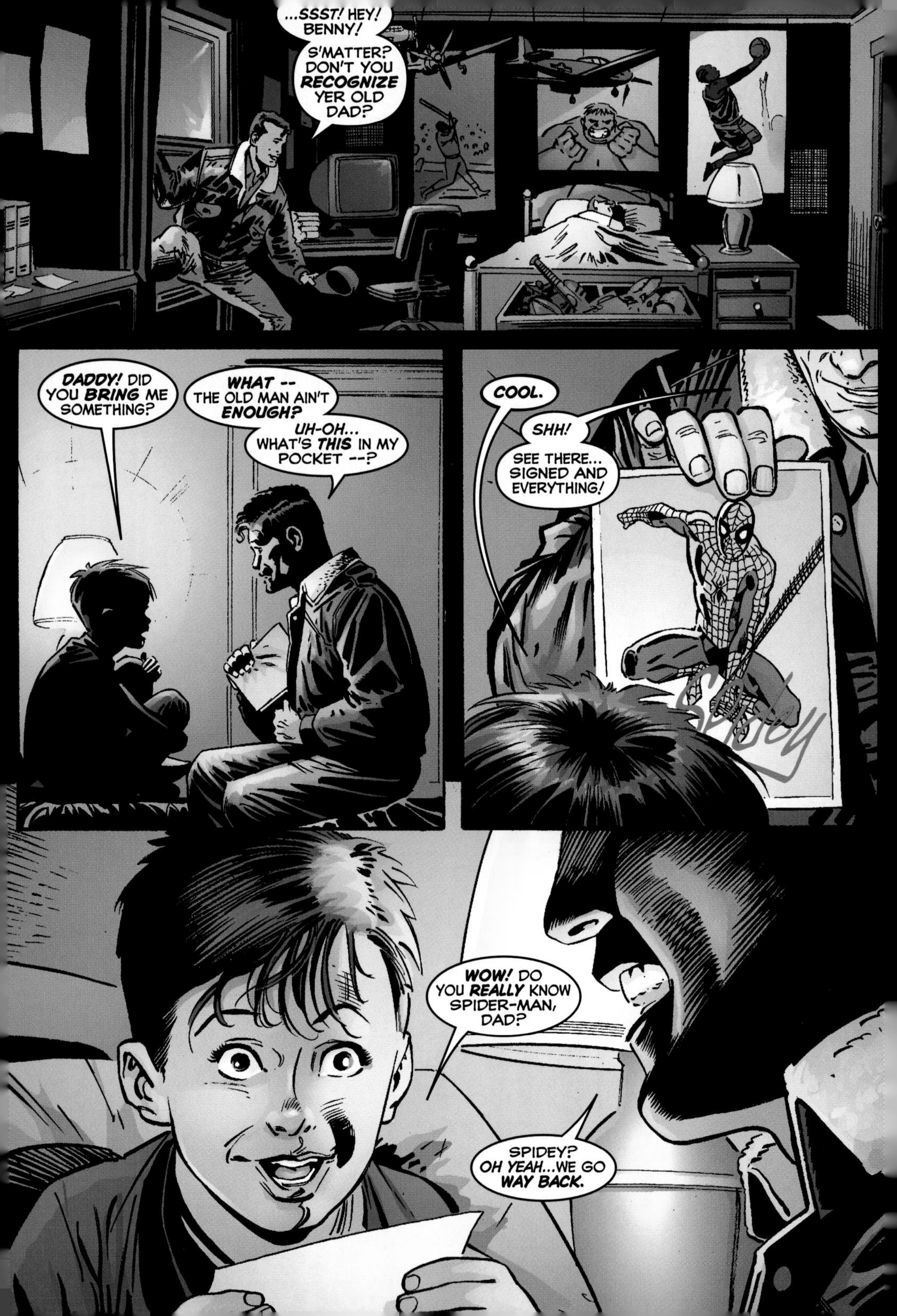
...SSST! HEY! BENNY!
S'MATTER? DON'T YOU RECOGNIZE YER OLD DAD?
DADDY! DID YOU BRING ME SOMETHING?
WHAT -- THE OLD MAN AIN'T ENOUGH?
UH-OH... WHAT'S THIS IN MY POCKET --?
COOL.
SHH!
SEE THERE... SIGNED AND EVERYTHING!
Spidey
WOW! DO YOU REALLY KNOW SPIDER-MAN, DAD?
SPIDEY? OH YEAH...WE GO WAY BACK.

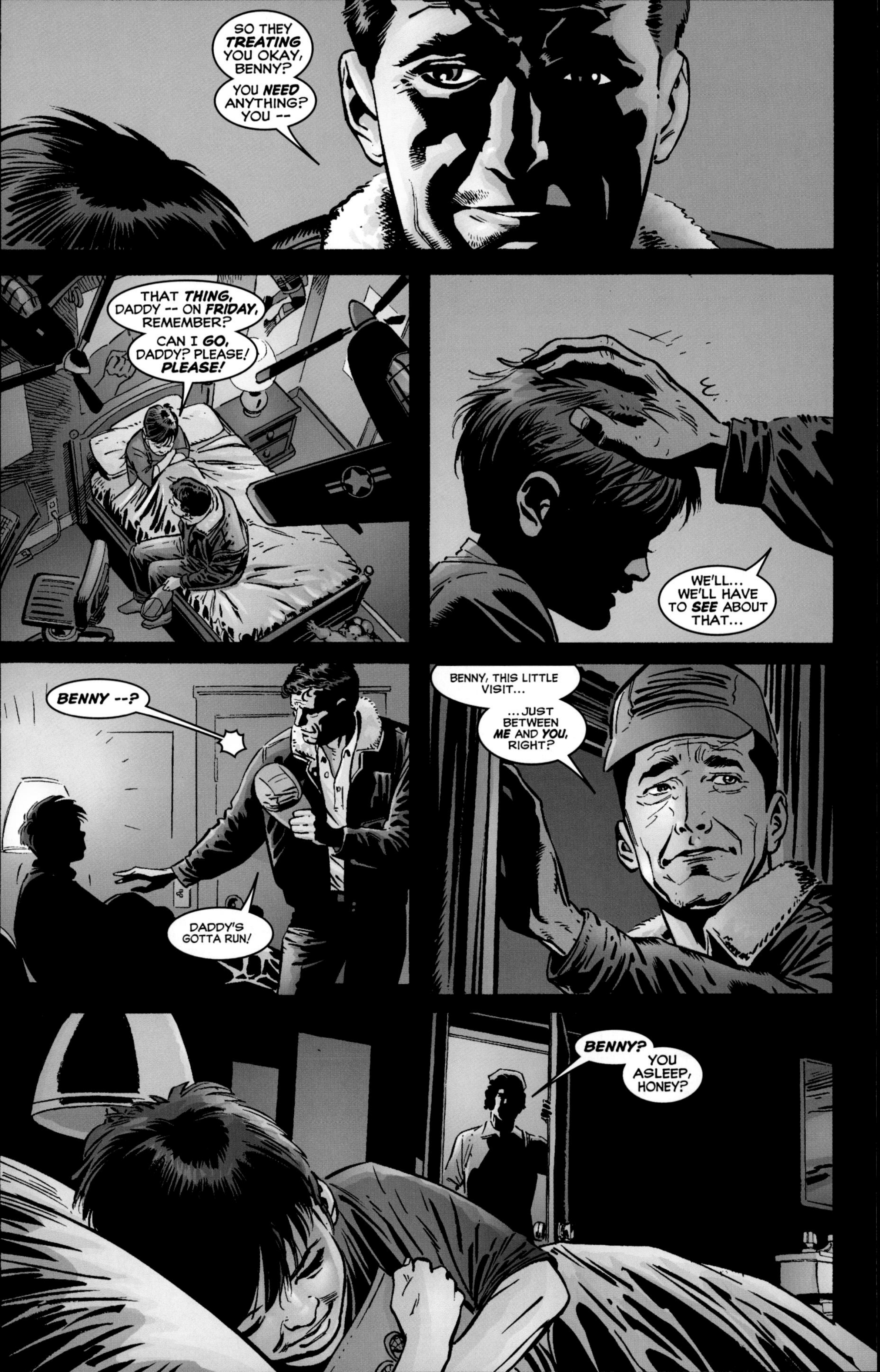
SO THEY TREATING YOU OKAY, BENNY?
YOU NEED ANYTHING? YOU --
THAT THING, DADDY -- ON FRIDAY, REMEMBER?
CAN I GO, DADDY? PLEASE! PLEASE!
WE'LL... WE'LL HAVE TO SEE ABOUT THAT...
BENNY --?
DADDY'S GOTTA RUN!
BENNY, THIS LITTLE VISIT...
...JUST BETWEEN ME AND YOU, RIGHT?
BENNY? YOU ASLEEP, HONEY?

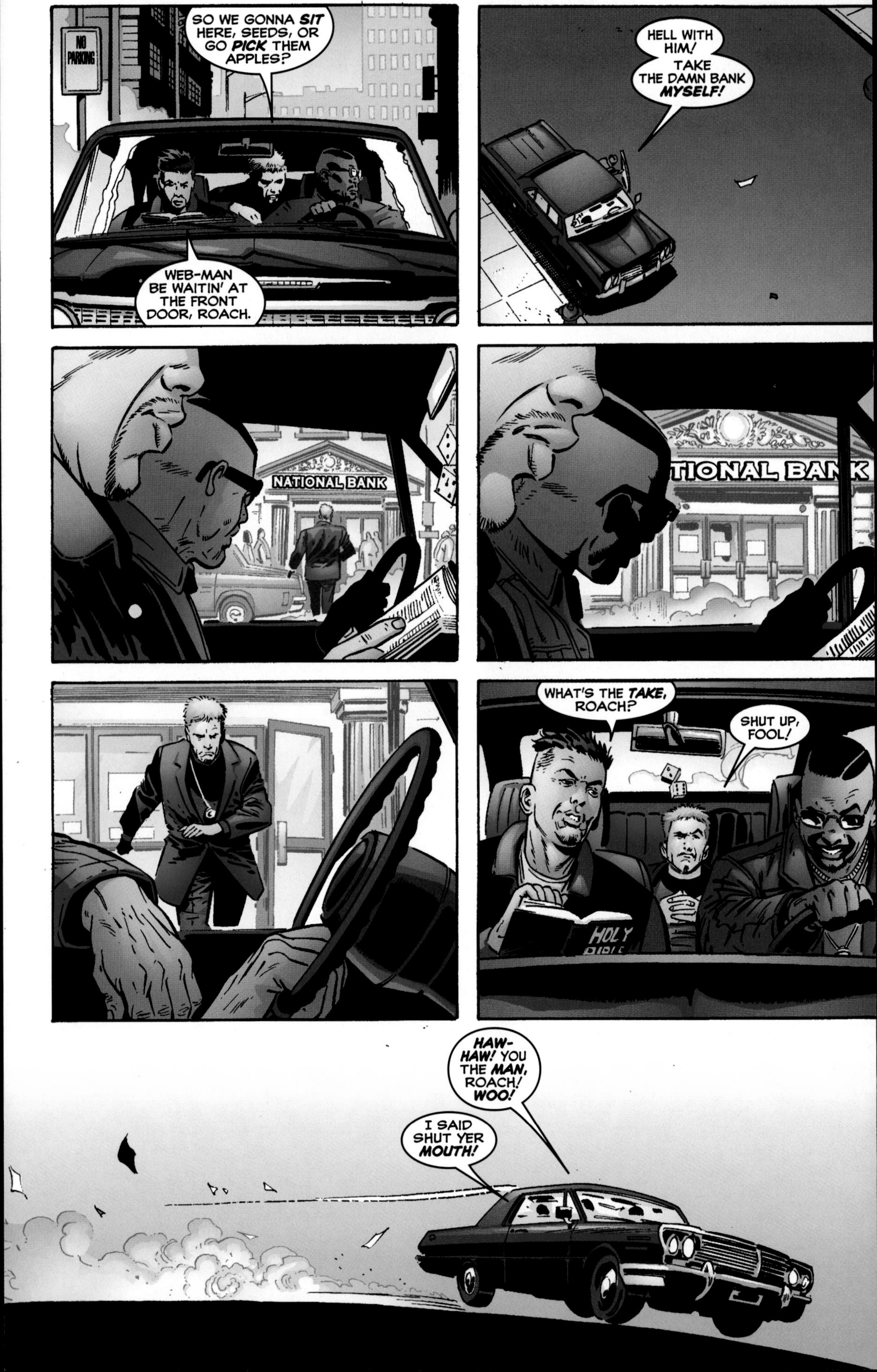
NO PARKING
SO WE GONNA SIT HERE, SEEDS, OR GO PICK THEM APPLES?
WEB-MAN BE WAITIN' AT THE FRONT DOOR, ROACH.
HELL WITH HIM! TAKE THE DAMN BANK MYSELF!
NATIONAL BANK
TIONAL BANK
WHAT'S THE TAKE, ROACH?
SHUT UP, FOOL!
HOLY
HAW-HAW! YOU THE MAN, ROACH! WOO!
I SAID SHUT YER MOUTH!

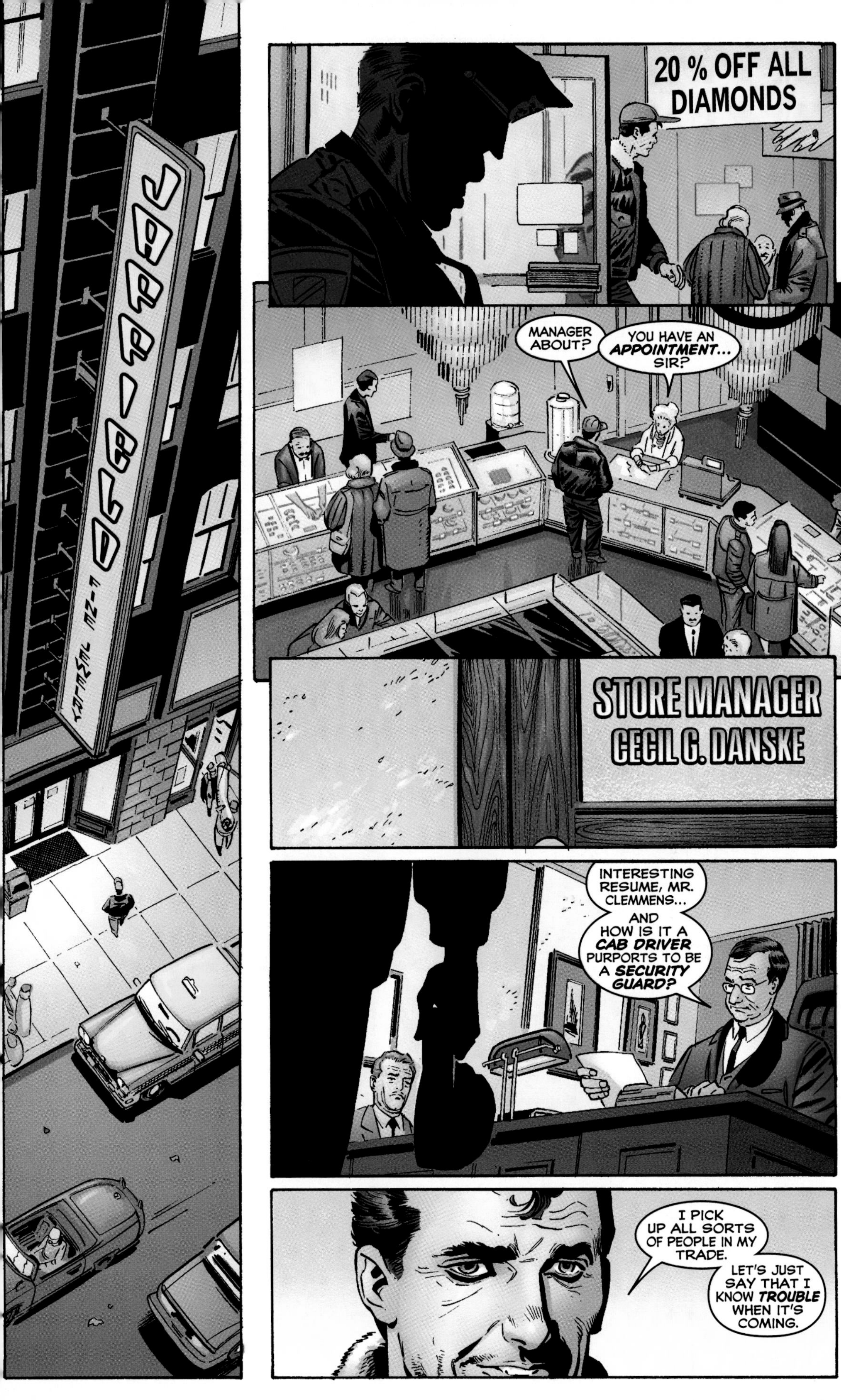
20 % OFF ALL DIAMONDS
MANAGER ABOUT?
YOU HAVE AN APPOINTMENT... SIR?
STORE MANAGER
CECIL G. DANSKE
INTERESTING RESUME, MR. CLEMMENS...
AND HOW IS IT A CAB DRIVER PURPORTS TO BE A SECURITY GUARD?
I PICK UP ALL SORTS OF PEOPLE IN MY TRADE.
LET'S JUST SAY THAT I KNOW TROUBLE WHEN IT'S COMING.

INDEED...HOW... *"EDIFYING."*

YOUR MAN OUT FRONT, FOR INSTANCE -- HE'S ASLEEP ON HIS FEET.

TOOK THAT RIGHT UNDER HIS *NOSE.*

THAT'S *STEALING,* MR. CLEMMENS!

THAT'S WHAT THEY *CALL* IT!

GIVE ME *SECURITY!*

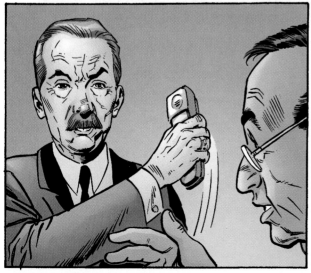

CAN YOU START *MONDAY,* MR. CLEMMENS?

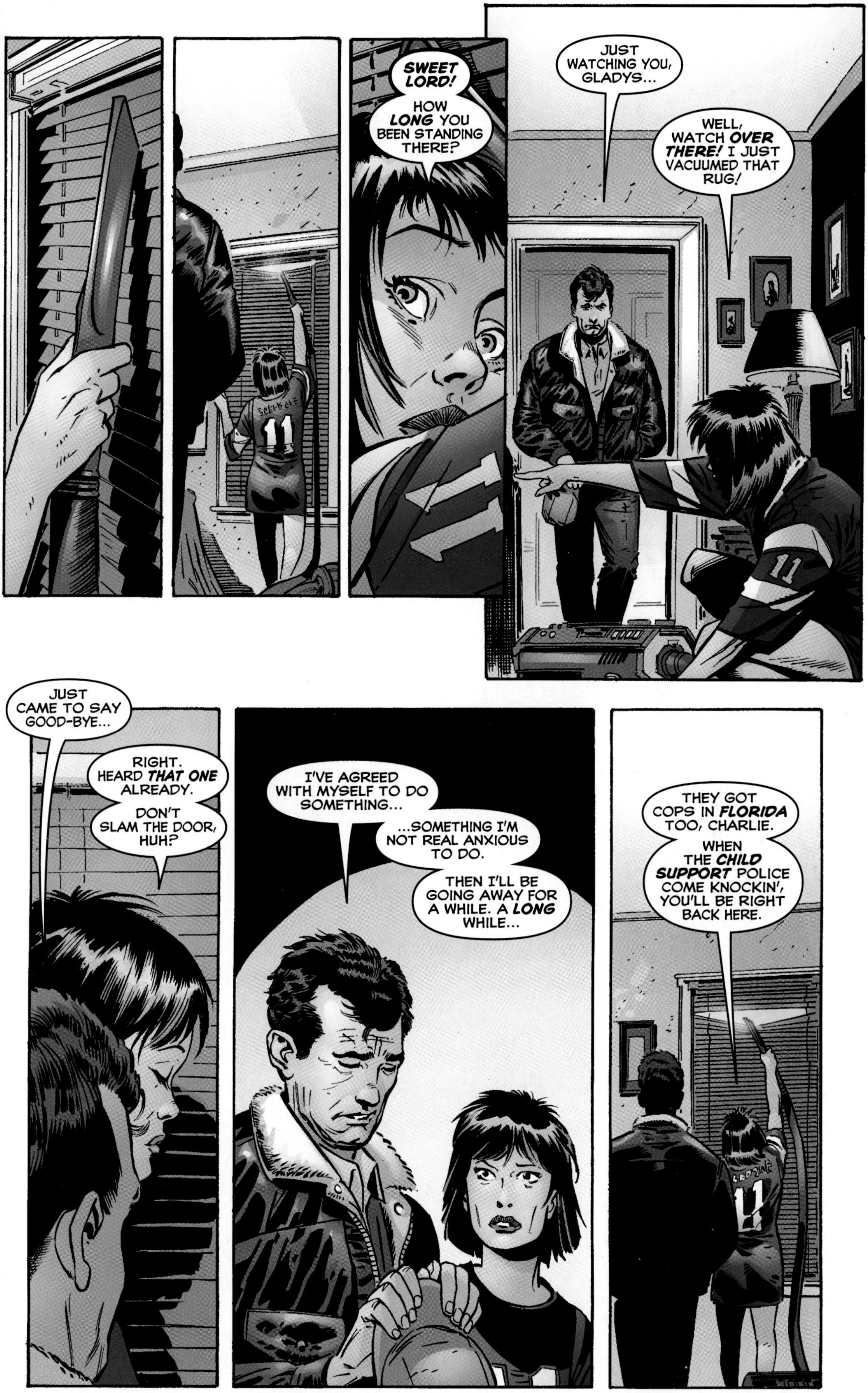

SWEET LORD!
HOW LONG YOU BEEN STANDING THERE?
JUST WATCHING YOU, GLADYS...
WELL, WATCH OVER THERE! I JUST VACUUMED THAT RUG!
JUST CAME TO SAY GOOD-BYE...
RIGHT. HEARD THAT ONE ALREADY.
DON'T SLAM THE DOOR, HUH?
I'VE AGREED WITH MYSELF TO DO SOMETHING...
...SOMETHING I'M NOT REAL ANXIOUS TO DO.
THEN I'LL BE GOING AWAY FOR A WHILE. A LONG WHILE...
THEY GOT COPS IN FLORIDA TOO, CHARLIE.
WHEN THE CHILD SUPPORT POLICE COME KNOCKIN', YOU'LL BE RIGHT BACK HERE.

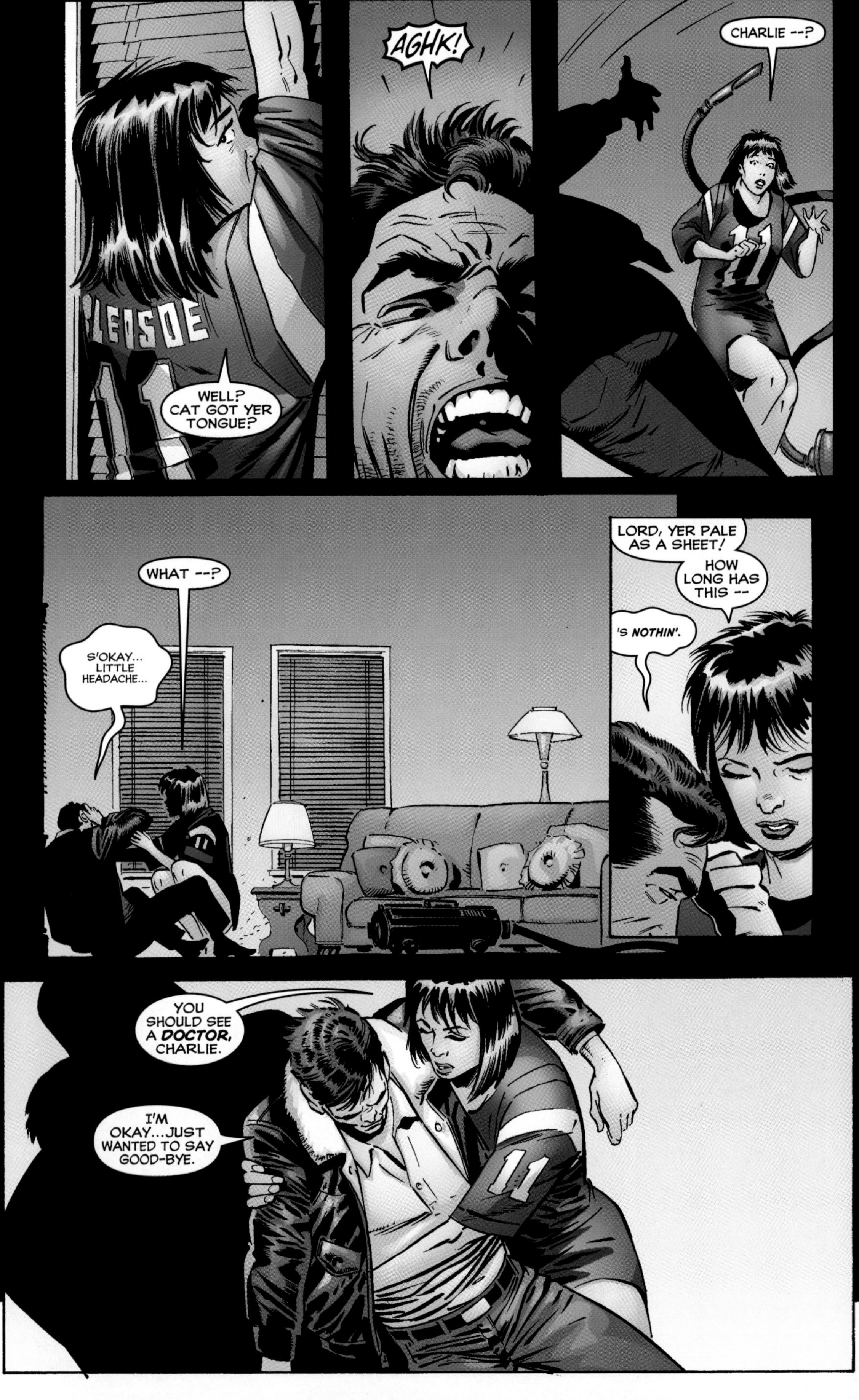
WELL? CAT GOT YER TONGUE?
AGHK!
CHARLIE --?
WHAT --?
S'OKAY... LITTLE HEADACHE...
LORD, YER PALE AS A SHEET!
HOW LONG HAS THIS --
'S NOTHIN'.
YOU SHOULD SEE A DOCTOR, CHARLIE.
I'M OKAY...JUST WANTED TO SAY GOOD-BYE.

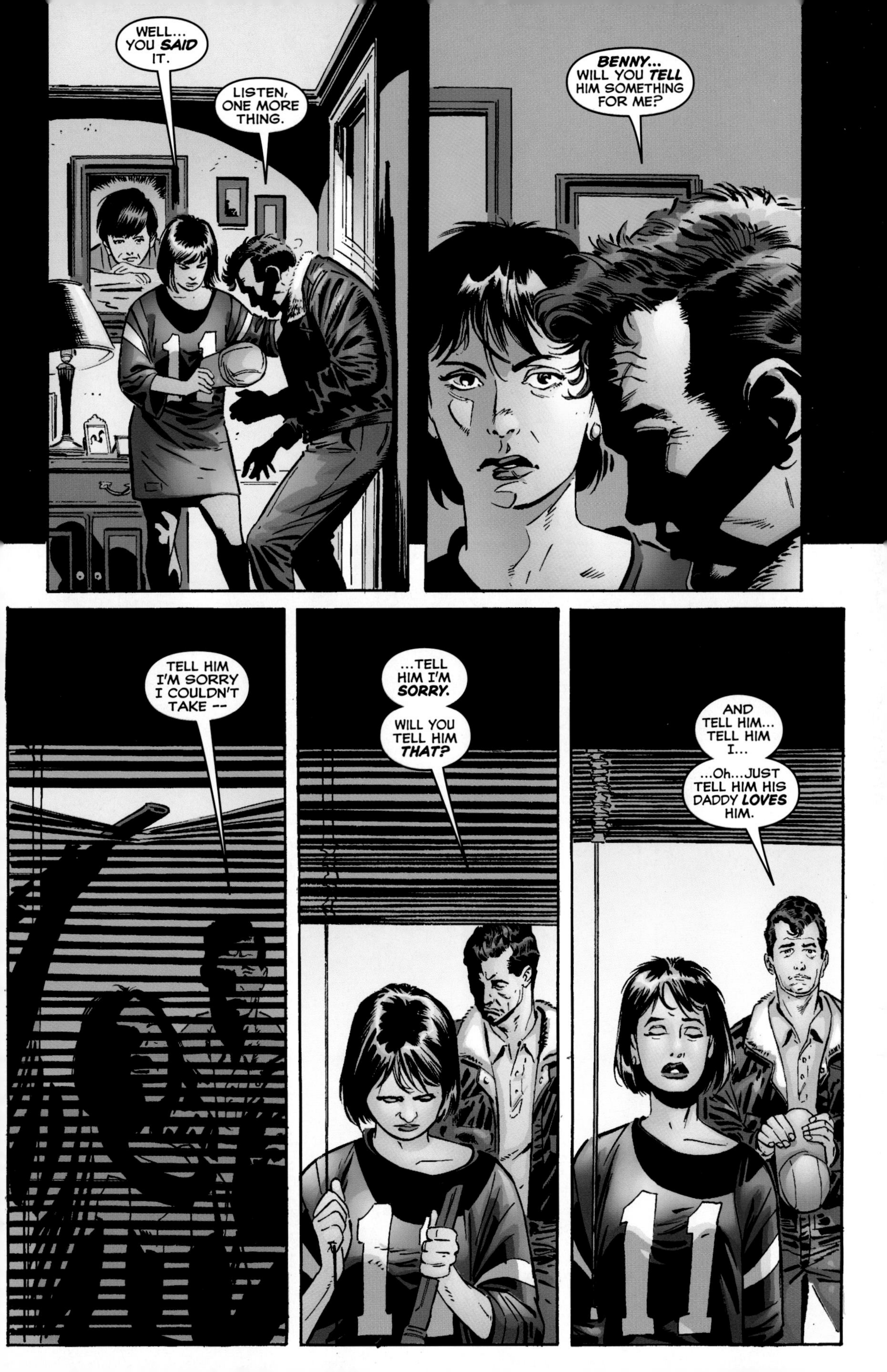
WELL... YOU **SAID** IT.
LISTEN, ONE MORE THING.
BENNY... WILL YOU **TELL** HIM SOMETHING FOR ME?
TELL HIM I'M SORRY I COULDN'T TAKE --
...TELL HIM I'M **SORRY.**
WILL YOU TELL HIM **THAT?**
AND TELL HIM... TELL HIM I...
...Oh...JUST TELL HIM HIS DADDY **LOVES** HIM.

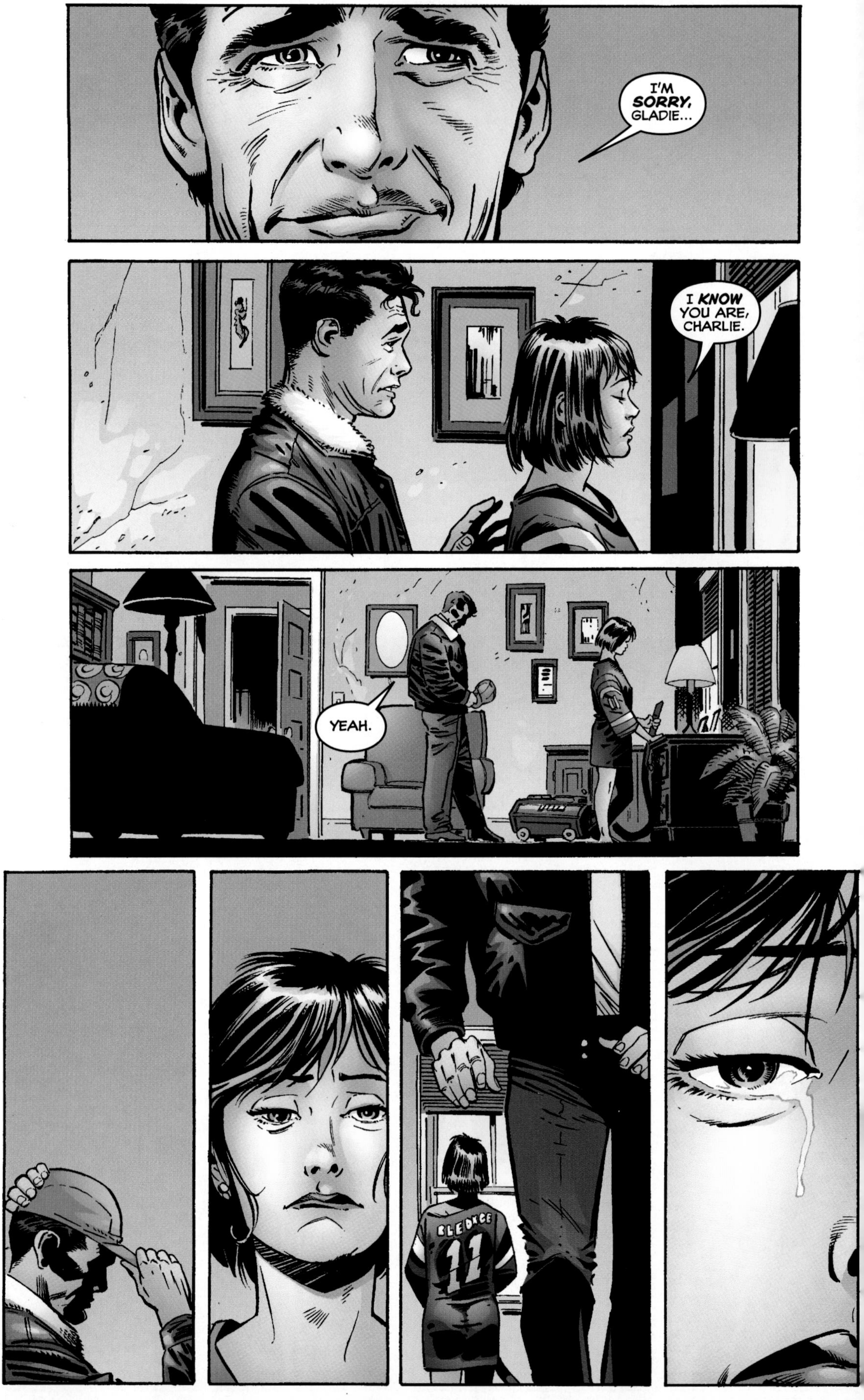
I'M **SORRY,** GLADIE...
I **KNOW** YOU ARE, CHARLIE.
YEAH.

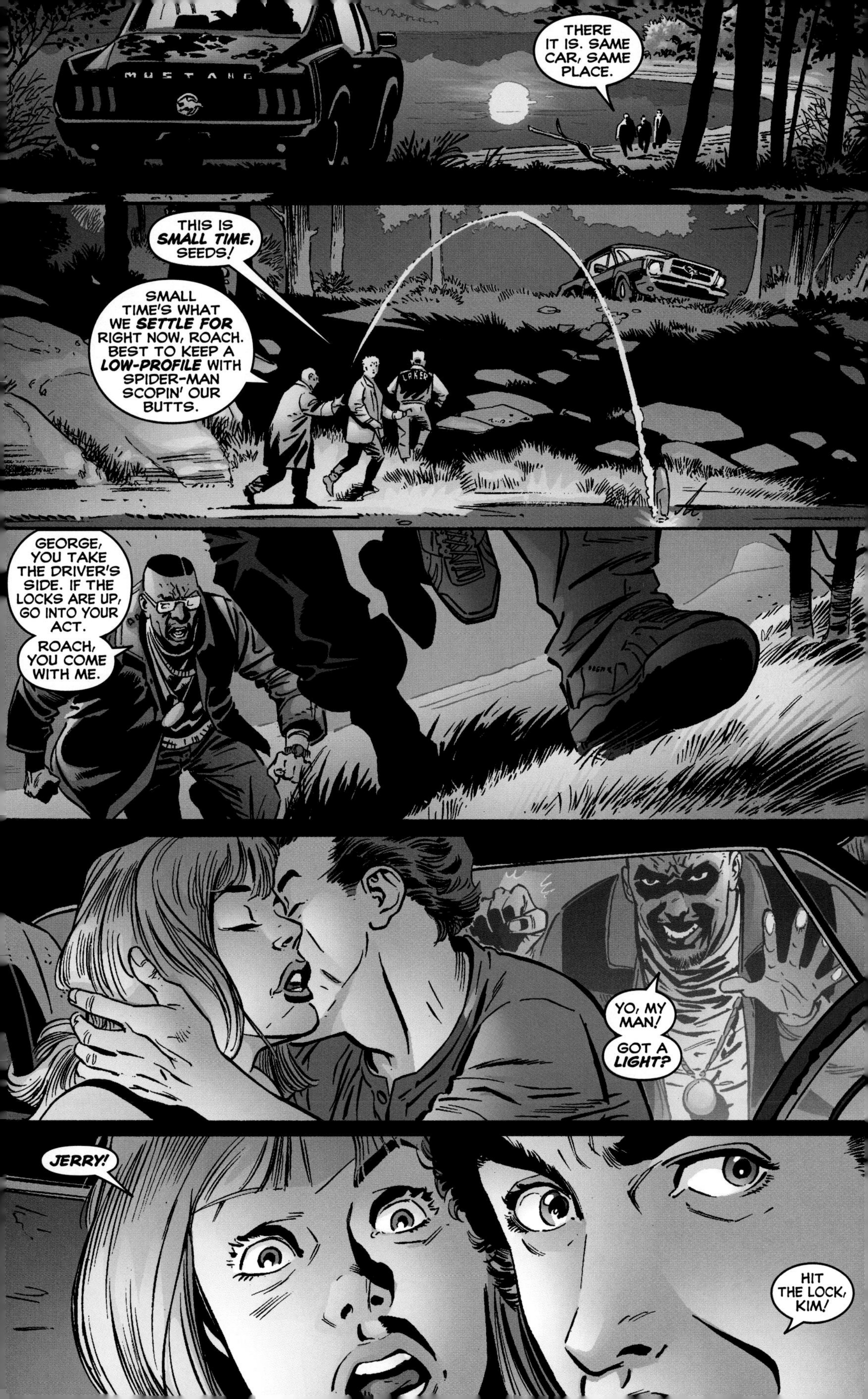
THERE IT IS. SAME CAR, SAME PLACE.
THIS IS SMALL TIME, SEEDS!
SMALL TIME'S WHAT WE SETTLE FOR RIGHT NOW, ROACH. BEST TO KEEP A LOW-PROFILE WITH SPIDER-MAN SCOPIN' OUR BUTTS.
GEORGE, YOU TAKE THE DRIVER'S SIDE. IF THE LOCKS ARE UP, GO INTO YOUR ACT.
ROACH, YOU COME WITH ME.
YO, MY MAN!
GOT A LIGHT?
JERRY!
HIT THE LOCK, KIM!

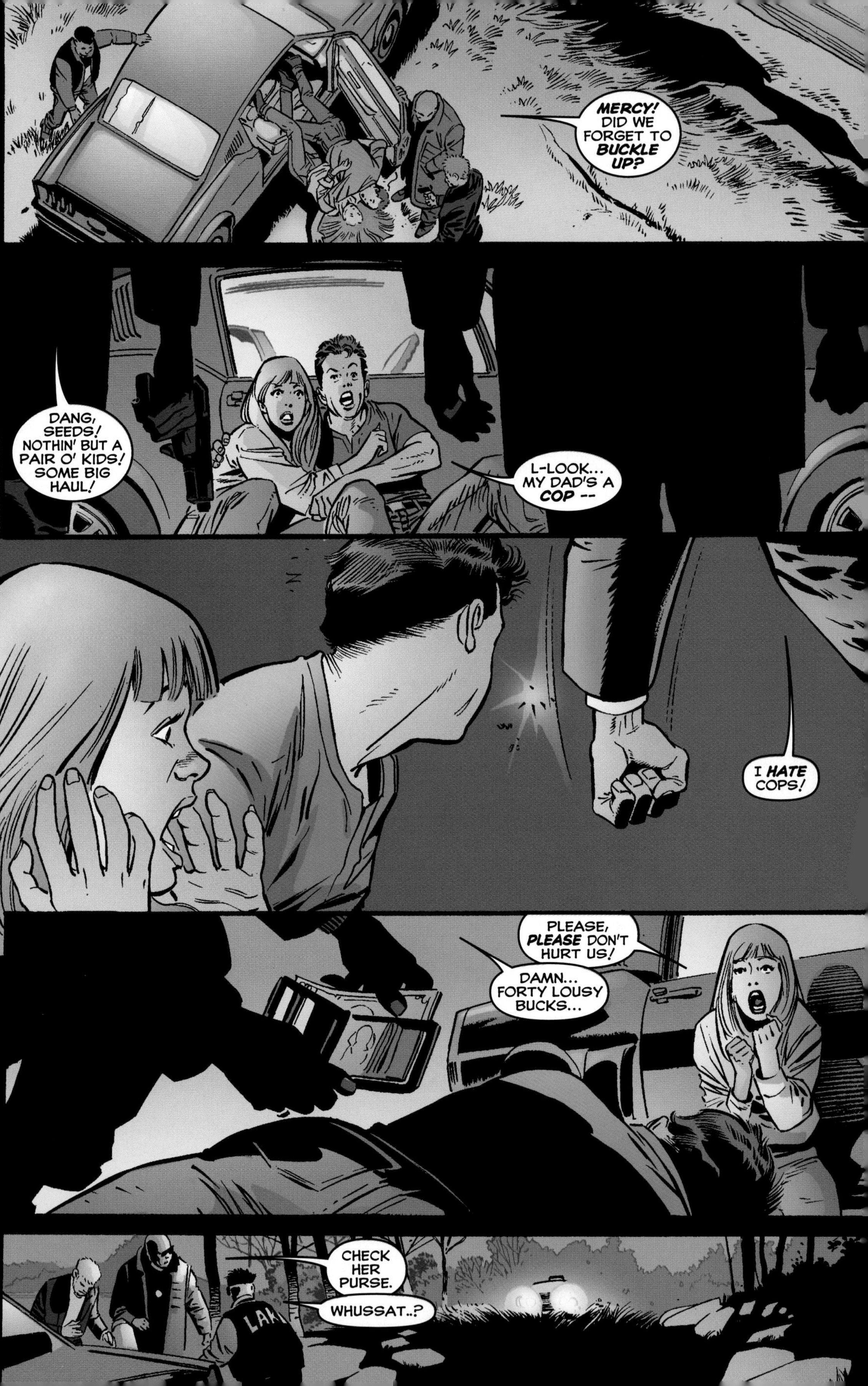
MERCY! DID WE FORGET TO BUCKLE UP?
DANG, SEEDS! NOTHIN' BUT A PAIR O' KIDS! SOME BIG HAUL!
L-LOOK... MY DAD'S A COP --
I HATE COPS!
PLEASE, PLEASE DON'T HURT US!
DAMN... FORTY LOUSY BUCKS...
CHECK HER PURSE.
WHUSSAT..?

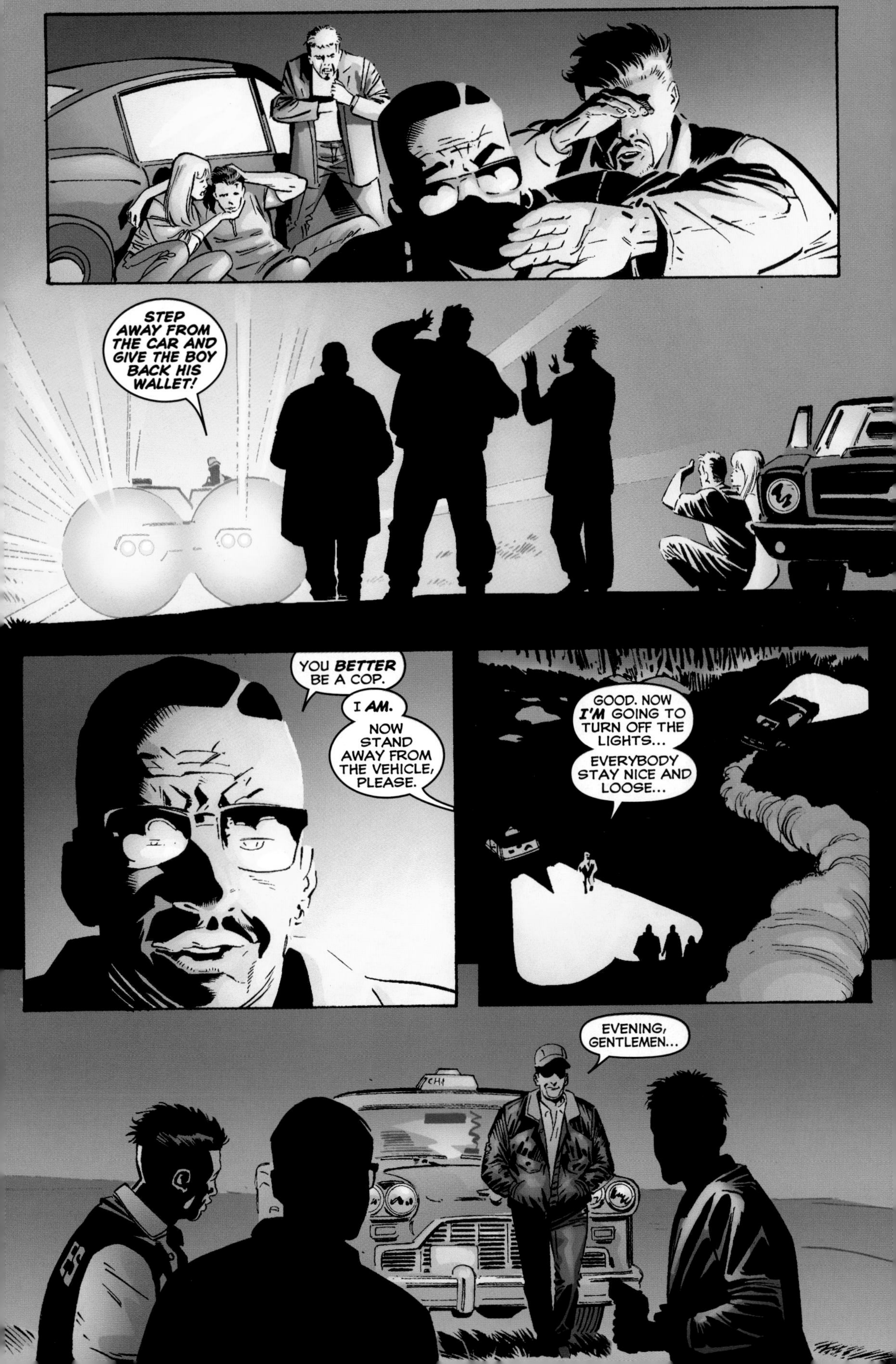
STEP AWAY FROM THE CAR AND GIVE THE BOY BACK HIS WALLET!
YOU BETTER BE A COP.
I AM.
NOW STAND AWAY FROM THE VEHICLE, PLEASE.
GOOD. NOW I'M GOING TO TURN OFF THE LIGHTS...
EVERYBODY STAY NICE AND LOOSE...
EVENING, GENTLEMEN...

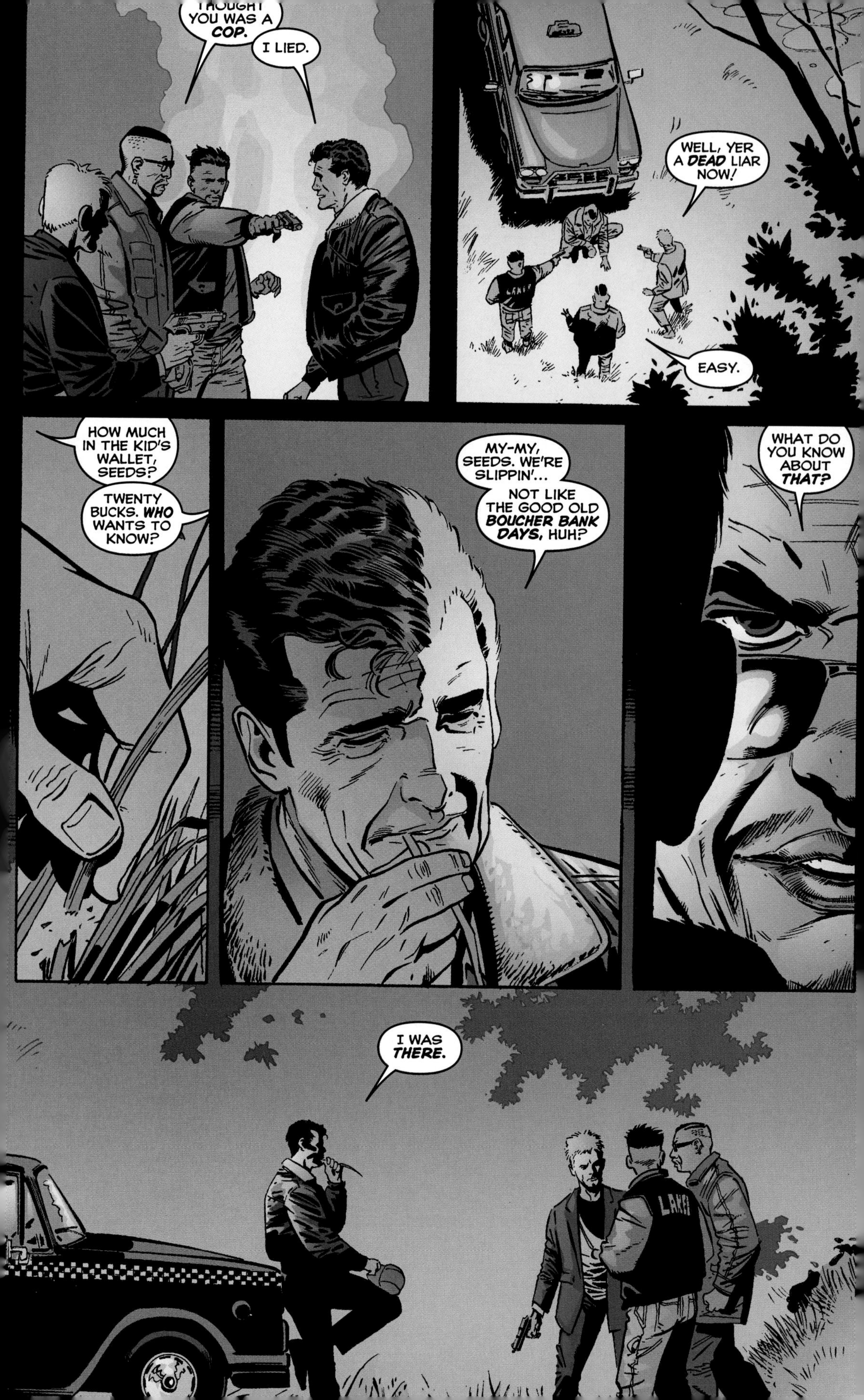
THOUGHT YOU WAS A COP.
I LIED.
WELL, YER A DEAD LIAR NOW!
EASY.
HOW MUCH IN THE KID'S WALLET, SEEDS?
TWENTY BUCKS. WHO WANTS TO KNOW?
MY-MY, SEEDS. WE'RE SLIPPIN'...
NOT LIKE THE GOOD OLD BOUCHER BANK DAYS, HUH?
WHAT DO YOU KNOW ABOUT THAT?
I WAS THERE.

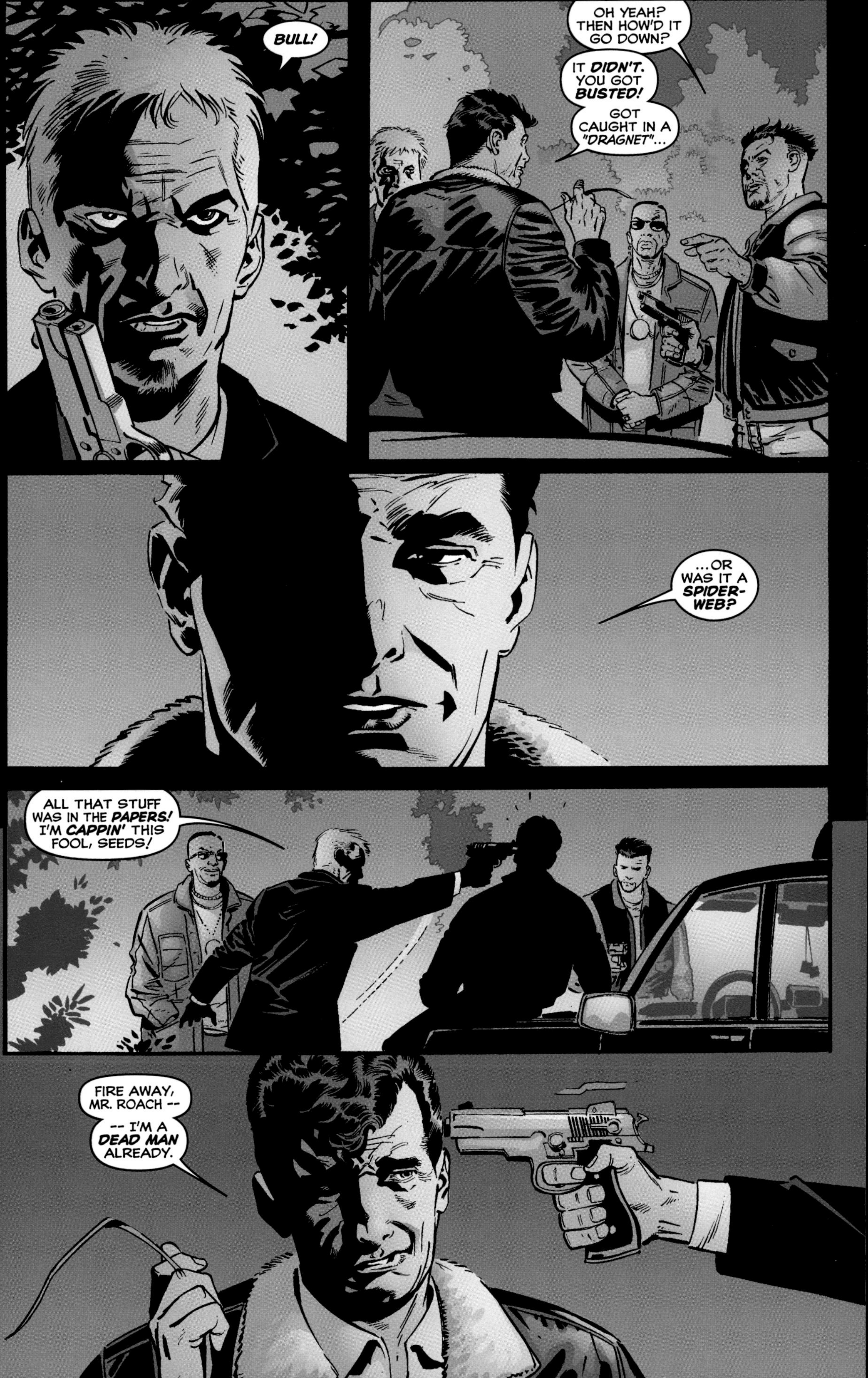
BULL!
OH YEAH? THEN HOW'D IT GO DOWN?
IT DIDN'T. YOU GOT BUSTED!
GOT CAUGHT IN A "DRAGNET"...
...OR WAS IT A SPIDER-WEB?
ALL THAT STUFF WAS IN THE PAPERS! I'M CAPPIN' THIS FOOL, SEEDS!
FIRE AWAY, MR. ROACH --
-- I'M A DEAD MAN ALREADY.

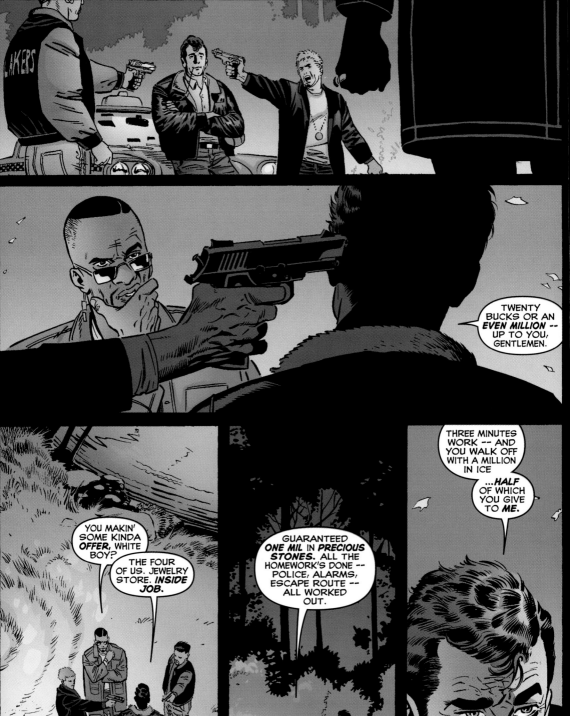

TWENTY BUCKS OR AN *EVEN MILLION* -- UP TO YOU, GENTLEMEN.

THREE MINUTES WORK -- AND YOU WALK OFF WITH A MILLION IN ICE

...*HALF* OF WHICH YOU GIVE TO *ME*.

YOU MAKIN' SOME KINDA *OFFER,* WHITE BOY?

THE FOUR OF US. JEWELRY STORE. *INSIDE JOB.*

GUARANTEED *ONE MIL* IN *PRECIOUS STONES.* ALL THE HOMEWORK'S DONE -- POLICE, ALARMS, ESCAPE ROUTE -- ALL WORKED OUT.

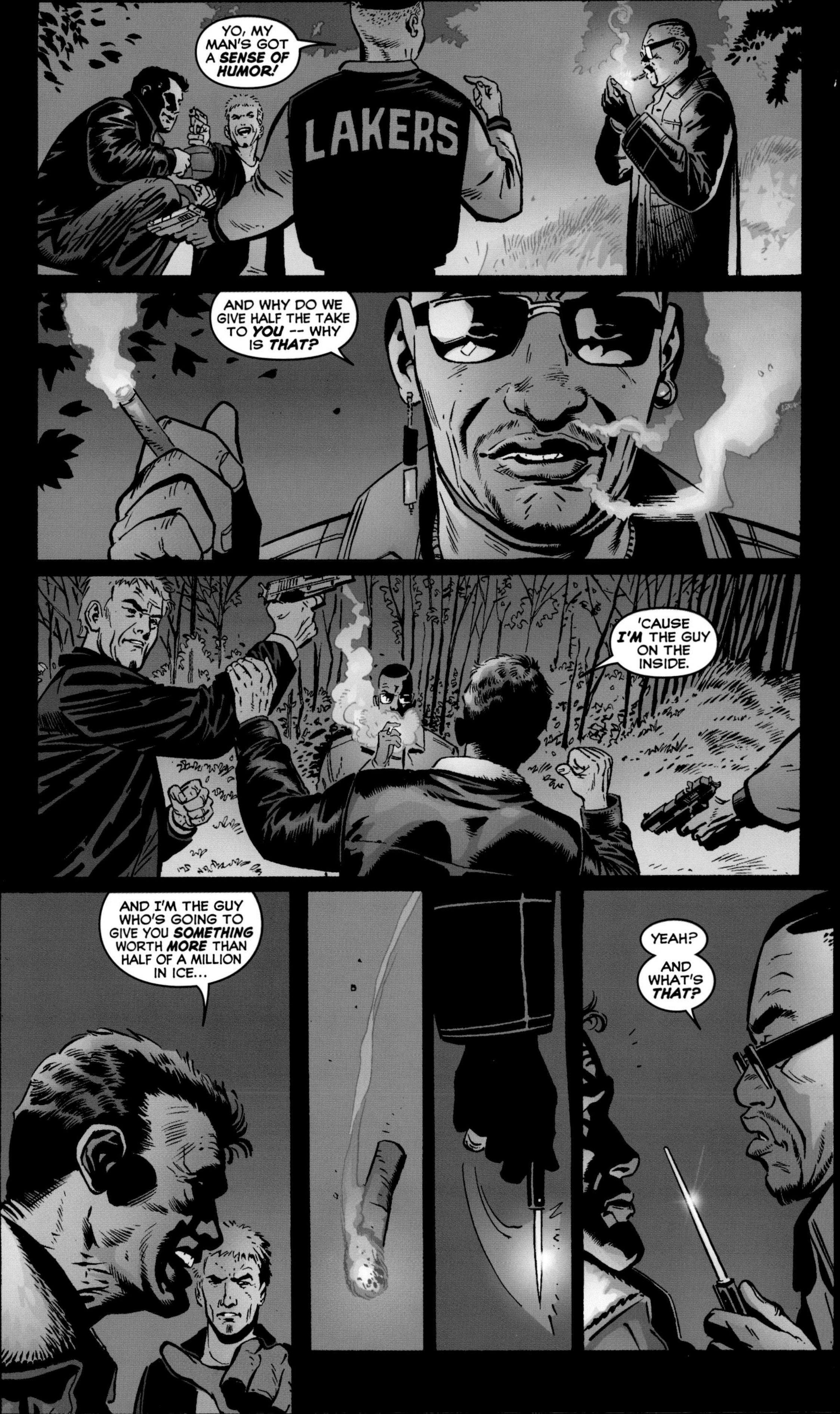
LAKERS
YO, MY MAN'S GOT A SENSE OF HUMOR!
AND WHY DO WE GIVE HALF THE TAKE TO YOU -- WHY IS THAT?
'CAUSE I'M THE GUY ON THE INSIDE.
AND I'M THE GUY WHO'S GOING TO GIVE YOU SOMETHING WORTH MORE THAN HALF OF A MILLION IN ICE...
YEAH?
AND WHAT'S THAT?

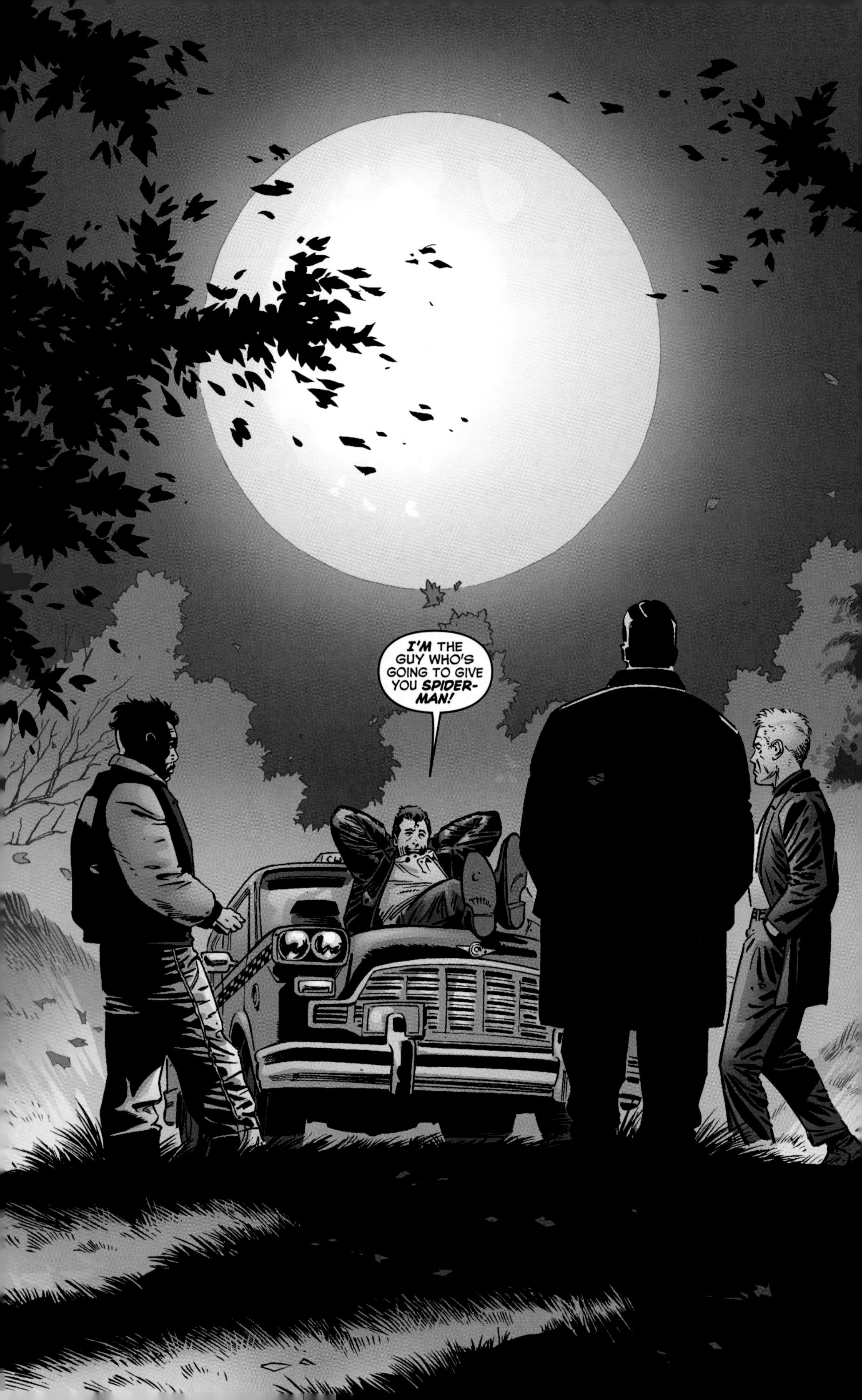
I'M THE GUY WHO'S GOING TO GIVE YOU SPIDER-MAN!

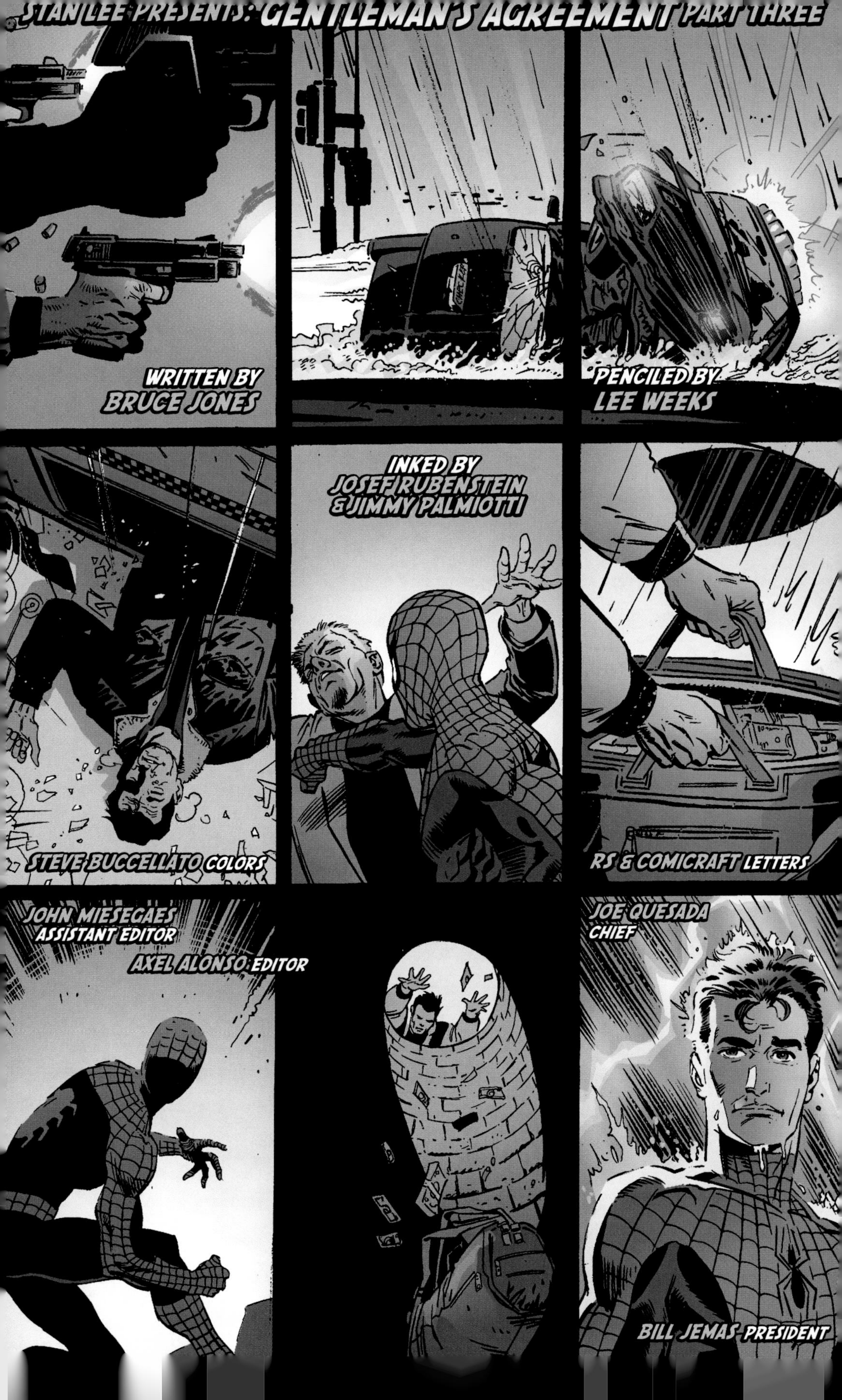
STAN LEE PRESENTS: GENTLEMAN'S AGREEMENT PART THREE
WRITTEN BY BRUCE JONES
PENCILED BY LEE WEEKS
INKED BY JOSEF RUBENSTEIN & JIMMY PALMIOTTI
STEVE BUCCELLATO COLORS
RS & COMICRAFT LETTERS
JOHN MIESEGAES ASSISTANT EDITOR
AXEL ALONSO EDITOR
JOE QUESADA CHIEF
BILL JEMAS PRESIDENT

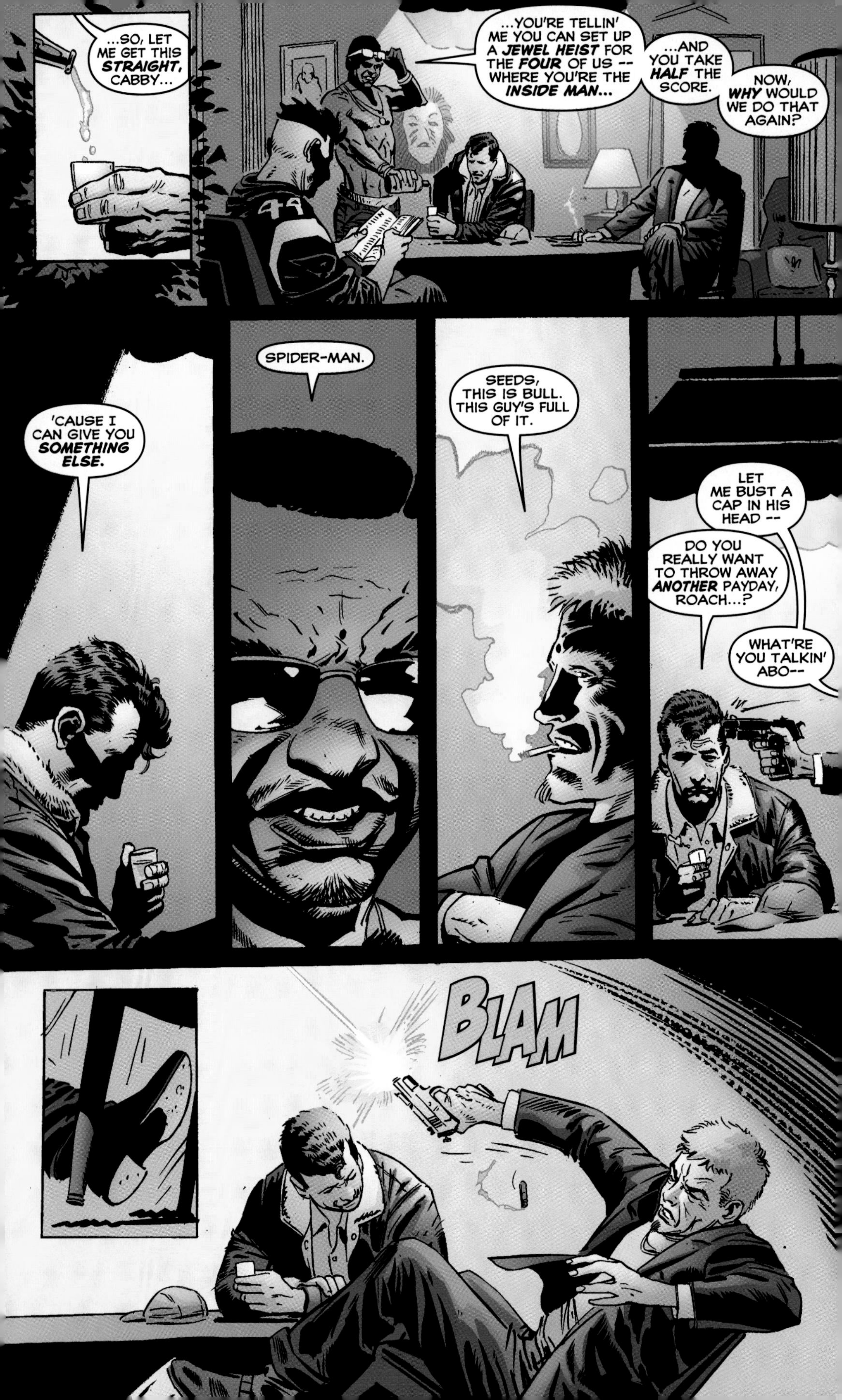

...SO, LET ME GET THIS STRAIGHT, CABBY...
...YOU'RE TELLIN' ME YOU CAN SET UP A JEWEL HEIST FOR THE FOUR OF US -- WHERE YOU'RE THE INSIDE MAN...
...AND YOU TAKE HALF THE SCORE.
NOW, WHY WOULD WE DO THAT AGAIN?
'CAUSE I CAN GIVE YOU SOMETHING ELSE.
SPIDER-MAN.
SEEDS, THIS IS BULL. THIS GUY'S FULL OF IT.
LET ME BUST A CAP IN HIS HEAD --
DO YOU REALLY WANT TO THROW AWAY ANOTHER PAYDAY, ROACH...?
WHAT'RE YOU TALKIN' ABO--
BLAM

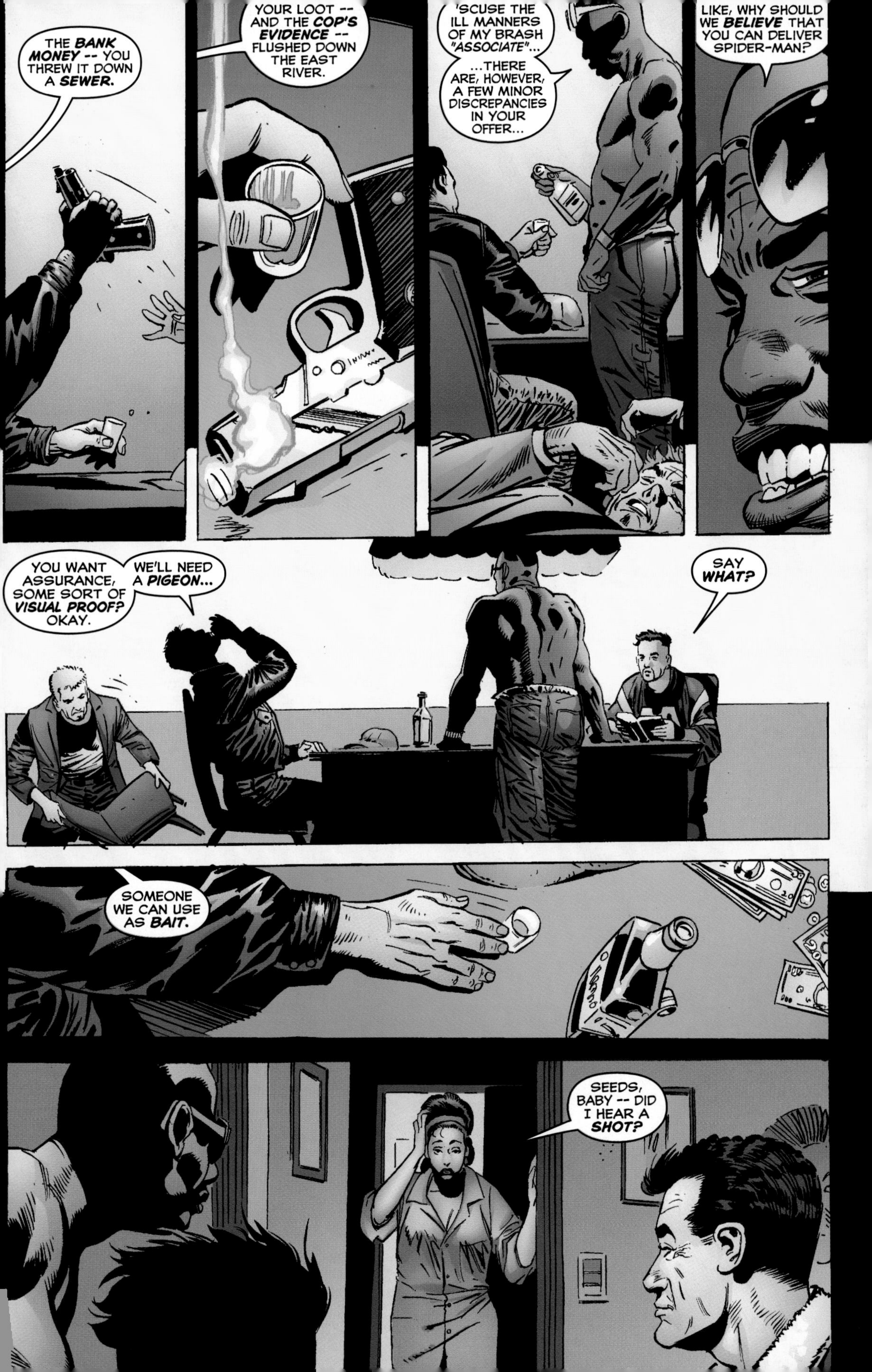
THE BANK MONEY -- YOU THREW IT DOWN A SEWER.
YOUR LOOT -- AND THE COP'S EVIDENCE -- FLUSHED DOWN THE EAST RIVER.
'SCUSE THE ILL MANNERS OF MY BRASH "ASSOCIATE"...
...THERE ARE, HOWEVER, A FEW MINOR DISCREPANCIES IN YOUR OFFER...
LIKE, WHY SHOULD WE BELIEVE THAT YOU CAN DELIVER SPIDER-MAN?
YOU WANT ASSURANCE, SOME SORT OF VISUAL PROOF? OKAY.
WE'LL NEED A PIGEON...
SAY WHAT?
SOMEONE WE CAN USE AS BAIT.
SEEDS, BABY -- DID I HEAR A SHOT?

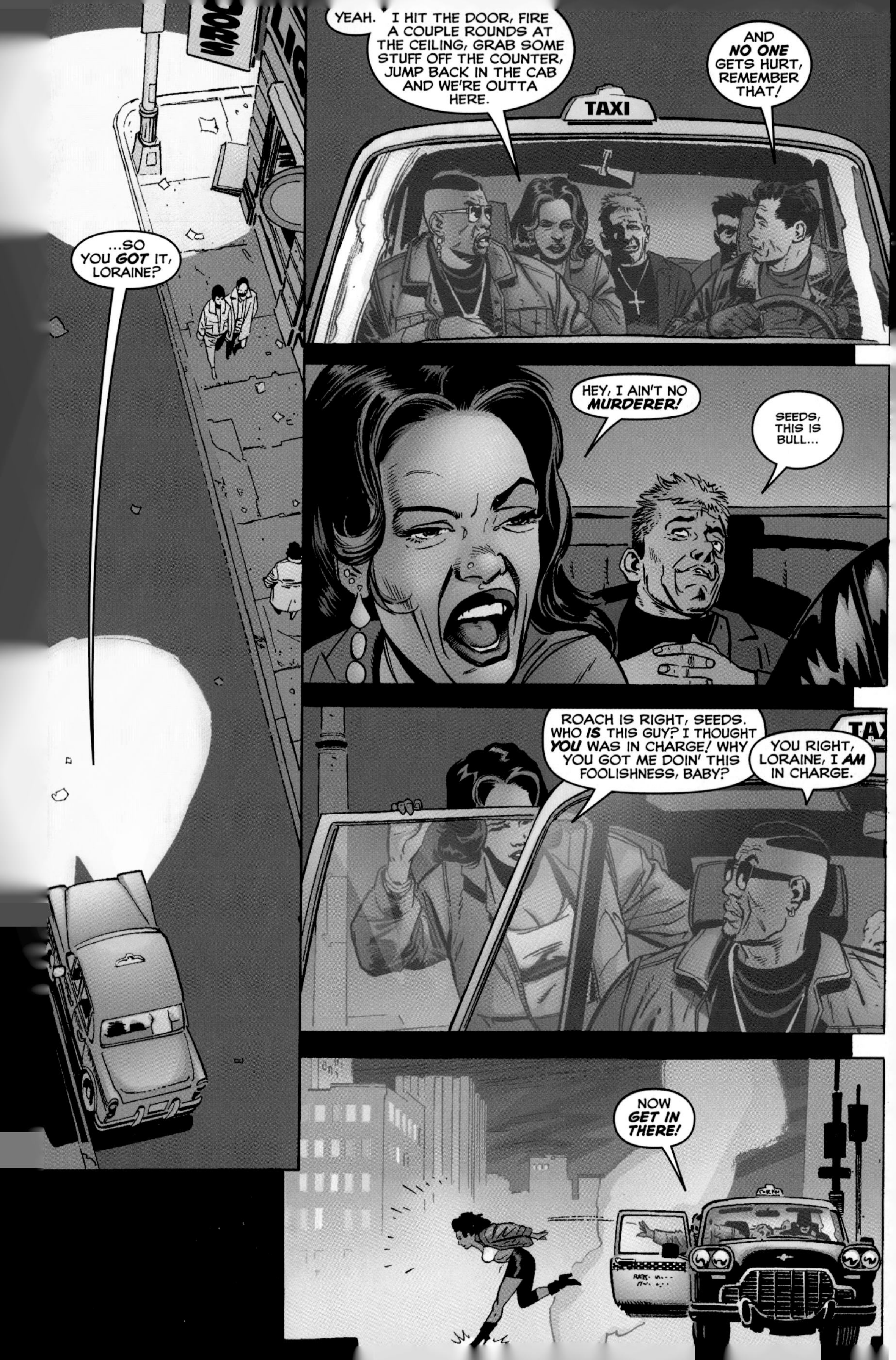

...SO YOU GOT IT, LORAINE?
YEAH. I HIT THE DOOR, FIRE A COUPLE ROUNDS AT THE CEILING, GRAB SOME STUFF OFF THE COUNTER, JUMP BACK IN THE CAB AND WE'RE OUTTA HERE.
AND NO ONE GETS HURT, REMEMBER THAT!
TAXI
HEY, I AIN'T NO MURDERER!
SEEDS, THIS IS BULL...
ROACH IS RIGHT, SEEDS. WHO IS THIS GUY? I THOUGHT YOU WAS IN CHARGE! WHY YOU GOT ME DOIN' THIS FOOLISHNESS, BABY?
YOU RIGHT, LORAINE, I AM IN CHARGE.
NOW GET IN THERE!

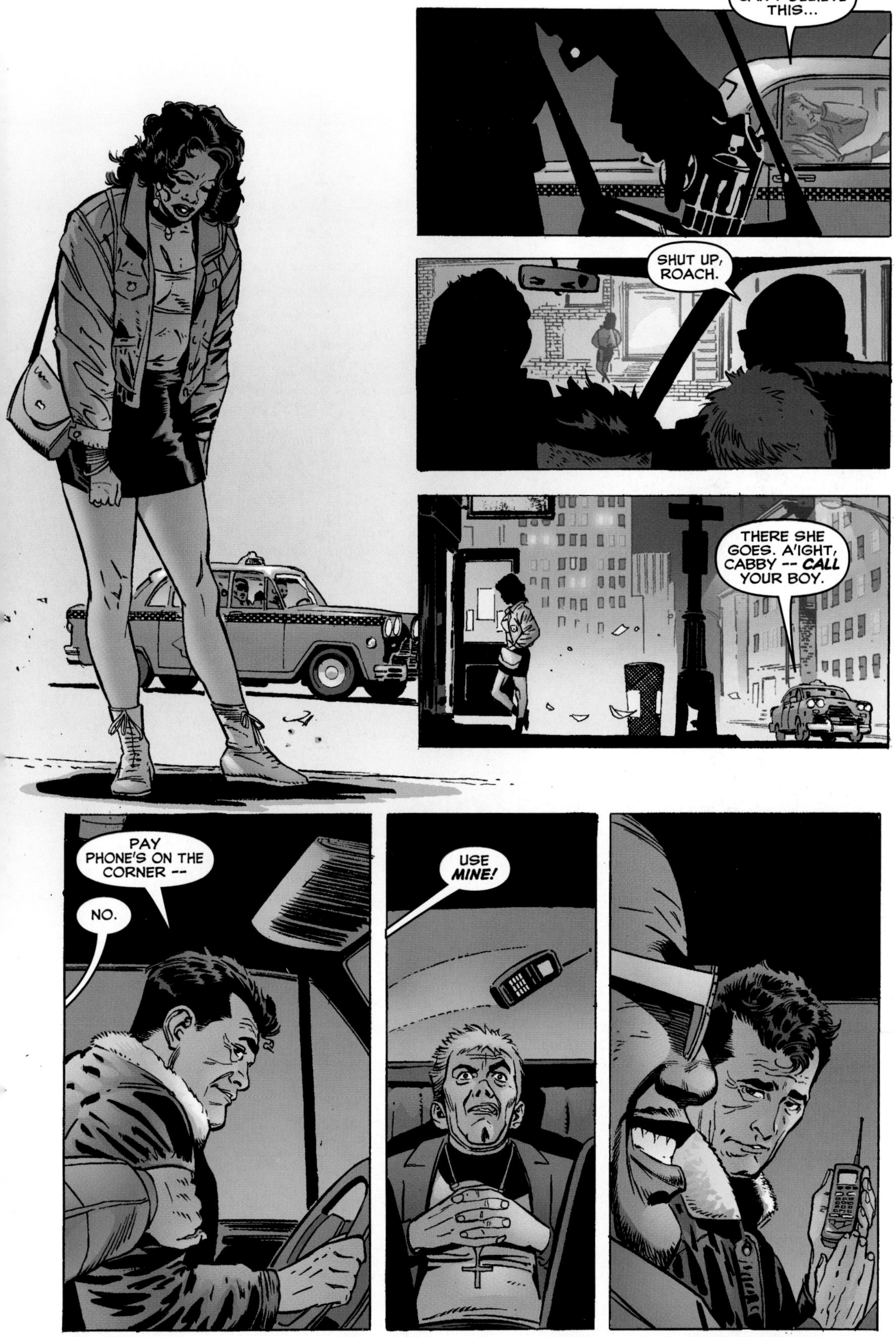
SEEDS, I CAN'T BELIEVE THIS...
SHUT UP, ROACH.
THERE SHE GOES. A'IGHT, CABBY -- CALL YOUR BOY.
PAY PHONE'S ON THE CORNER --
NO.
USE MINE!

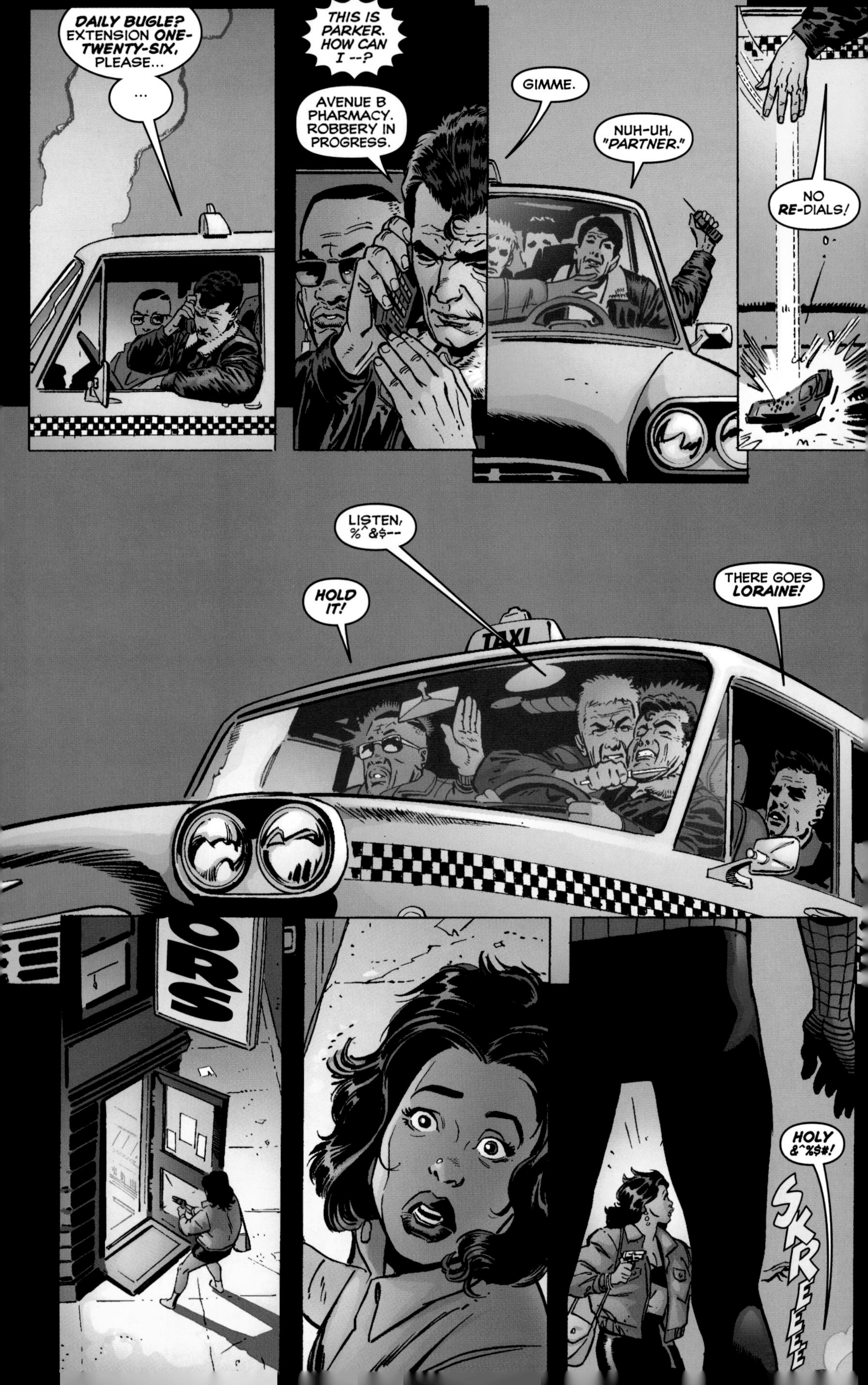
DAILY BUGLE? EXTENSION ONE-TWENTY-SIX, PLEASE...
...
THIS IS PARKER. HOW CAN I --?
AVENUE B PHARMACY. ROBBERY IN PROGRESS.
GIMME.
NUH-UH, "PARTNER."
NO RE-DIALS!
LISTEN, %^&$--
HOLD IT!
THERE GOES LORAINE!
HOLY &^%$#!
SKREEEE

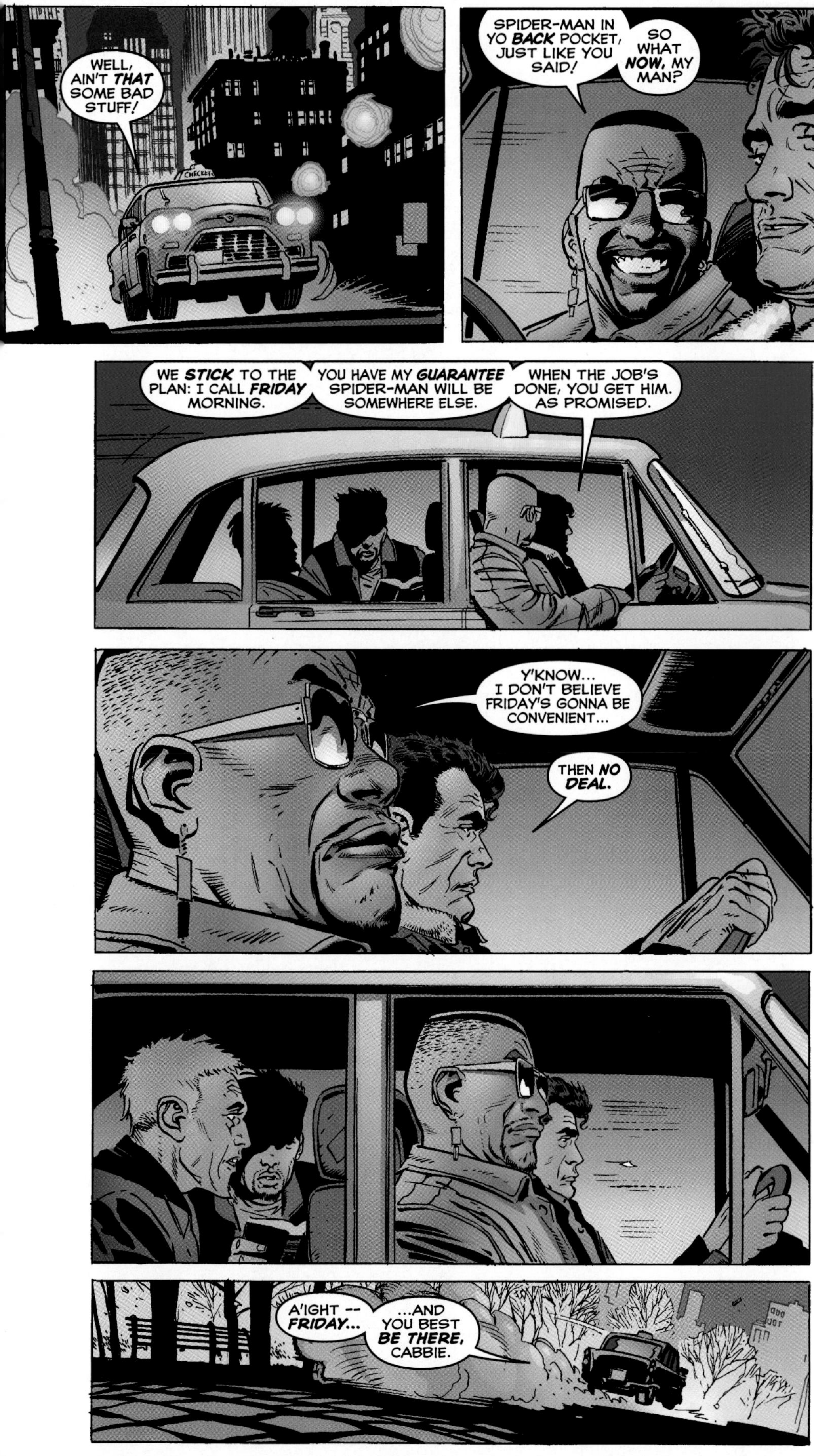
WELL, AIN'T THAT SOME BAD STUFF!
CHECKER
SPIDER-MAN IN YO BACK POCKET, JUST LIKE YOU SAID!
SO WHAT NOW, MY MAN?
WE STICK TO THE PLAN: I CALL FRIDAY MORNING.
YOU HAVE MY GUARANTEE SPIDER-MAN WILL BE SOMEWHERE ELSE.
WHEN THE JOB'S DONE, YOU GET HIM. AS PROMISED.
Y'KNOW... I DON'T BELIEVE FRIDAY'S GONNA BE CONVENIENT...
THEN NO DEAL.
A'IGHT -- FRIDAY...
...AND YOU BEST BE THERE, CABBIE.

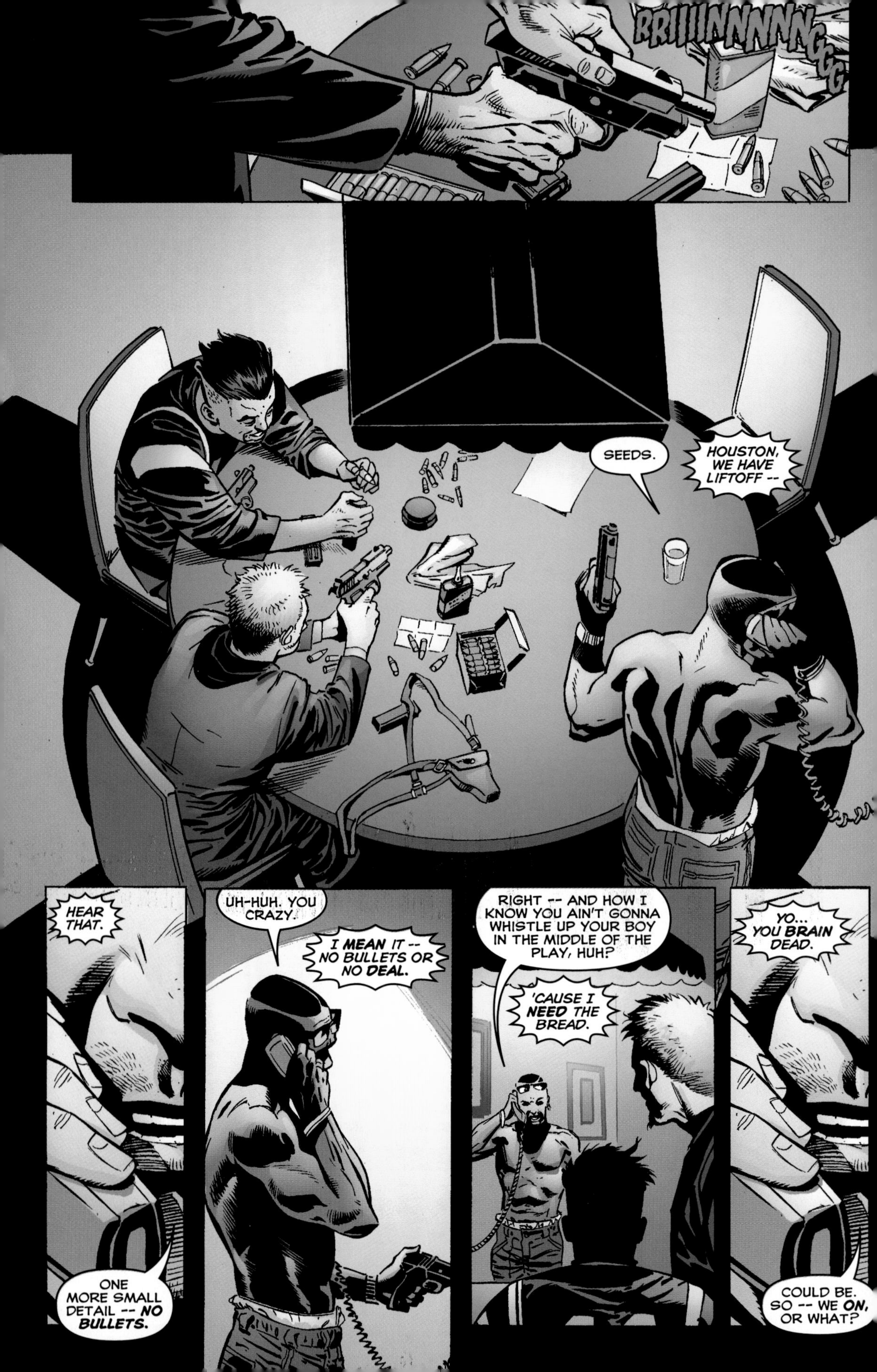
RRIIIINNNNNGGG
SEEDS.
HOUSTON, WE HAVE LIFTOFF --
HEAR THAT.
ONE MORE SMALL DETAIL -- NO BULLETS.
UH-HUH. YOU CRAZY.
I MEAN IT -- NO BULLETS OR NO DEAL.
RIGHT -- AND HOW I KNOW YOU AIN'T GONNA WHISTLE UP YOUR BOY IN THE MIDDLE OF THE PLAY, HUH?
'CAUSE I NEED THE BREAD.
YO... YOU BRAIN DEAD.
COULD BE. SO -- WE ON, OR WHAT?

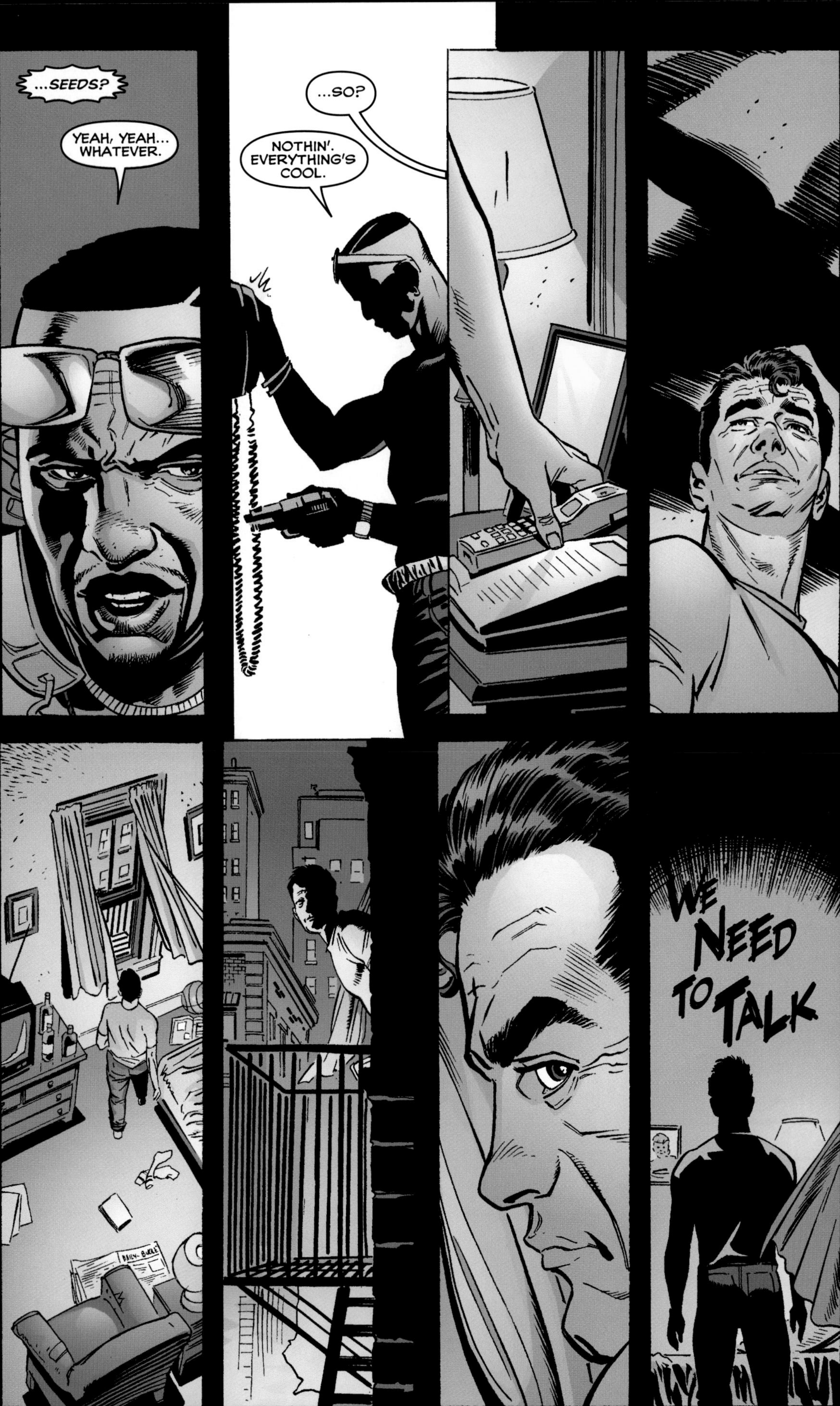
...SEEDS?
YEAH, YEAH... WHATEVER.
...SO?
NOTHIN'. EVERYTHING'S COOL.
DAILY BUGLE
WE NEED TO TALK

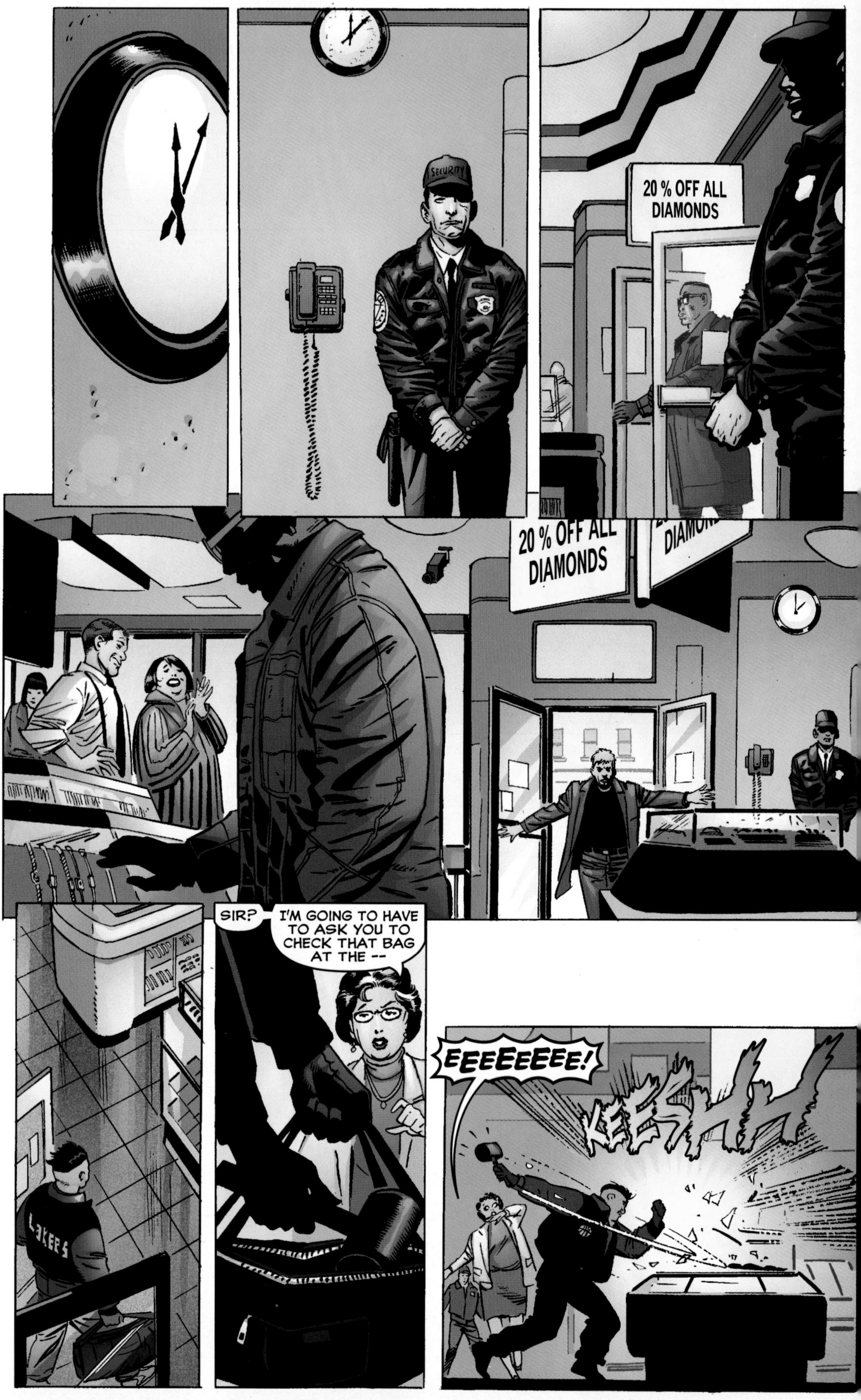
SECURITY
20 % OFF ALL DIAMONDS
20 % OFF ALL DIAMONDS
SIR?
I'M GOING TO HAVE TO ASK YOU TO CHECK THAT BAG AT THE --
EEEEEEEE!
KEESHH

AWRIGHT, PEOPLE, YOU KNOW THE DRILL!

ON YER *FACES!* NOBODY GETS CUTE AND WE'LL GET THROUGH THIS!

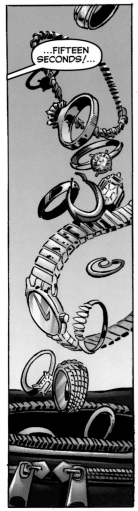

...FIFTEEN SECONDS!...

HEY, MAN! YOU IN LOVE WITH ME?

...N-NO, SIR!

THEN WHY YOU *LOOKIN'* AT ME?

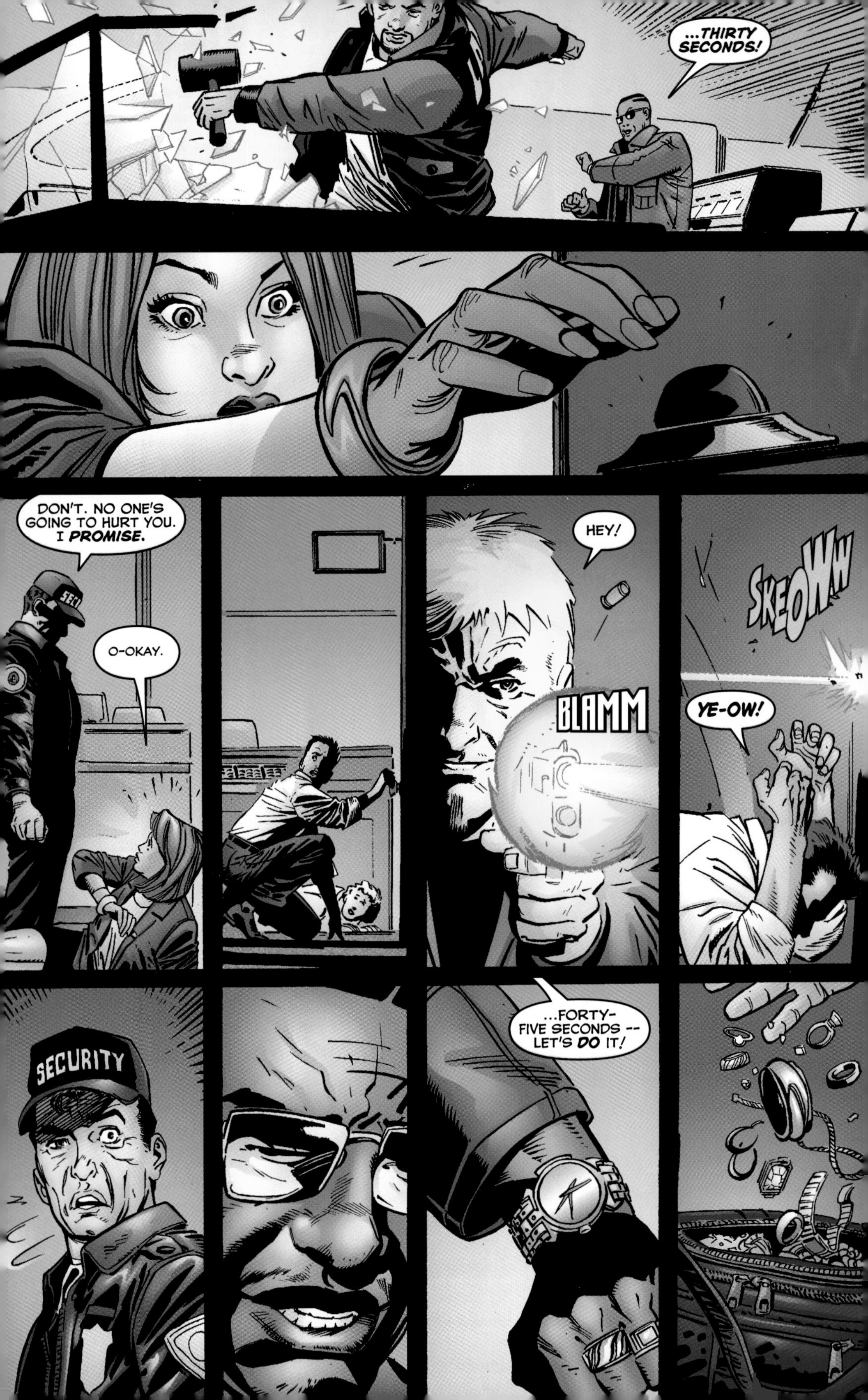
...THIRTY SECONDS!
DON'T. NO ONE'S GOING TO HURT YOU. I PROMISE.
O-OKAY.
HEY!
BLAMM
SKEOWW
YE-OW!
SECURITY
...FORTY-FIVE SECONDS -- LET'S DO IT!

CLANGCLANGCLANGCLANG

MOVE!

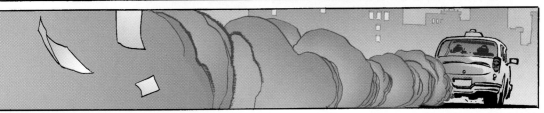

RIGHT NOW! GIVE! SPIDER-MAN -- WHO is he?

DAMMIT, SEEDS -- WE AGREED NO BULLETS!

I WON'T ASK TWICE...

I'M MEETING HIM TONIGHT AT THIS ADDRESS.

NINE SHARP.

GIVE THIS MAN HIS SHARE...

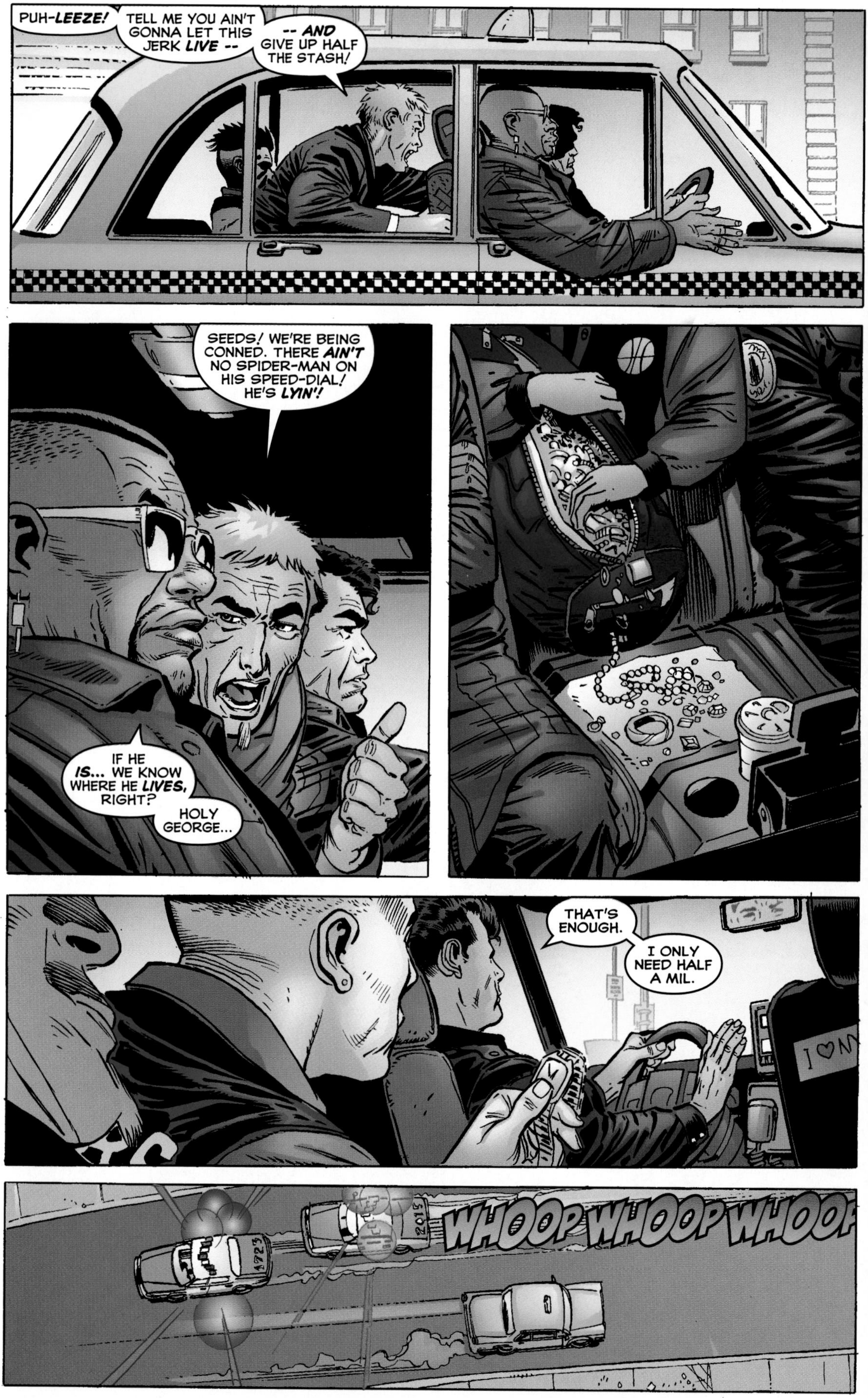
PUH-**LEEZE!**
TELL ME YOU AIN'T GONNA LET THIS JERK **LIVE** --
-- **AND** GIVE UP HALF THE STASH!
SEEDS! WE'RE BEING CONNED. THERE **AIN'T** NO SPIDER-MAN ON HIS SPEED-DIAL! HE'S **LYIN'!**
IF HE **IS...** WE KNOW WHERE HE **LIVES,** RIGHT?
HOLY GEORGE...
THAT'S ENOUGH.
I ONLY NEED HALF A MIL.
WHOOP WHOOP WHOOP

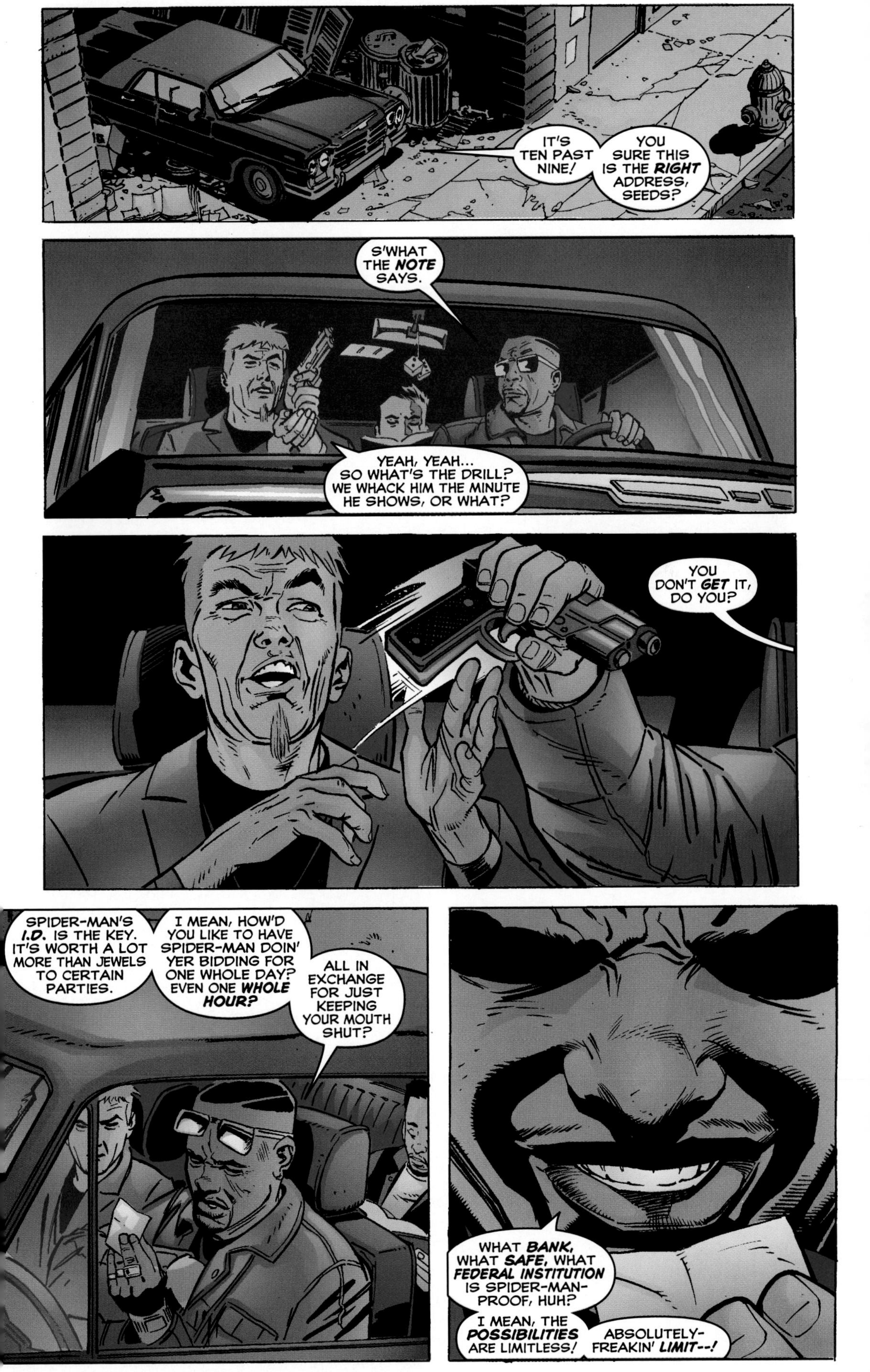
IT'S TEN PAST NINE!
YOU SURE THIS IS THE RIGHT ADDRESS, SEEDS?
S'WHAT THE NOTE SAYS.
YEAH, YEAH... SO WHAT'S THE DRILL? WE WHACK HIM THE MINUTE HE SHOWS, OR WHAT?
YOU DON'T GET IT, DO YOU?
SPIDER-MAN'S I.D. IS THE KEY. IT'S WORTH A LOT MORE THAN JEWELS TO CERTAIN PARTIES.
I MEAN, HOW'D YOU LIKE TO HAVE SPIDER-MAN DOIN' YER BIDDING FOR ONE WHOLE DAY? EVEN ONE WHOLE HOUR?
ALL IN EXCHANGE FOR JUST KEEPING YOUR MOUTH SHUT?
WHAT BANK, WHAT SAFE, WHAT FEDERAL INSTITUTION IS SPIDER-MAN-PROOF, HUH?
I MEAN, THE POSSIBILITIES ARE LIMITLESS!
ABSOLUTELY-FREAKIN' LIMIT--!

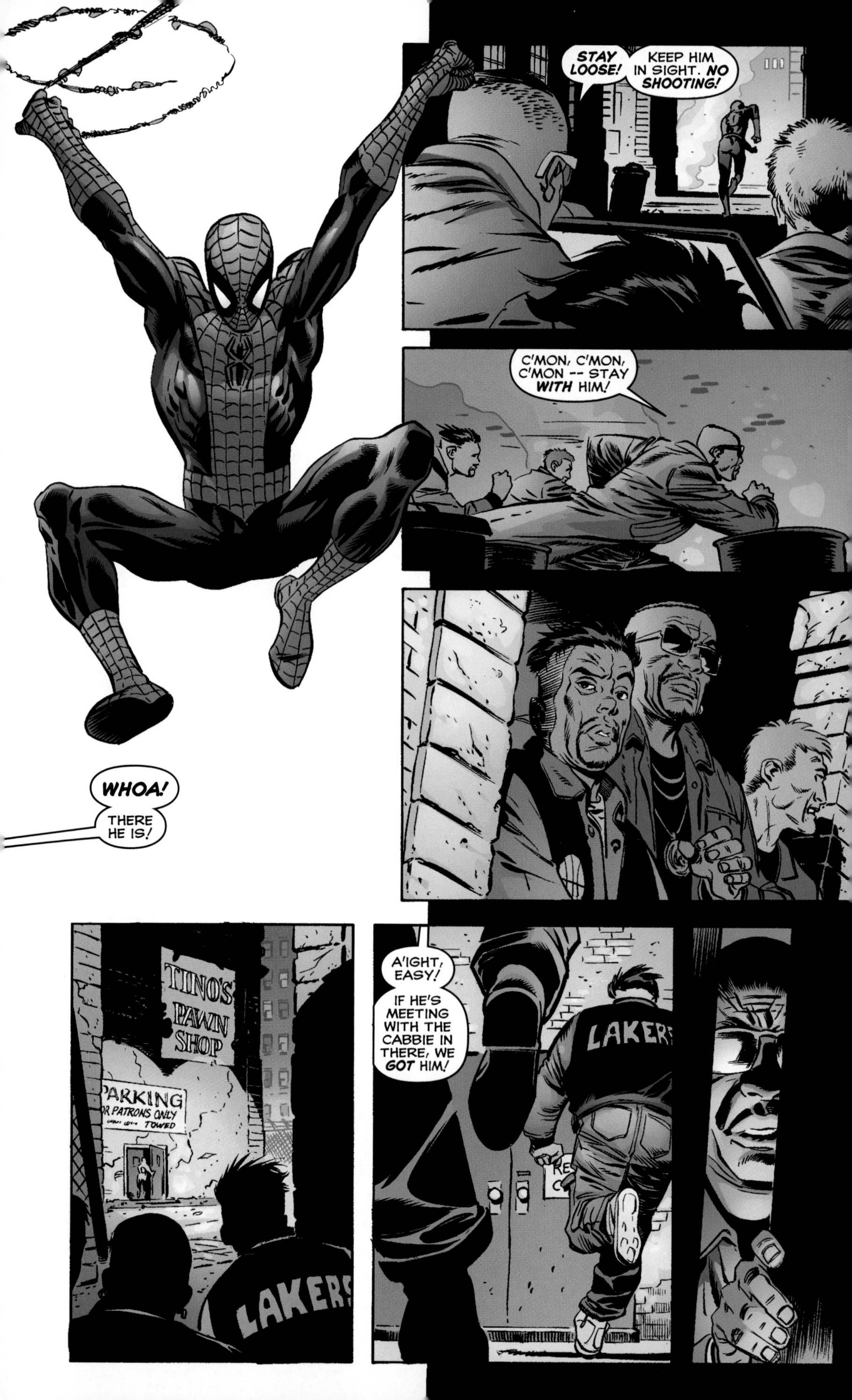
STAY LOOSE!
KEEP HIM IN SIGHT. NO SHOOTING!
C'MON, C'MON, C'MON -- STAY WITH HIM!
WHOA!
THERE HE IS!
TINO'S PAWN SHOP
PARKING FOR PATRONS ONLY
TOWED
LAKERS
A'IGHT, EASY!
IF HE'S MEETING WITH THE CABBIE IN THERE, WE GOT HIM!
LAKERS

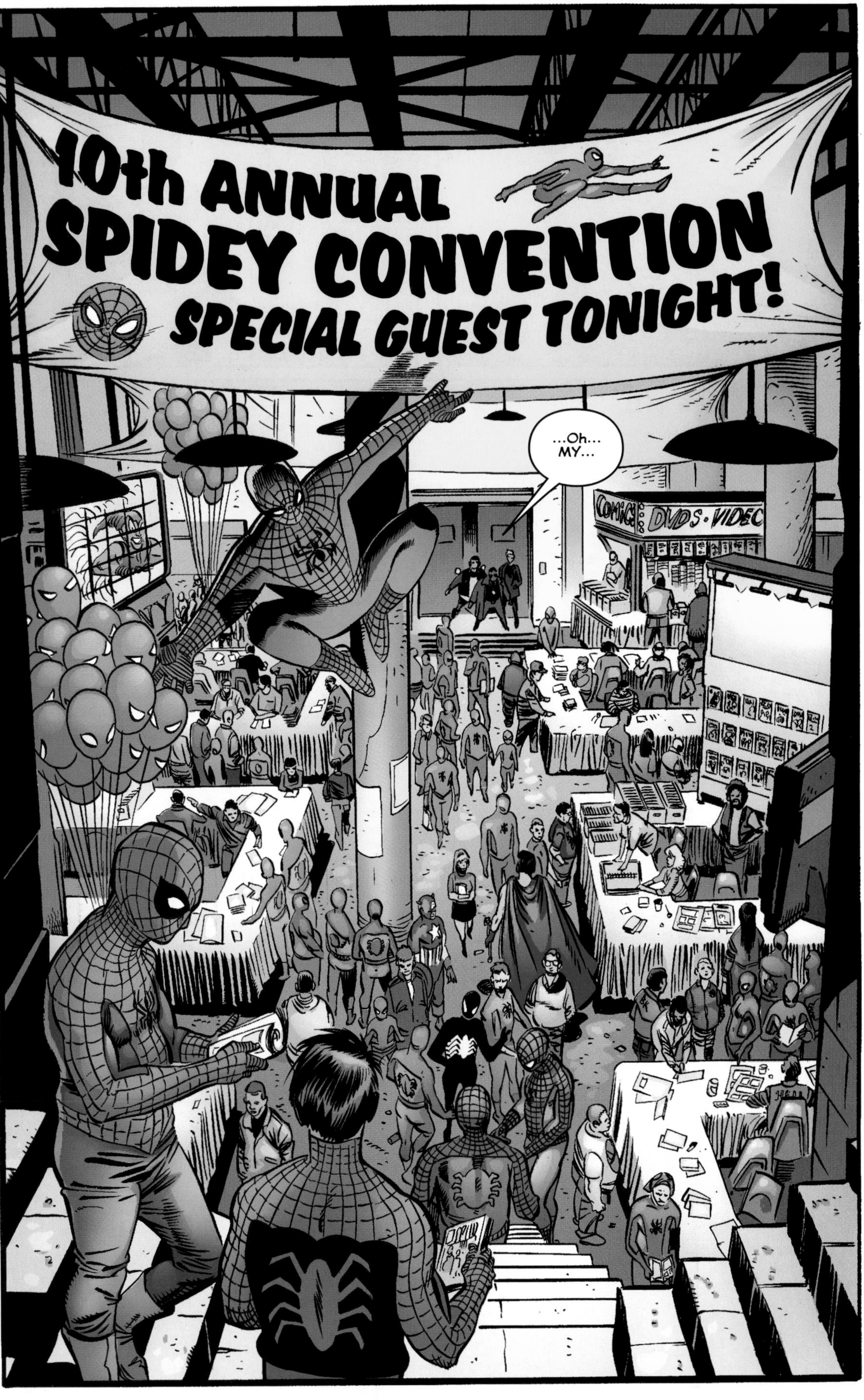
10th ANNUAL
SPIDEY CONVENTION
SPECIAL GUEST TONIGHT!
...Oh...
MY...
COMICS
DVDS · VIDEO

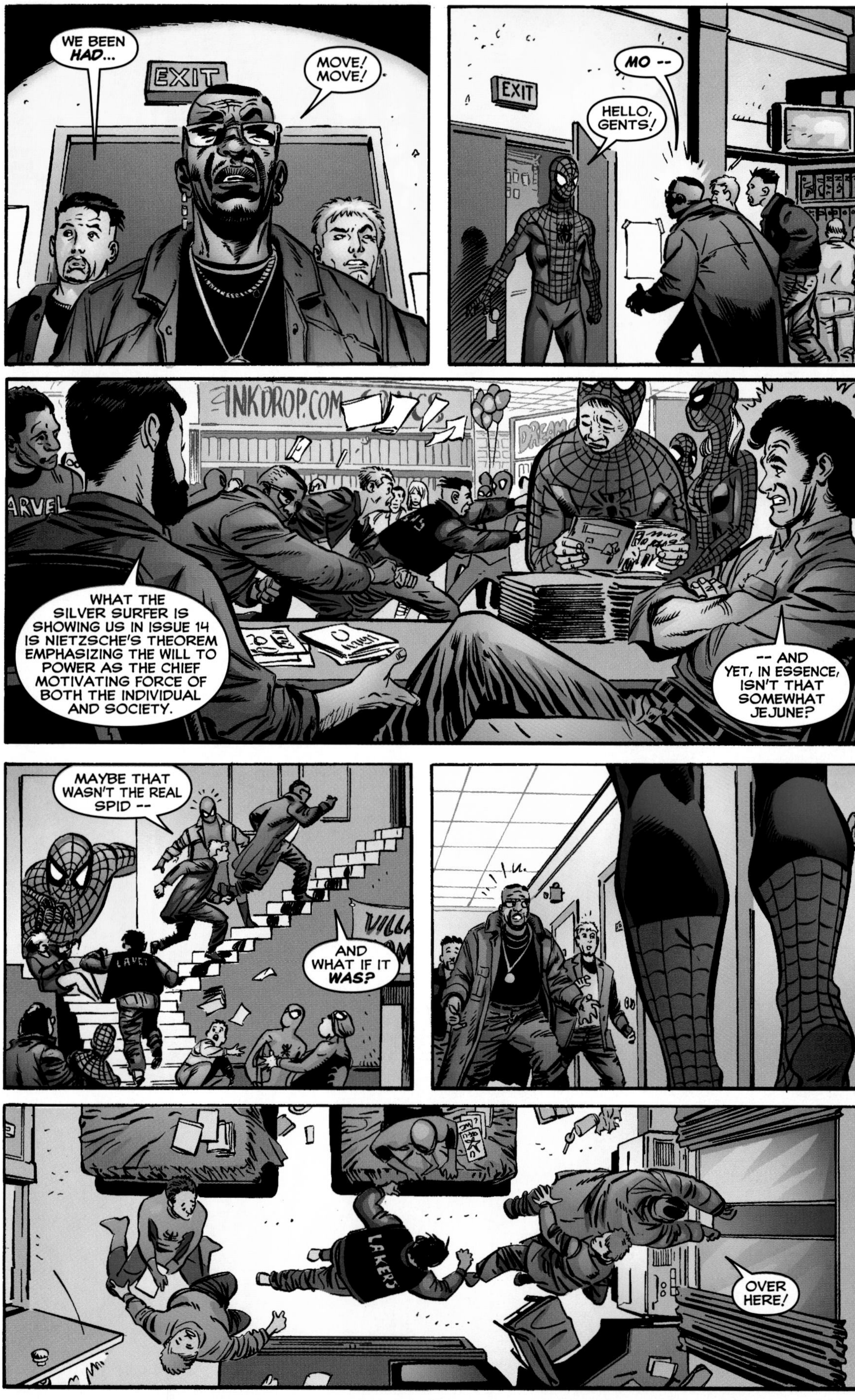
WE BEEN HAD...
EXIT
MOVE! MOVE!
EXIT
MO --
HELLO, GENTS!
INKDROP.COM
WHAT THE SILVER SURFER IS SHOWING US IN ISSUE 14 IS NIETZSCHE'S THEOREM EMPHASIZING THE WILL TO POWER AS THE CHIEF MOTIVATING FORCE OF BOTH THE INDIVIDUAL AND SOCIETY.
-- AND YET, IN ESSENCE, ISN'T THAT SOMEWHAT JEJUNE?
MAYBE THAT WASN'T THE REAL SPID --
AND WHAT IF IT WAS?
LAKERS
OVER HERE!

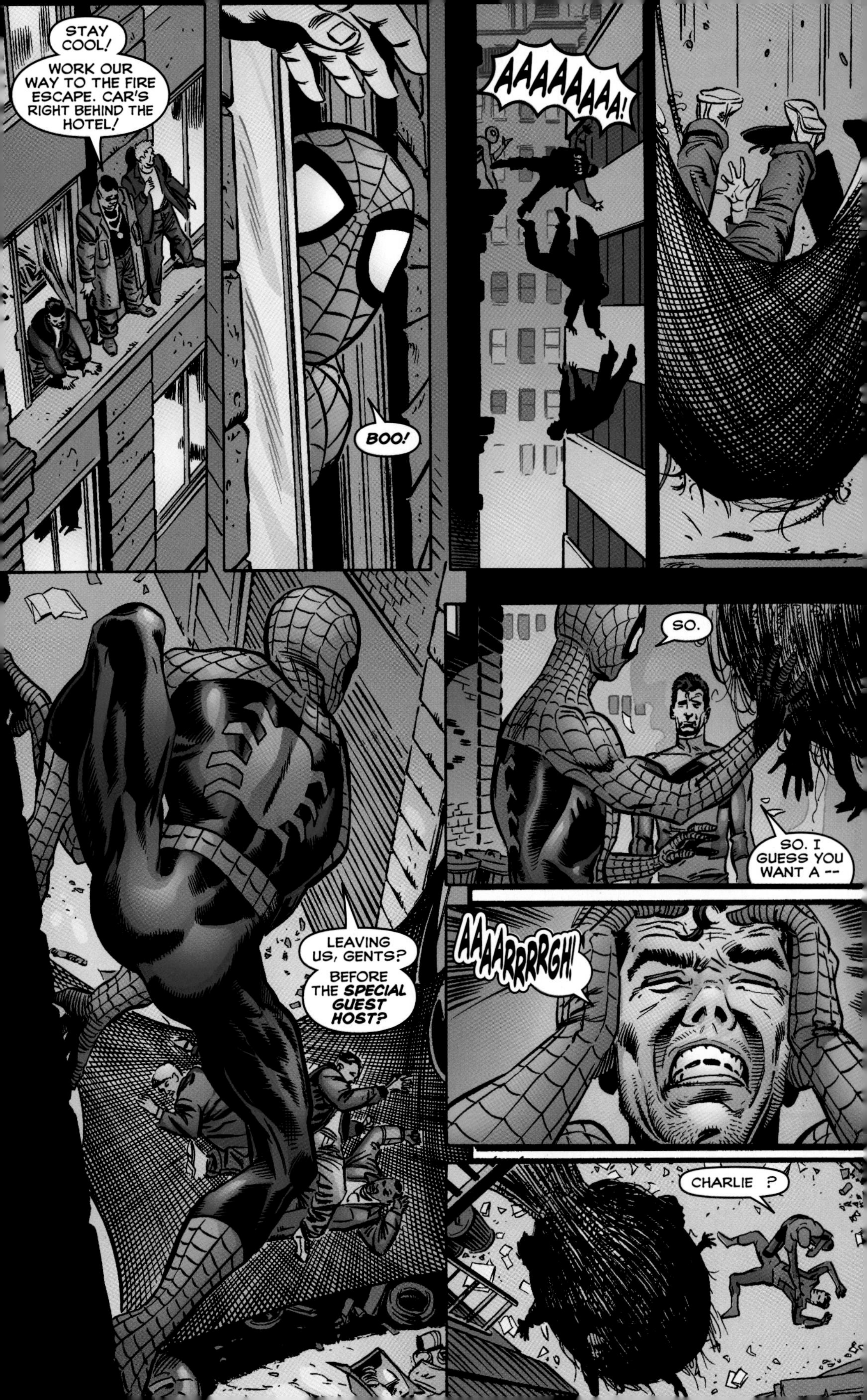
STAY COOL!
WORK OUR WAY TO THE FIRE ESCAPE. CAR'S RIGHT BEHIND THE HOTEL!
BOO!
AAAAAAAA!
LEAVING US, GENTS?
BEFORE THE SPECIAL GUEST HOST?
SO.
SO. I GUESS YOU WANT A --
AAAARRRRGH!
CHARLIE ?

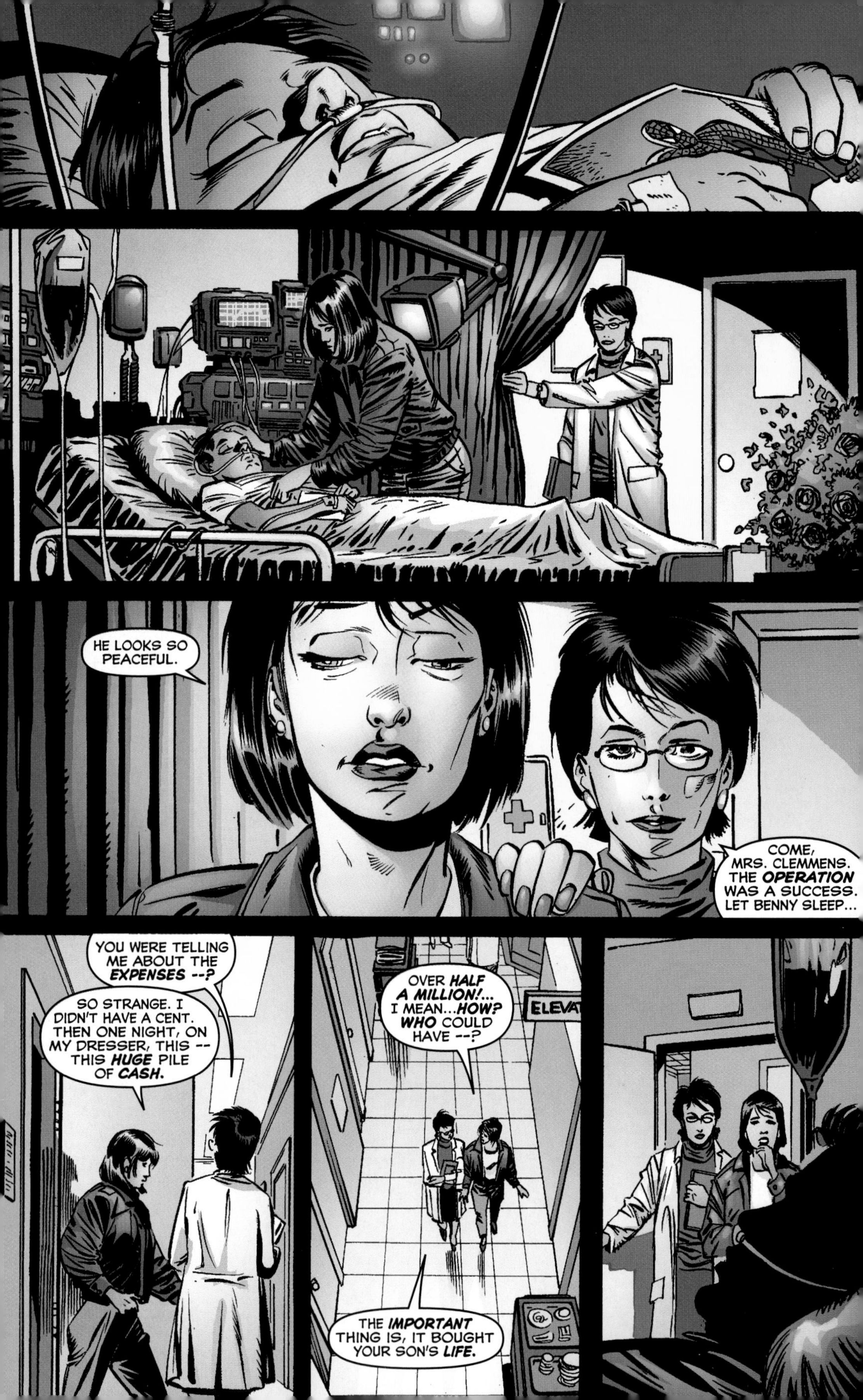
HE LOOKS SO PEACEFUL.
COME, MRS. CLEMMENS. THE OPERATION WAS A SUCCESS. LET BENNY SLEEP...
YOU WERE TELLING ME ABOUT THE EXPENSES --?
SO STRANGE. I DIDN'T HAVE A CENT. THEN ONE NIGHT, ON MY DRESSER, THIS -- THIS HUGE PILE OF CASH.
OVER HALF A MILLION!... I MEAN...HOW? WHO COULD HAVE --?
ELEVAT
THE IMPORTANT THING IS, IT BOUGHT YOUR SON'S LIFE.

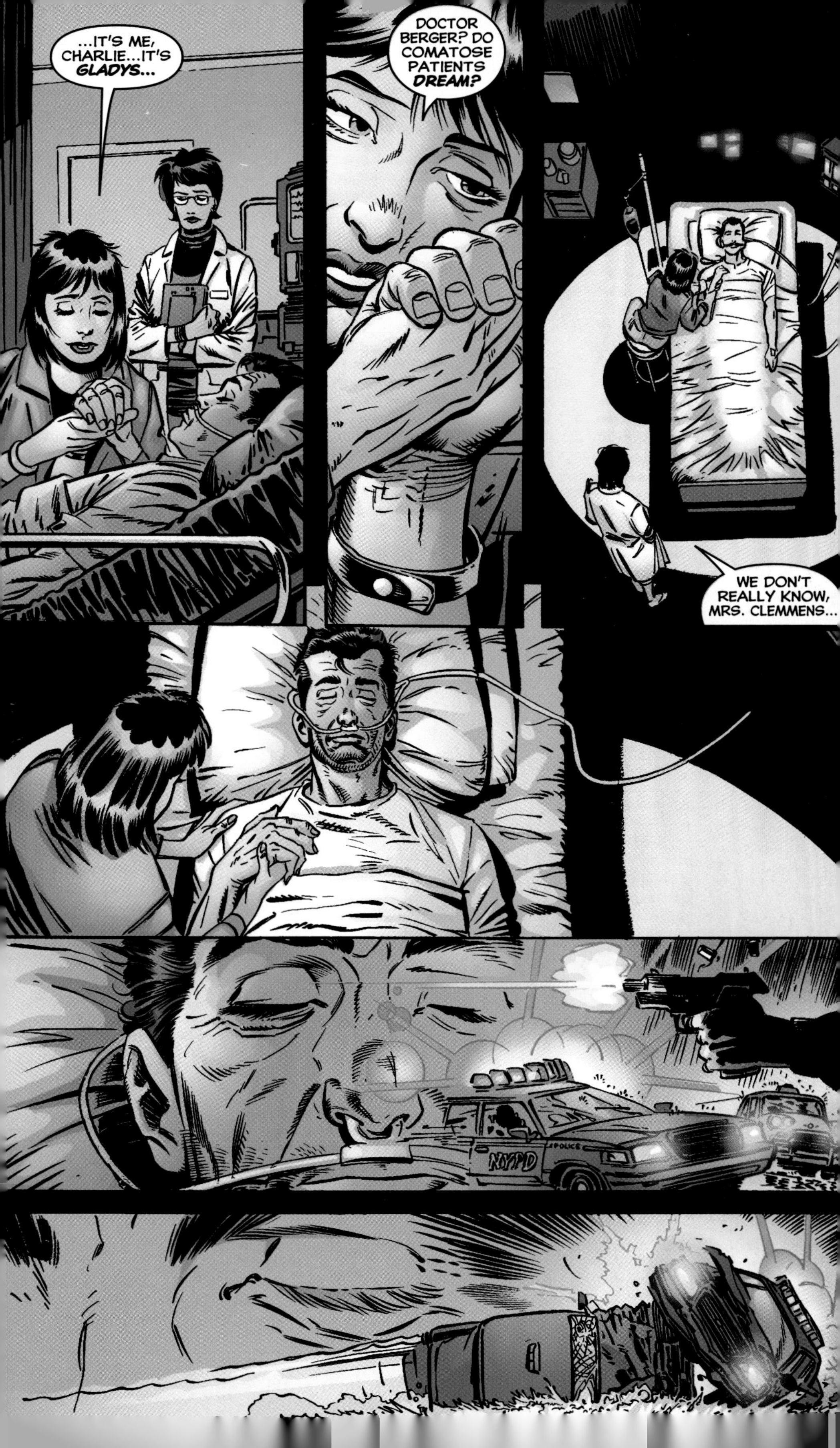
...IT'S ME, CHARLIE...IT'S GLADYS...
DOCTOR BERGER? DO COMATOSE PATIENTS DREAM?
WE DON'T REALLY KNOW, MRS. CLEMMENS...

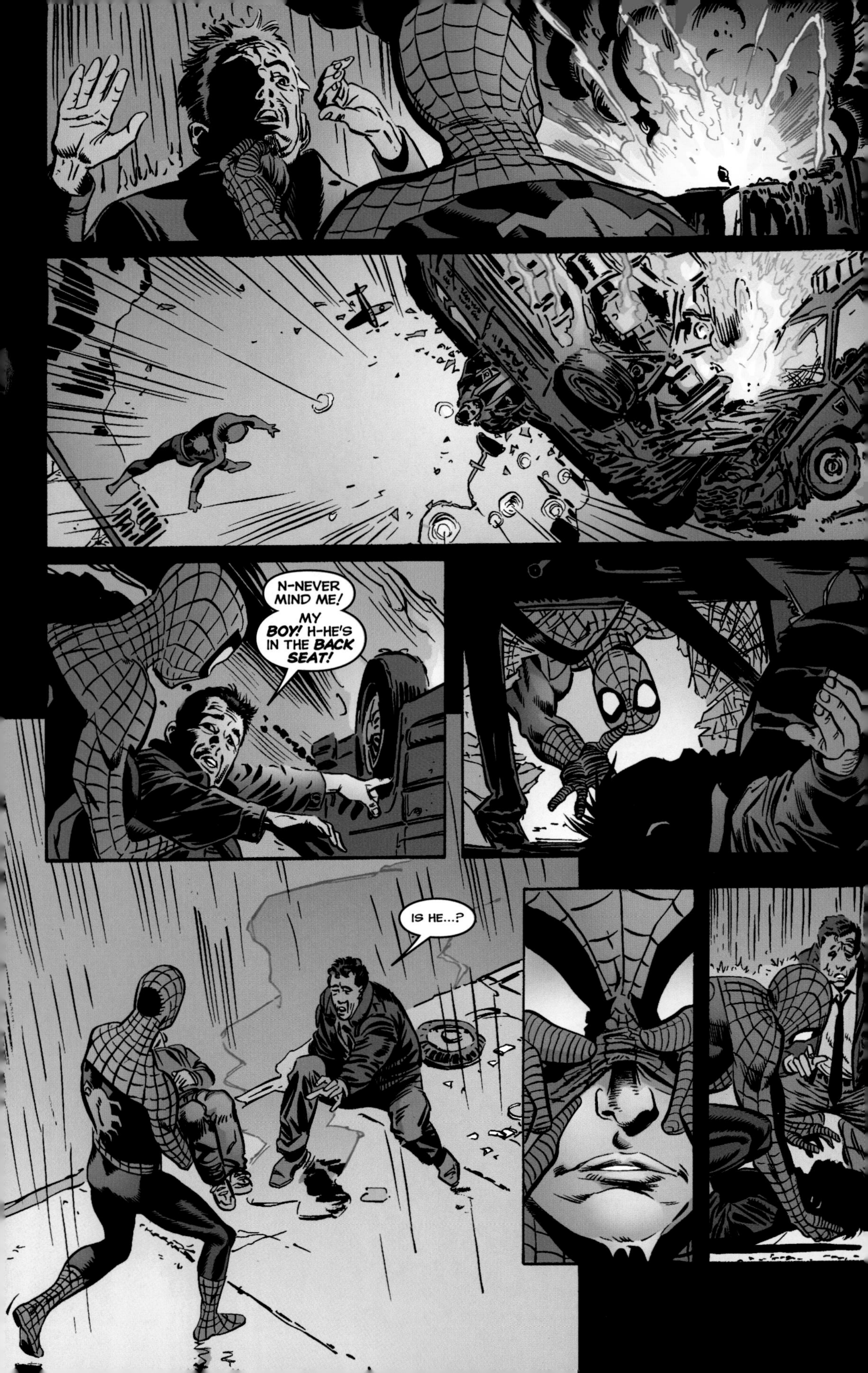
N-NEVER MIND ME! MY BOY! H-HE'S IN THE BACK SEAT!
IS HE...?

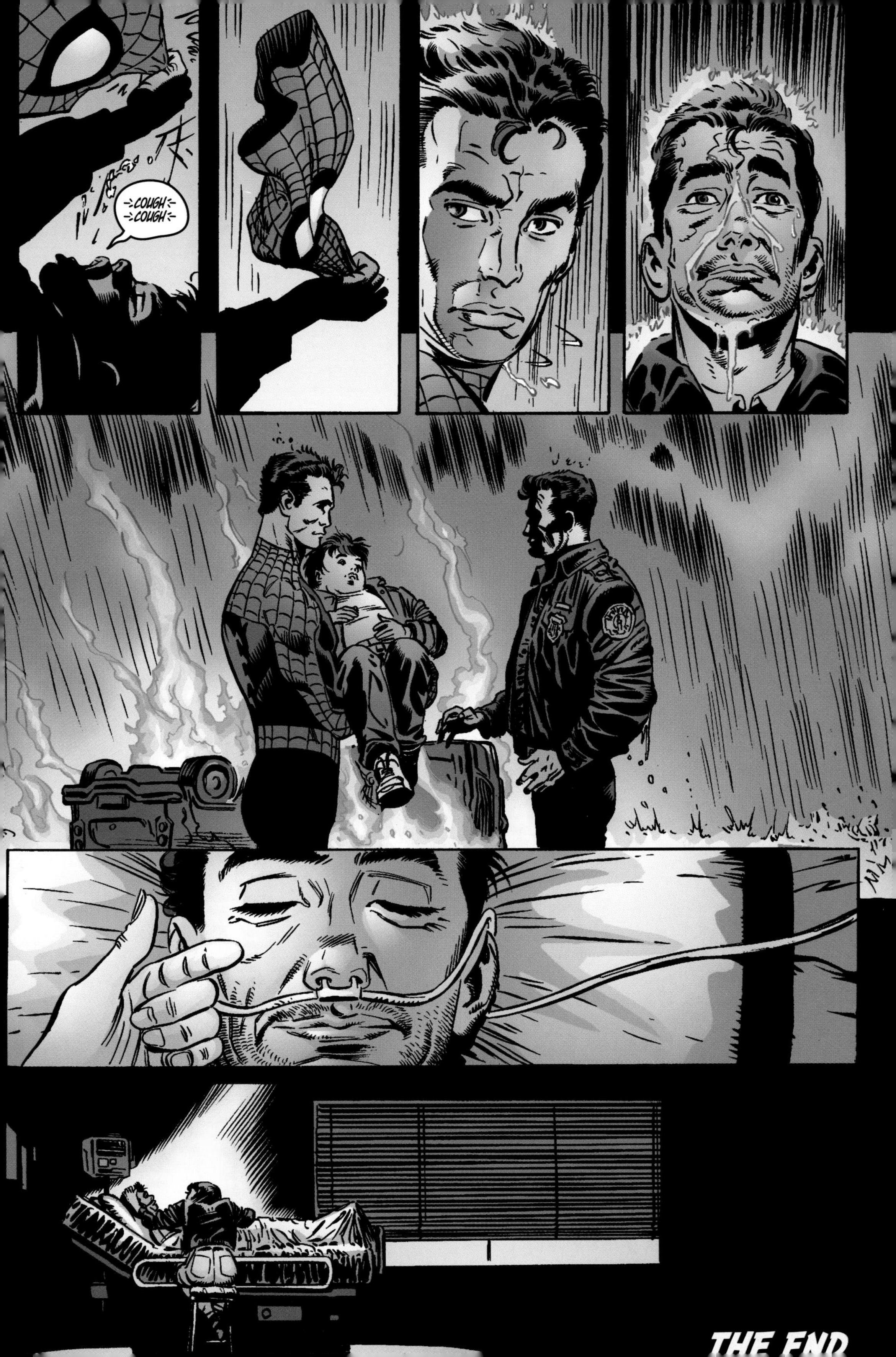

COUGH COUGH
THE END

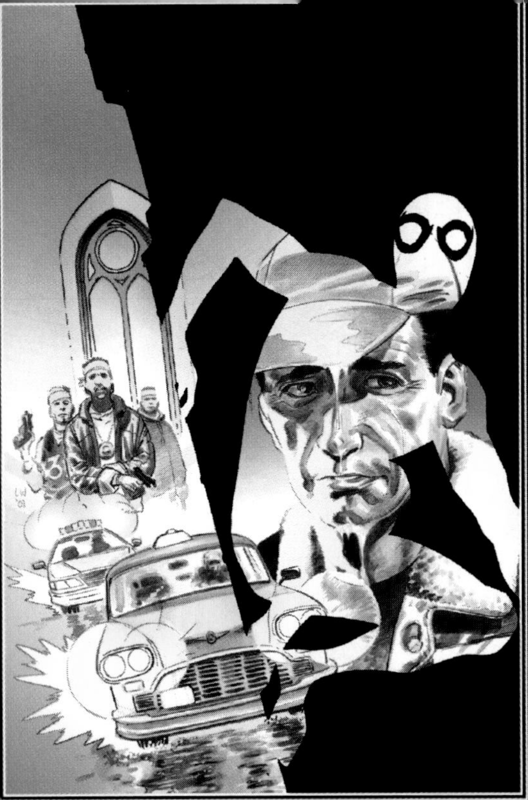

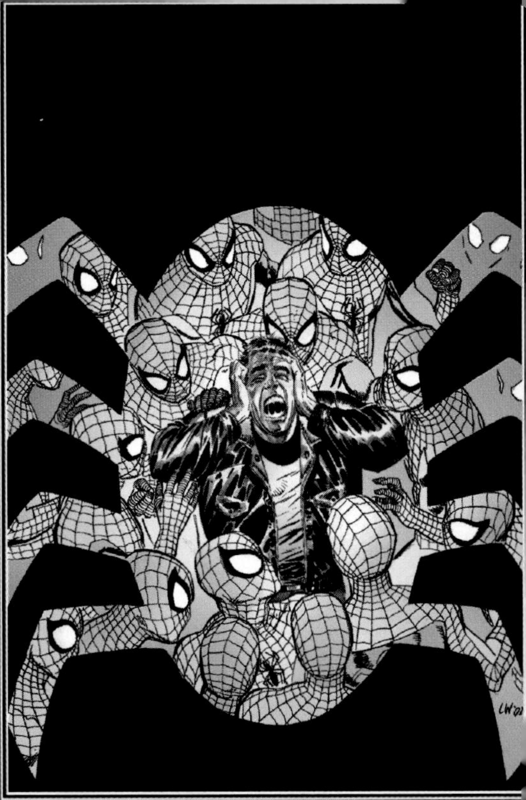

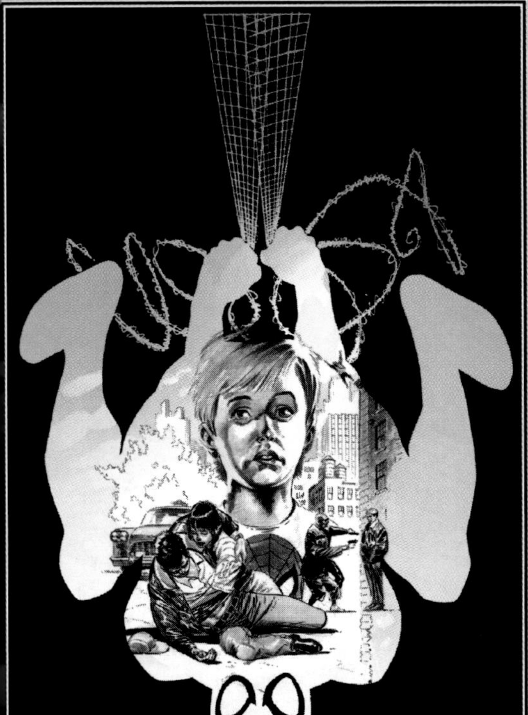

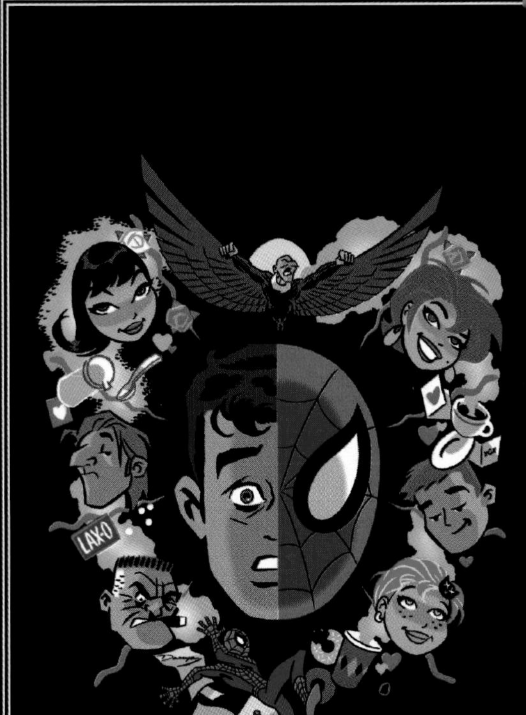

COVER GALLERY

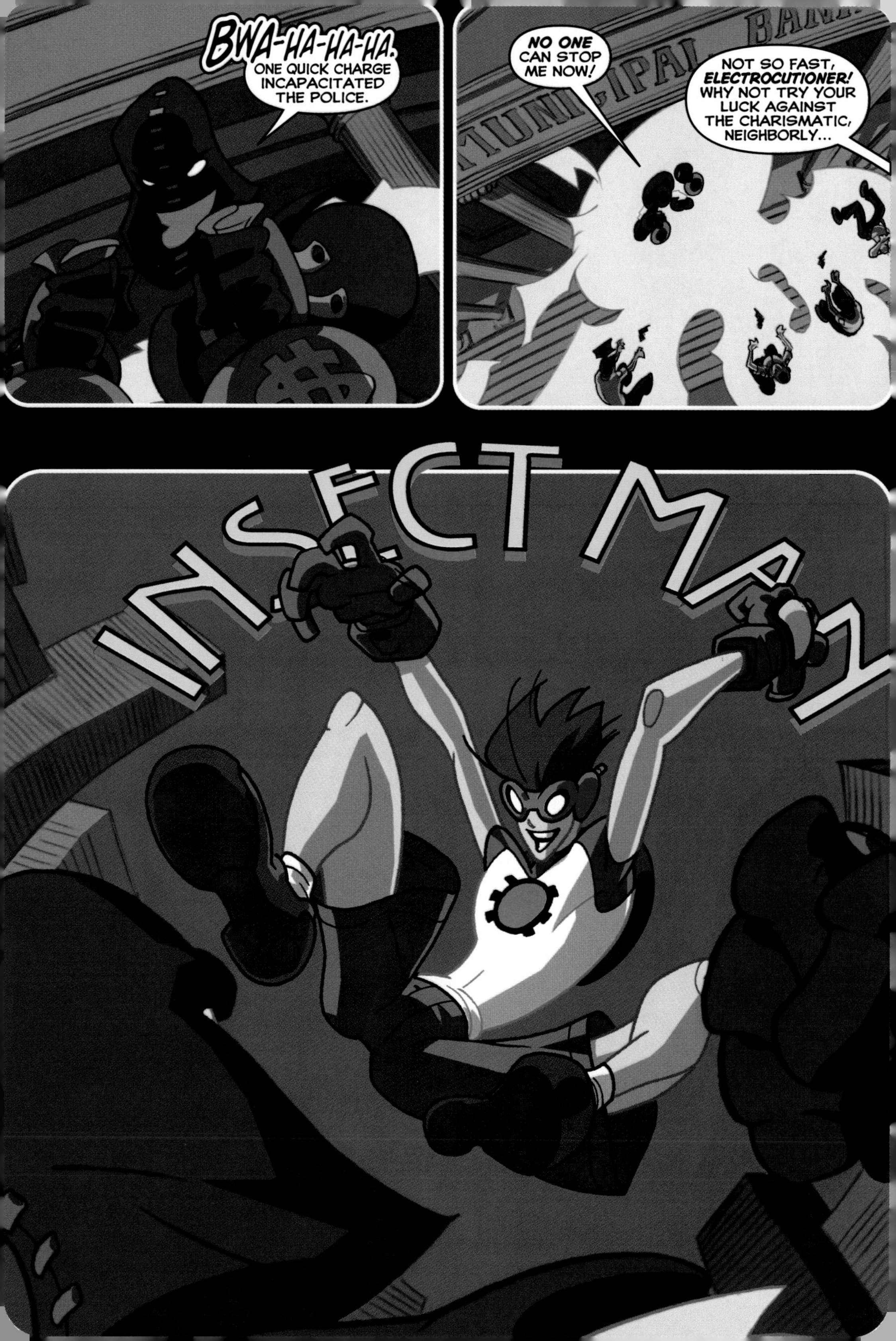
BWA-HA-HA-HA.
ONE QUICK CHARGE INCAPACITATED THE POLICE.
NO ONE CAN STOP ME NOW!
NOT SO FAST, ELECTROCUTIONER! WHY NOT TRY YOUR LUCK AGAINST THE CHARISMATIC, NEIGHBORLY...
INSECT MAN

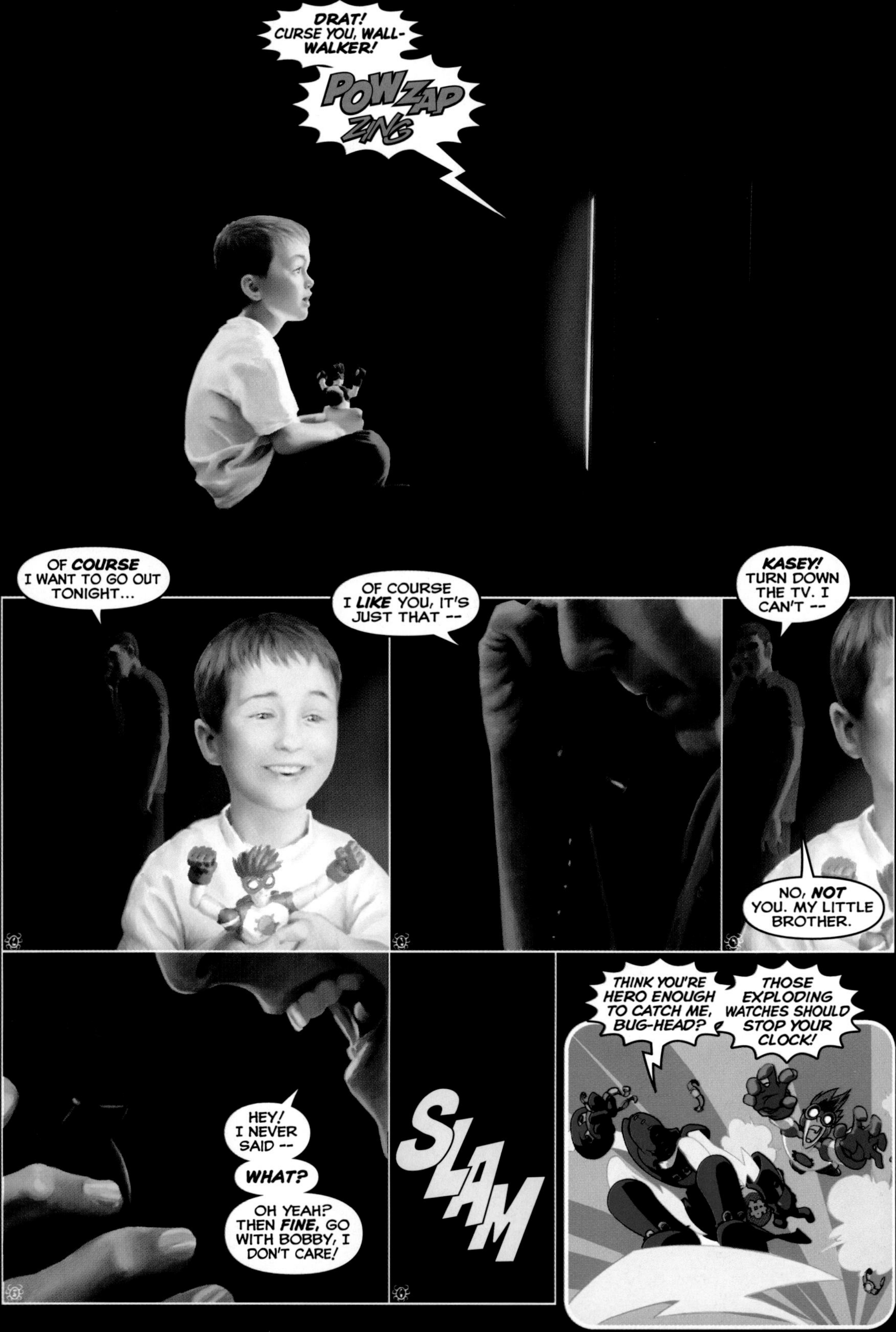
DRAT! CURSE YOU, WALL-WALKER!
POW ZAP ZING
OF COURSE I WANT TO GO OUT TONIGHT...
OF COURSE I LIKE YOU, IT'S JUST THAT --
KASEY! TURN DOWN THE TV. I CAN'T --
NO, NOT YOU. MY LITTLE BROTHER.
HEY! I NEVER SAID --
WHAT?
OH YEAH? THEN FINE, GO WITH BOBBY, I DON'T CARE!
SLAM
THINK YOU'RE HERO ENOUGH TO CATCH ME, BUG-HEAD?
THOSE EXPLODING WATCHES SHOULD STOP YOUR CLOCK!

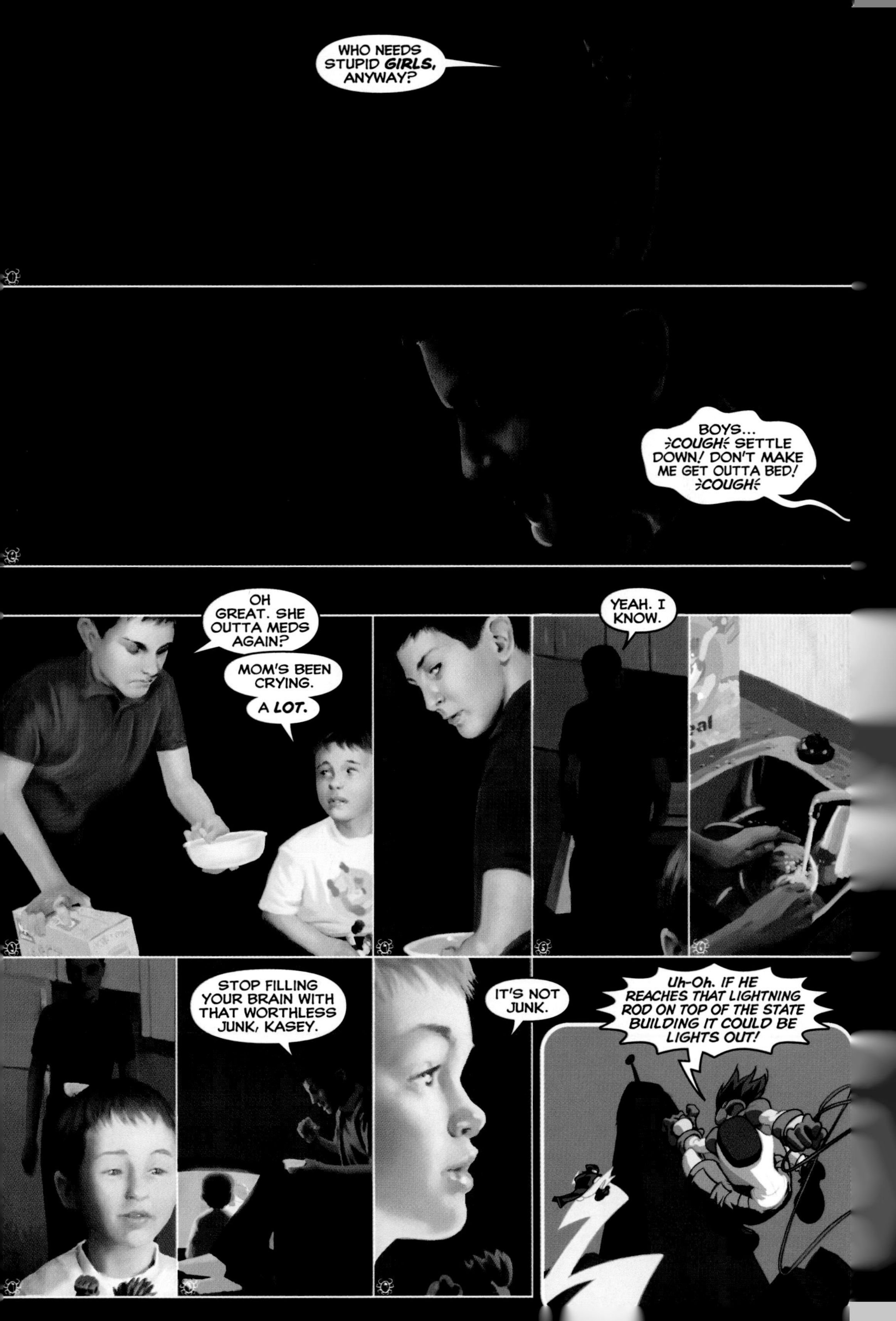
WHO NEEDS STUPID GIRLS, ANYWAY?
BOYS... ⁑COUGH⁑ SETTLE DOWN! DON'T MAKE ME GET OUTTA BED! ⁑COUGH⁑
OH GREAT. SHE OUTTA MEDS AGAIN?
MOM'S BEEN CRYING.
A LOT.
YEAH. I KNOW.
STOP FILLING YOUR BRAIN WITH THAT WORTHLESS JUNK, KASEY.
IT'S NOT JUNK.
Uh-Oh. IF HE REACHES THAT LIGHTNING ROD ON TOP OF THE STATE BUILDING IT COULD BE LIGHTS OUT!

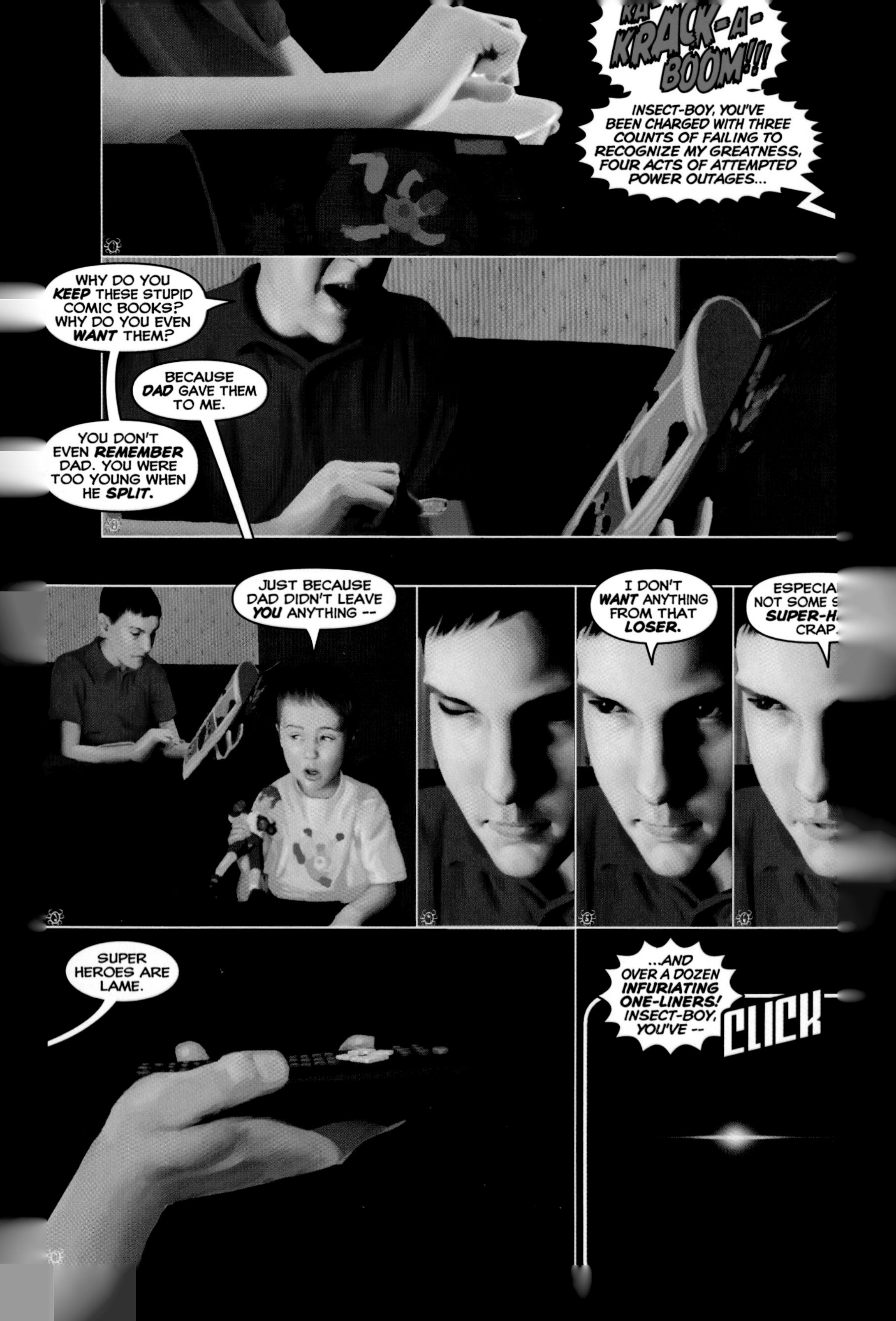

KRACK-A-BOOM!!!
INSECT-BOY, YOU'VE BEEN CHARGED WITH THREE COUNTS OF FAILING TO RECOGNIZE MY GREATNESS, FOUR ACTS OF ATTEMPTED POWER OUTAGES...
WHY DO YOU KEEP THESE STUPID COMIC BOOKS? WHY DO YOU EVEN WANT THEM?
BECAUSE DAD GAVE THEM TO ME.
YOU DON'T EVEN REMEMBER DAD. YOU WERE TOO YOUNG WHEN HE SPLIT.
JUST BECAUSE DAD DIDN'T LEAVE YOU ANYTHING --
I DON'T WANT ANYTHING FROM THAT LOSER.
ESPECIA NOT SOME S SUPER-H CRAP.
SUPER HEROES ARE LAME.
...AND OVER A DOZEN INFURIATING ONE-LINERS! INSECT-BOY, YOU'VE --
CLICK

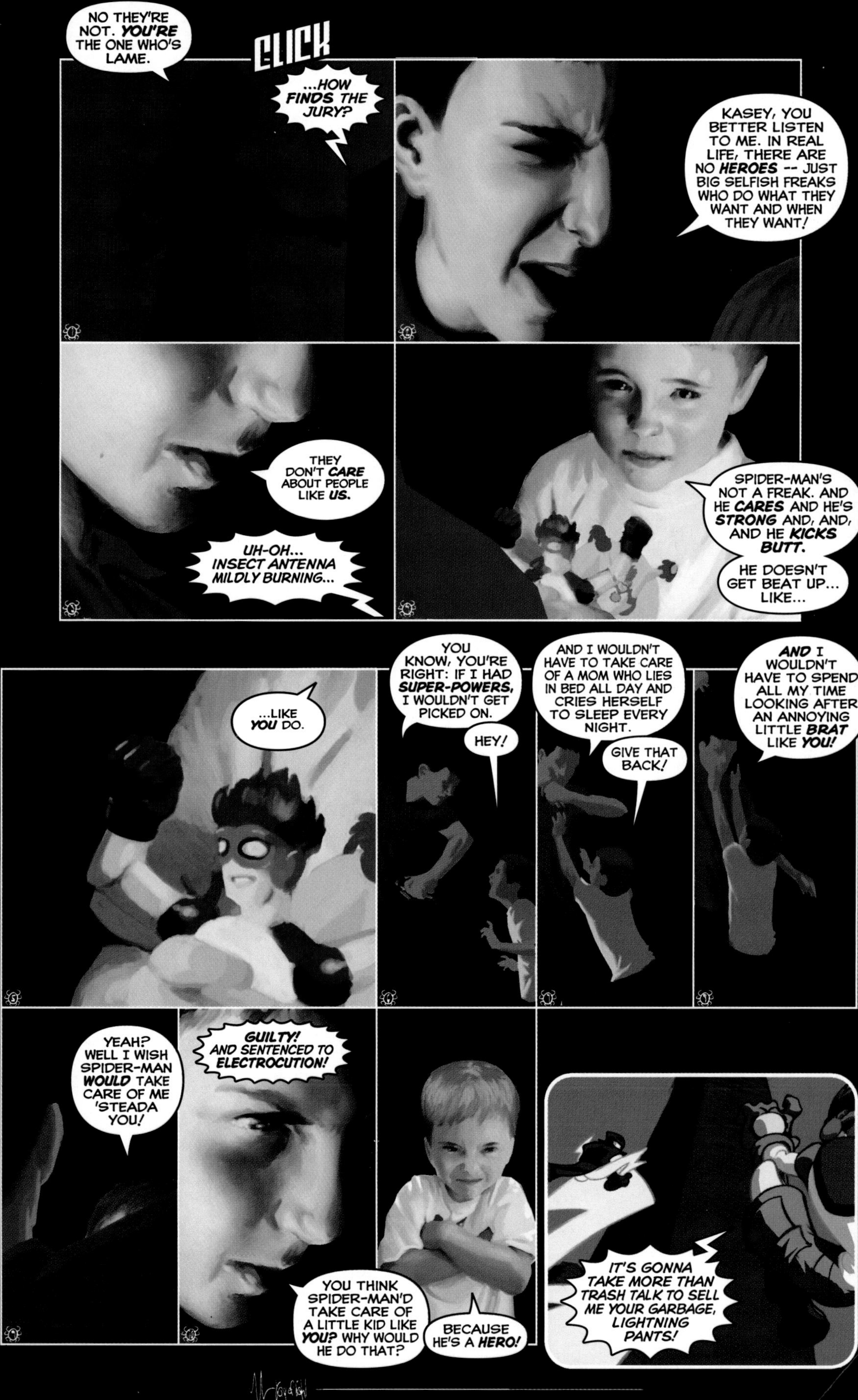
NO THEY'RE NOT. YOU'RE THE ONE WHO'S LAME.
CLICK
...HOW FINDS THE JURY?
KASEY, YOU BETTER LISTEN TO ME. IN REAL LIFE, THERE ARE NO HEROES -- JUST BIG SELFISH FREAKS WHO DO WHAT THEY WANT AND WHEN THEY WANT!
THEY DON'T CARE ABOUT PEOPLE LIKE US.
UH-OH... INSECT ANTENNA MILDLY BURNING...
SPIDER-MAN'S NOT A FREAK. AND HE CARES AND HE'S STRONG AND, AND, AND HE KICKS BUTT.
HE DOESN'T GET BEAT UP... LIKE...
...LIKE YOU DO.
YOU KNOW, YOU'RE RIGHT: IF I HAD SUPER-POWERS, I WOULDN'T GET PICKED ON.
HEY!
AND I WOULDN'T HAVE TO TAKE CARE OF A MOM WHO LIES IN BED ALL DAY AND CRIES HERSELF TO SLEEP EVERY NIGHT.
GIVE THAT BACK!
AND I WOULDN'T HAVE TO SPEND ALL MY TIME LOOKING AFTER AN ANNOYING LITTLE BRAT LIKE YOU!
YEAH? WELL I WISH SPIDER-MAN WOULD TAKE CARE OF ME 'STEADA YOU!
GUILTY! AND SENTENCED TO ELECTROCUTION!
YOU THINK SPIDER-MAN'D TAKE CARE OF A LITTLE KID LIKE YOU? WHY WOULD HE DO THAT?
BECAUSE HE'S A HERO!
IT'S GONNA TAKE MORE THAN TRASH TALK TO SELL ME YOUR GARBAGE, LIGHTNING PANTS!

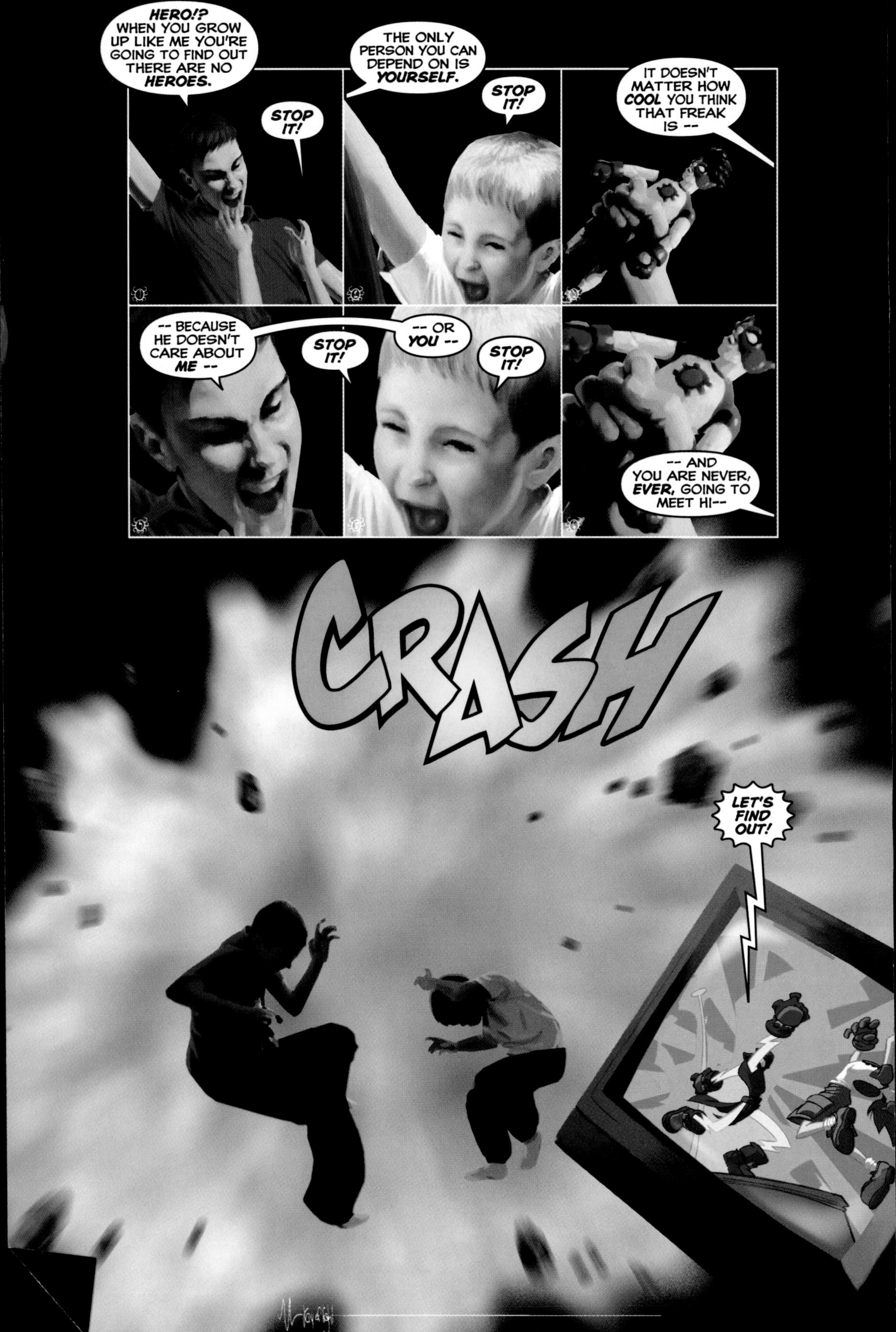

HERO!? WHEN YOU GROW UP LIKE ME YOU'RE GOING TO FIND OUT THERE ARE NO HEROES.
STOP IT!
THE ONLY PERSON YOU CAN DEPEND ON IS YOURSELF.
STOP IT!
IT DOESN'T MATTER HOW COOL YOU THINK THAT FREAK IS --
-- BECAUSE HE DOESN'T CARE ABOUT ME --
STOP IT!
-- OR YOU --
STOP IT!
-- AND YOU ARE NEVER, EVER, GOING TO MEET HI--
CRASH
LET'S FIND OUT!

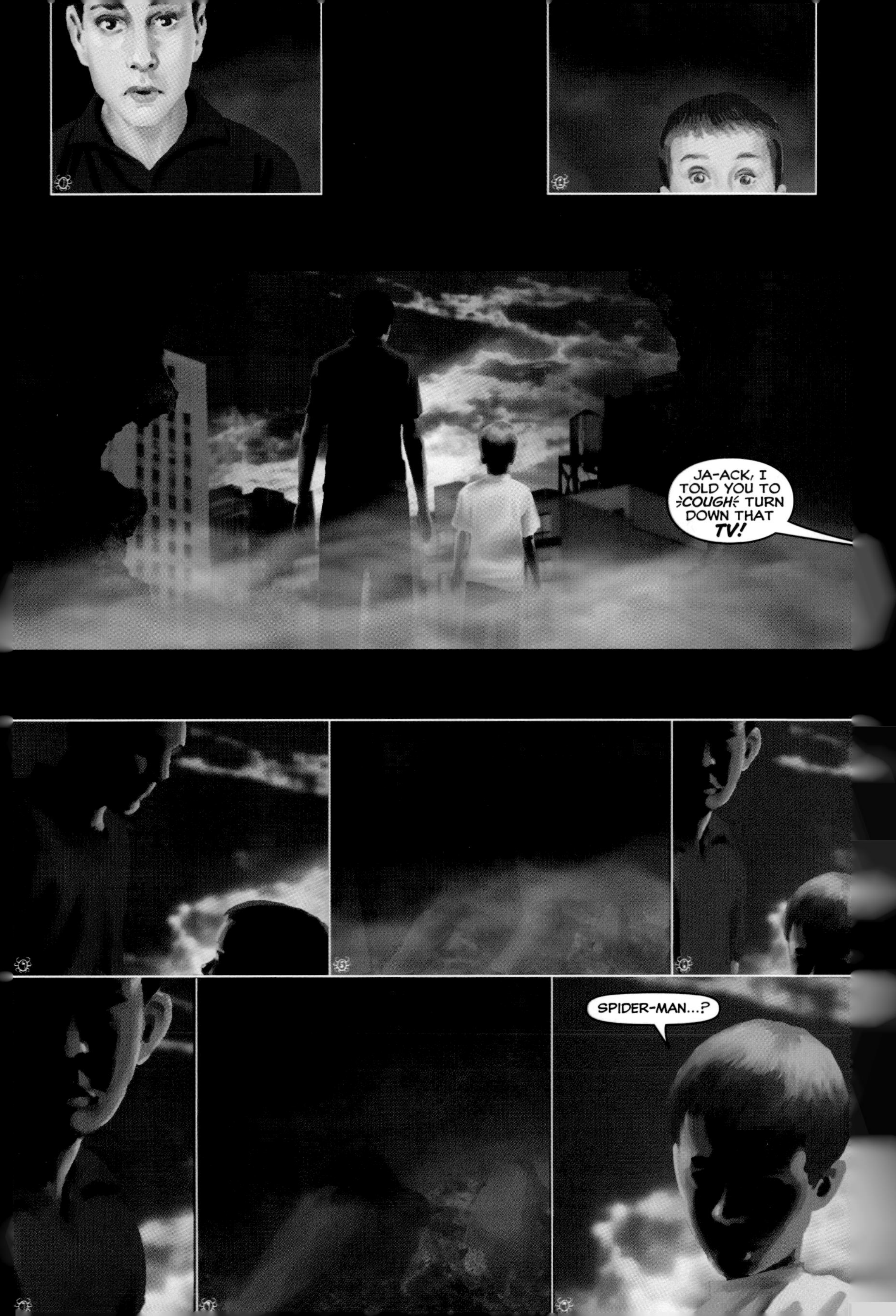
JA-ACK, I TOLD YOU TO *COUGH* TURN DOWN THAT TV!
SPIDER-MAN...?

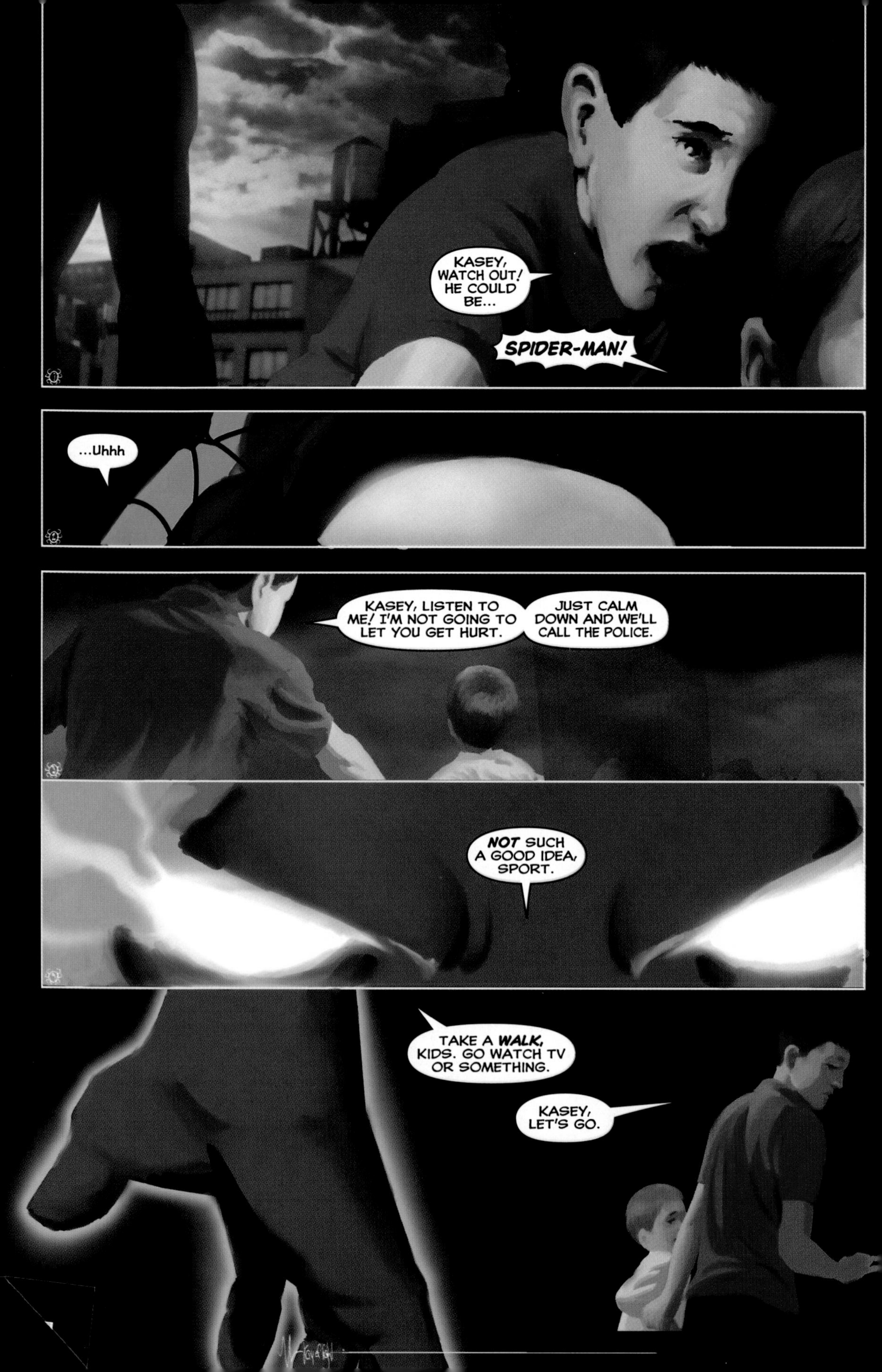

KASEY, WATCH OUT! HE COULD BE...
SPIDER-MAN!
...Uhhh
KASEY, LISTEN TO ME! I'M NOT GOING TO LET YOU GET HURT.
JUST CALM DOWN AND WE'LL CALL THE POLICE.
NOT SUCH A GOOD IDEA, SPORT.
TAKE A WALK, KIDS. GO WATCH TV OR SOMETHING.
KASEY, LET'S GO.

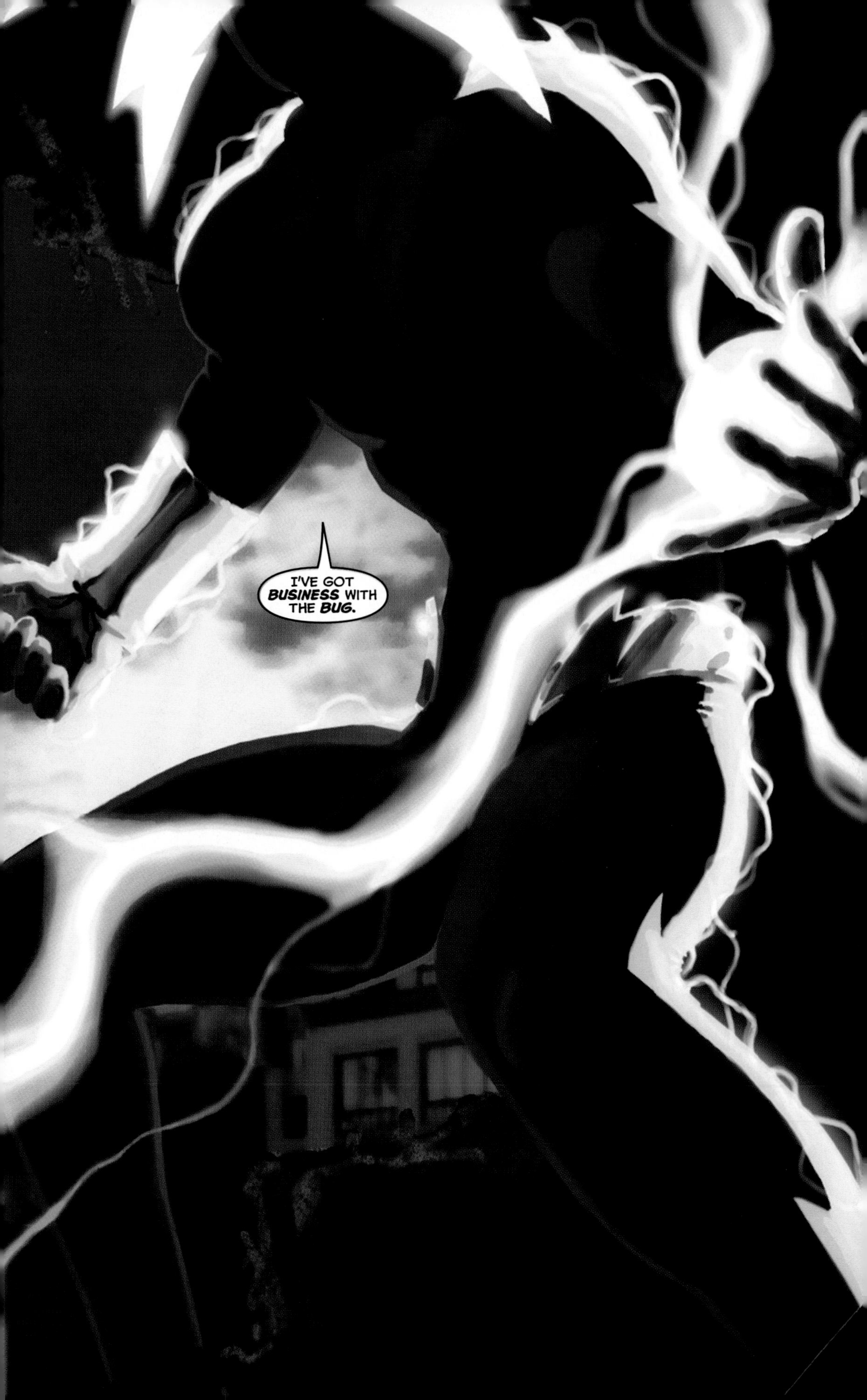
I'VE GOT BUSINESS WITH THE BUG.

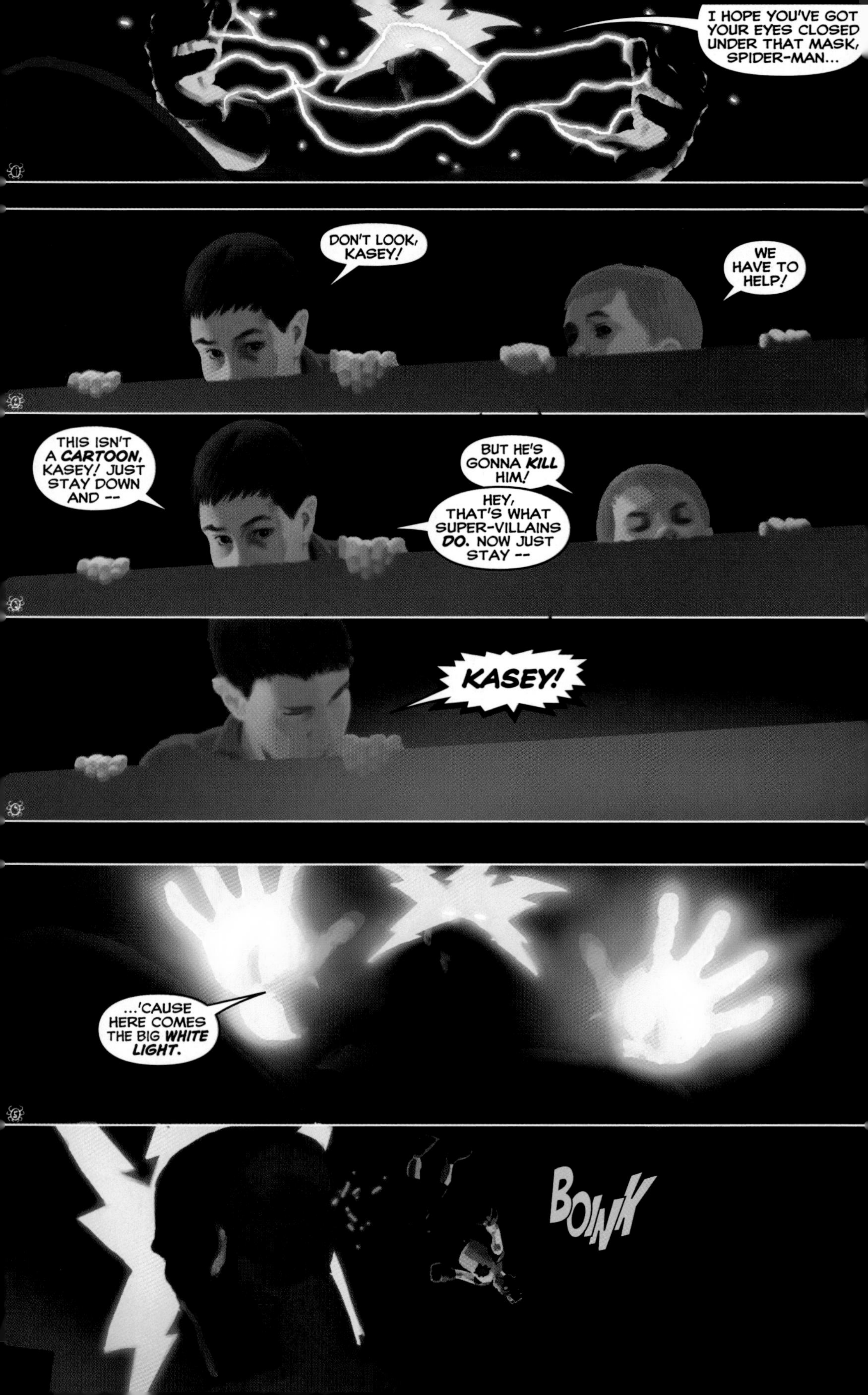
I HOPE YOU'VE GOT YOUR EYES CLOSED UNDER THAT MASK, SPIDER-MAN...
DON'T LOOK, KASEY!
WE HAVE TO HELP!
THIS ISN'T A **CARTOON,** KASEY! JUST STAY DOWN AND --
BUT HE'S GONNA **KILL** HIM!
HEY, THAT'S WHAT SUPER-VILLAINS **DO.** NOW JUST STAY --
KASEY!
...'CAUSE HERE COMES THE BIG **WHITE LIGHT.**
BOINK

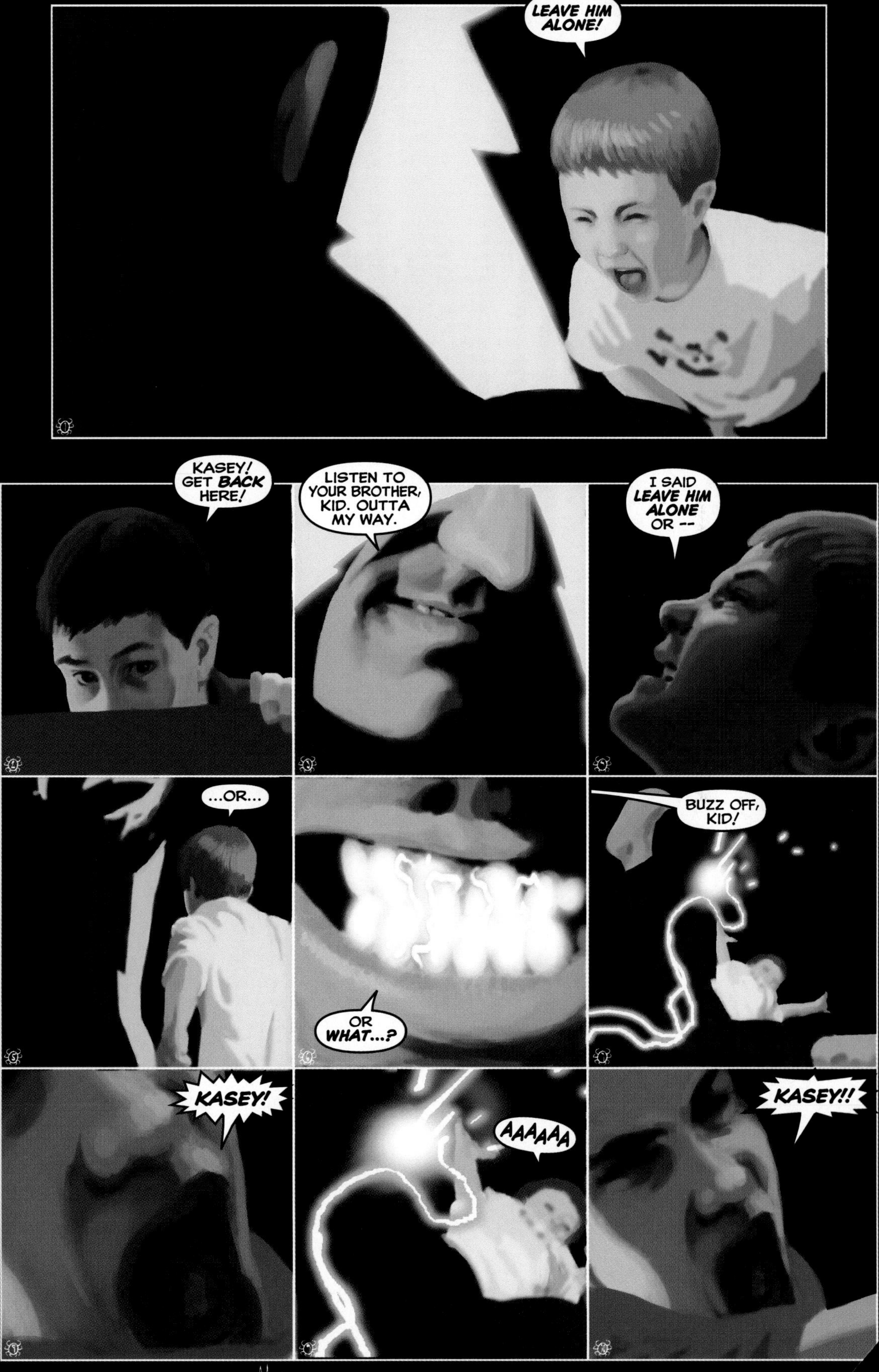
LEAVE HIM ALONE!
KASEY! GET BACK HERE!
LISTEN TO YOUR BROTHER, KID. OUTTA MY WAY.
I SAID LEAVE HIM ALONE OR --
...OR...
OR WHAT...?
BUZZ OFF, KID!
KASEY!
AAAAAA
KASEY!!

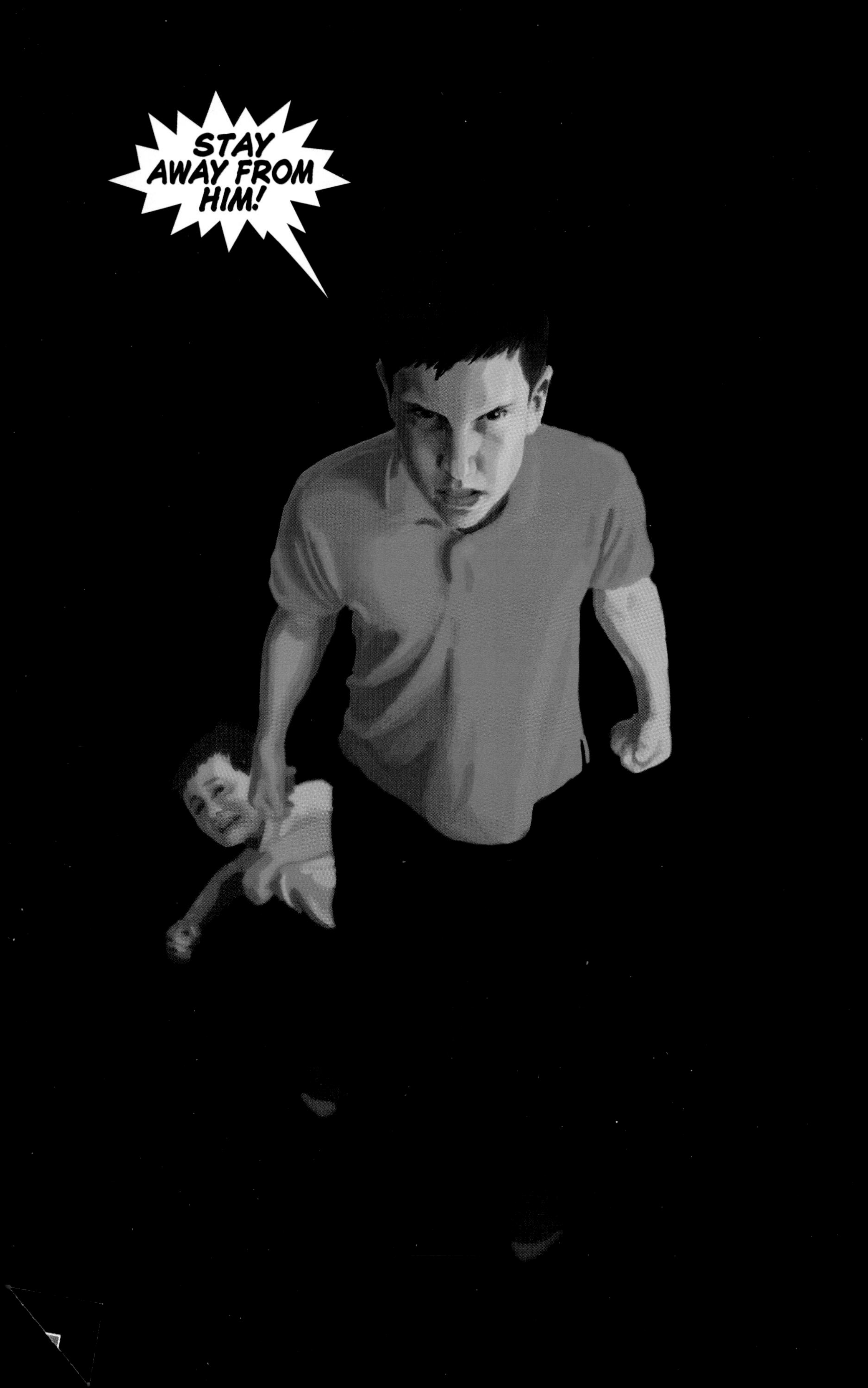
STAY AWAY FROM HIM!

WELL, BIG BROTHER TO THE RESCUE. A REAL, LIVE HERO.
TELL ME, LITTLE BOY, DO YOU PROTECT THE LITTLE GIRLS FROM BULLIES AT SCHOOL...?
DO THEY REWARD THEIR MIGHTY HERO WITH KISSES AND SECRET NOTES...?
DO YOU PLAY FOOTBALL WITH ALL YOUR OTHER FRIENDS, AND LAUGH AT THE LITTLE KID TOO SCRAWNY TO BE PICKED TO PLAY...?
DIDN'T THINK SO.

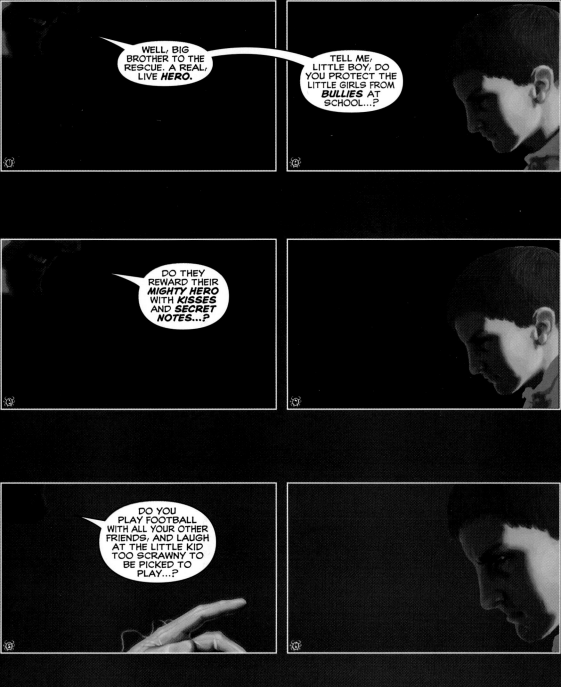

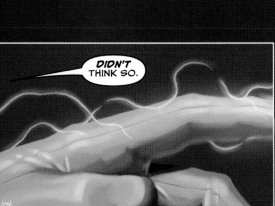

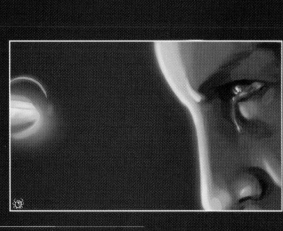

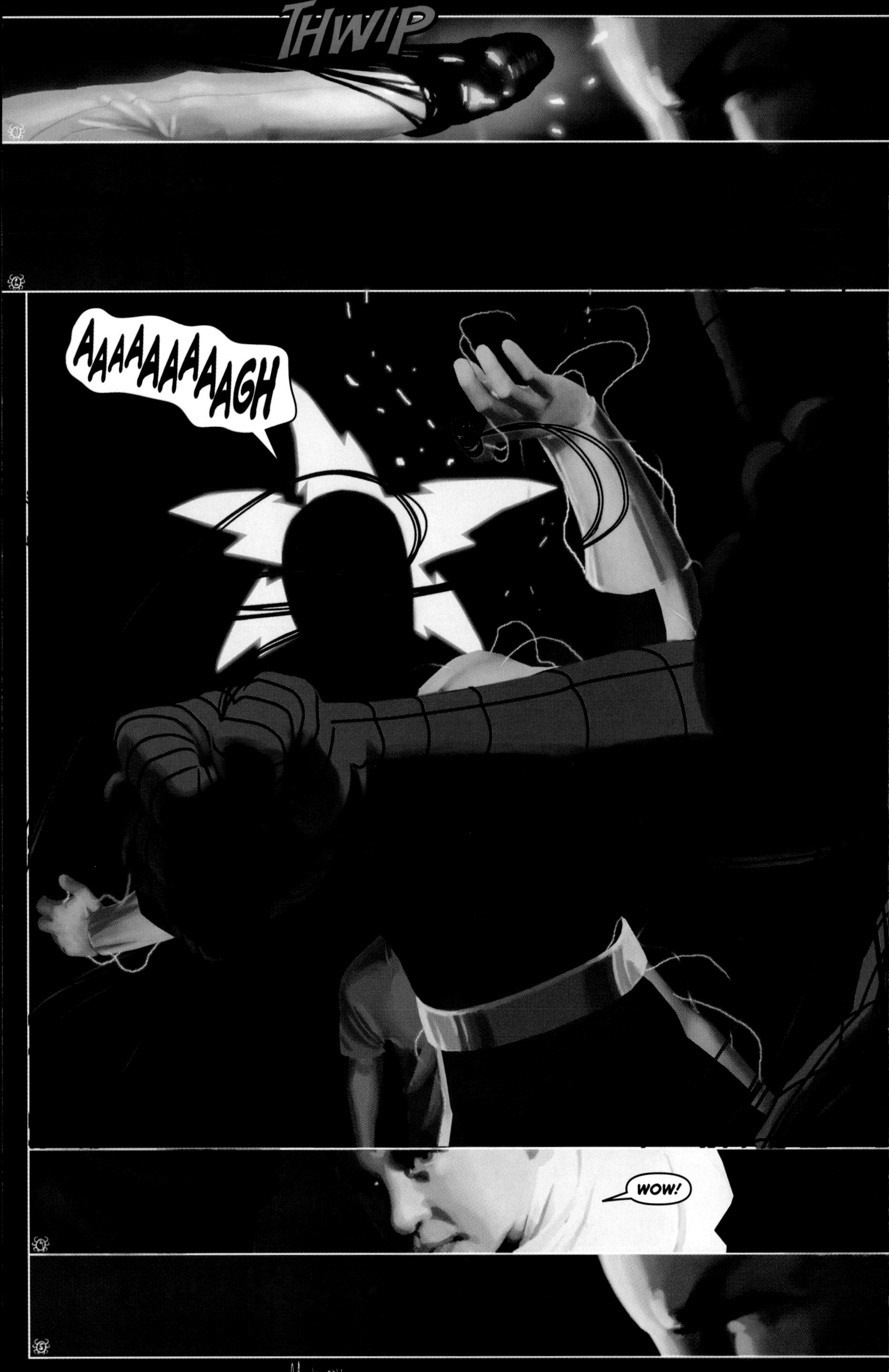
THWIP
AAAAAAAAAAGH
WOW!

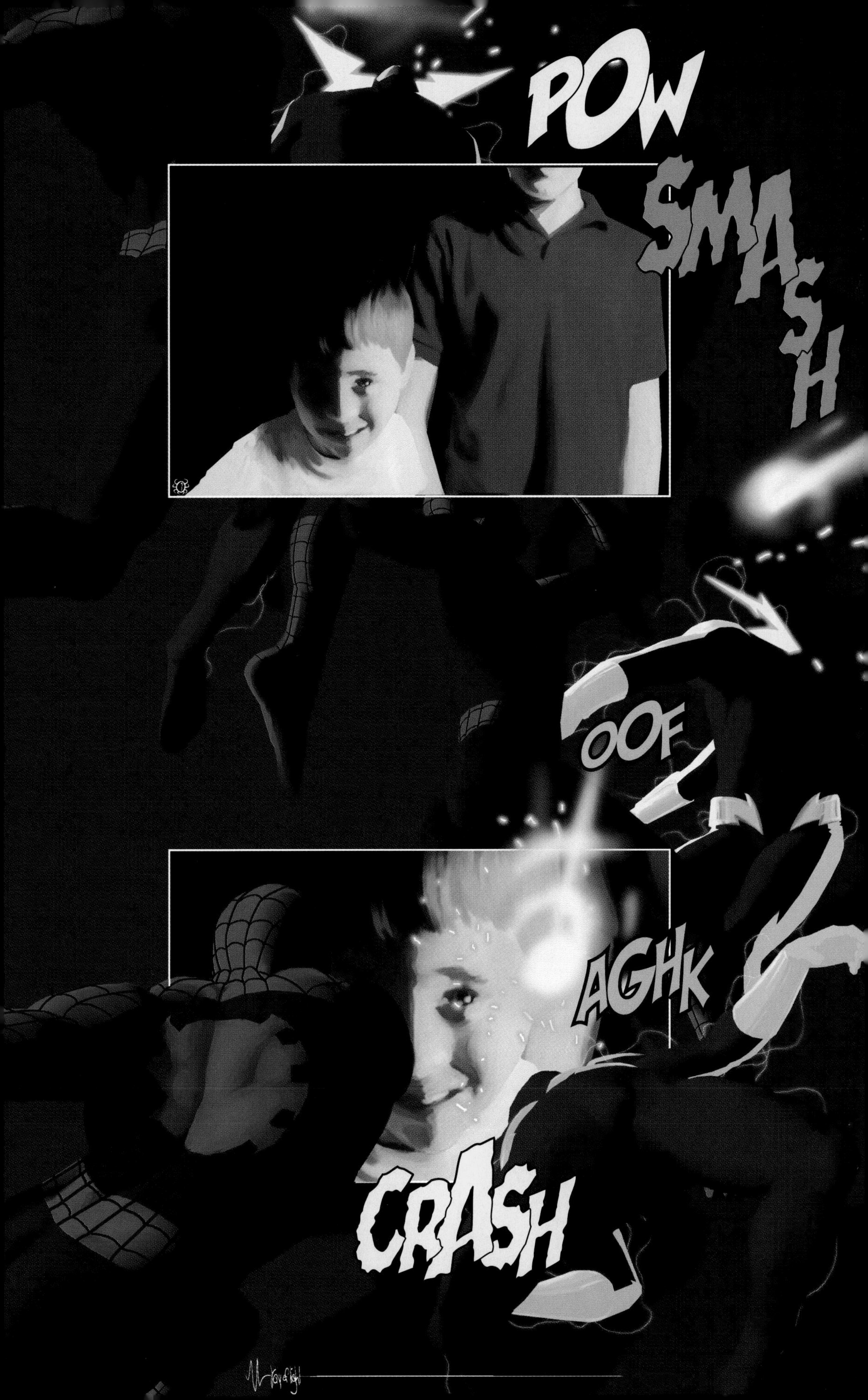
POW
SMASH
OOF
AGHK
CRASH

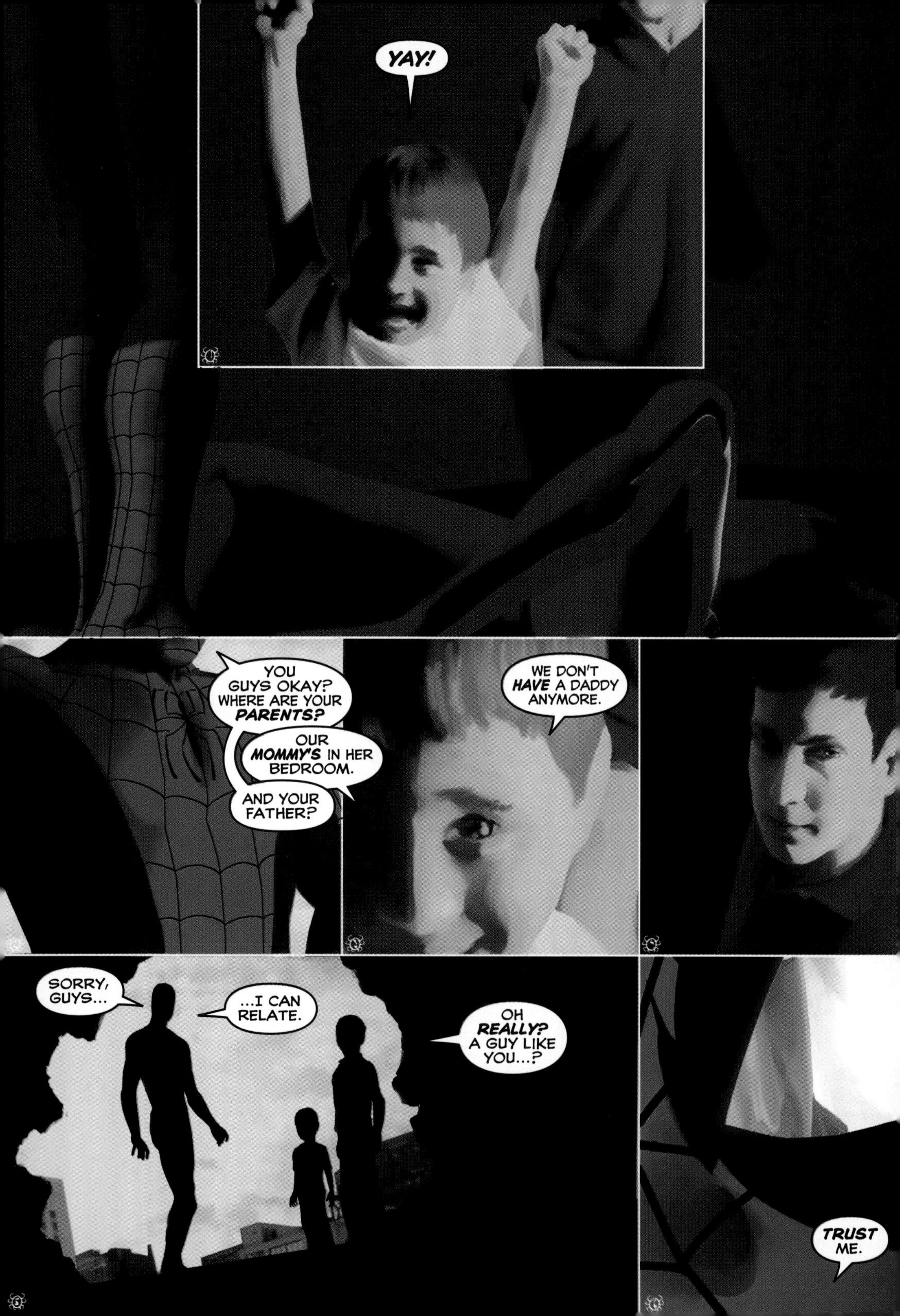
YAY!
YOU GUYS OKAY? WHERE ARE YOUR PARENTS?
OUR MOMMY'S IN HER BEDROOM.
AND YOUR FATHER?
WE DON'T HAVE A DADDY ANYMORE.
SORRY, GUYS...
...I CAN RELATE.
OH REALLY? A GUY LIKE YOU...?
TRUST ME.

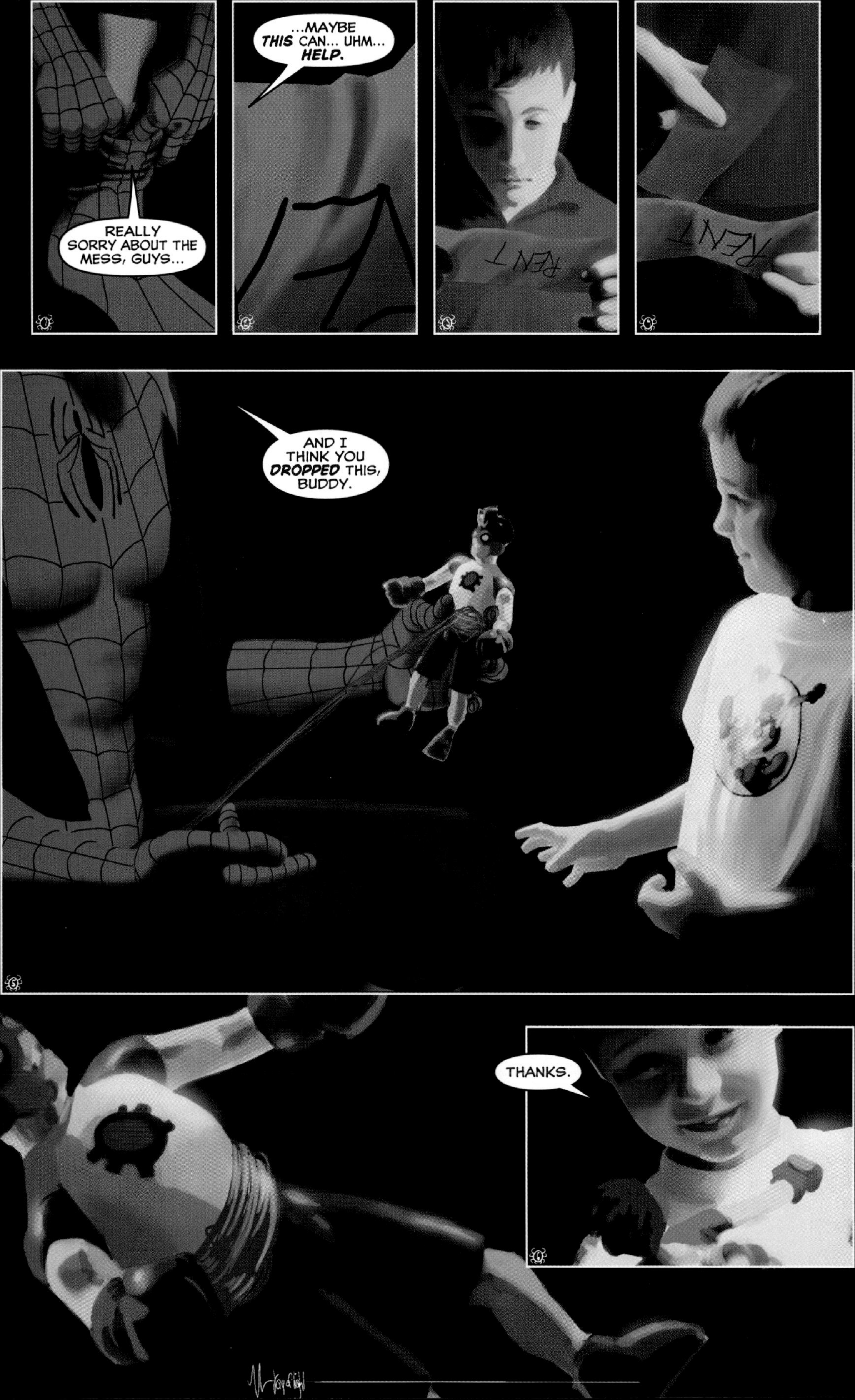
REALLY SORRY ABOUT THE MESS, GUYS...
...MAYBE THIS CAN... UHM... HELP.
RENT
RENT
AND I THINK YOU DROPPED THIS, BUDDY.
THANKS.

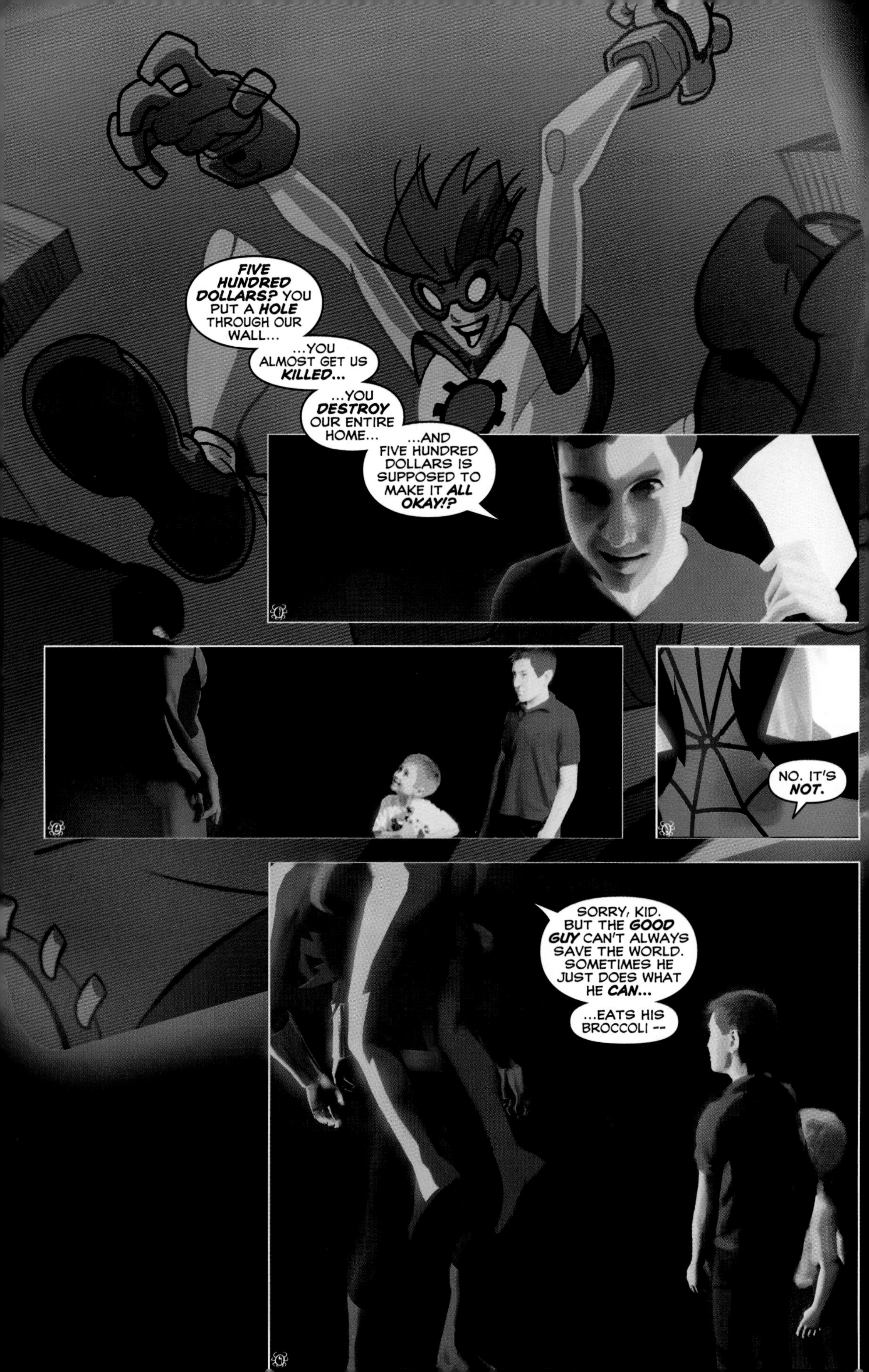
FIVE HUNDRED DOLLARS? YOU PUT A HOLE THROUGH OUR WALL...
...YOU ALMOST GET US KILLED...
...YOU DESTROY OUR ENTIRE HOME...
...AND FIVE HUNDRED DOLLARS IS SUPPOSED TO MAKE IT ALL OKAY!?
NO. IT'S NOT.
SORRY, KID. BUT THE GOOD GUY CAN'T ALWAYS SAVE THE WORLD. SOMETIMES HE JUST DOES WHAT HE CAN...
...EATS HIS BROCCOLI --

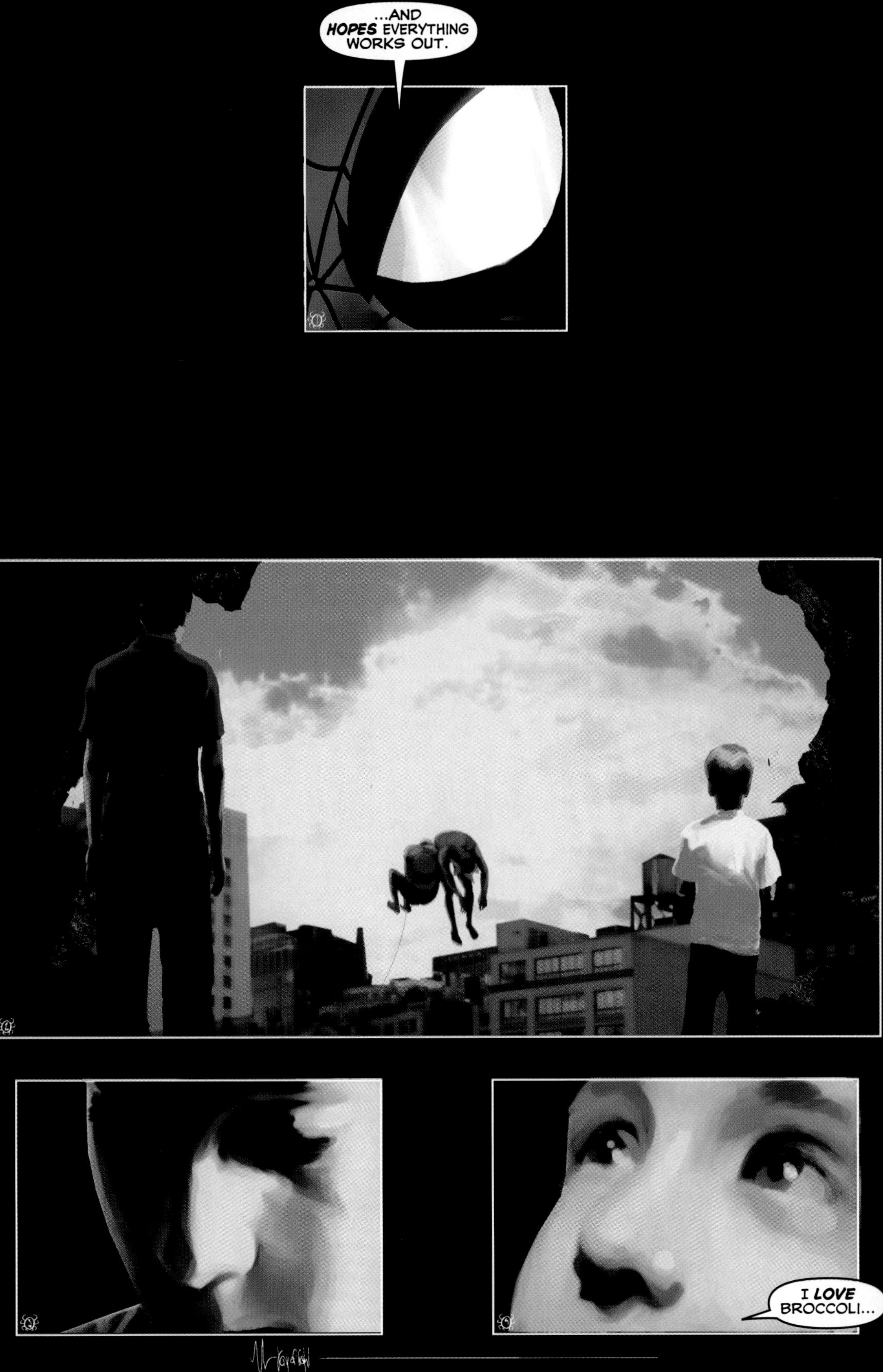
...AND HOPES EVERYTHING WORKS OUT.
I LOVE BROCCOLI...

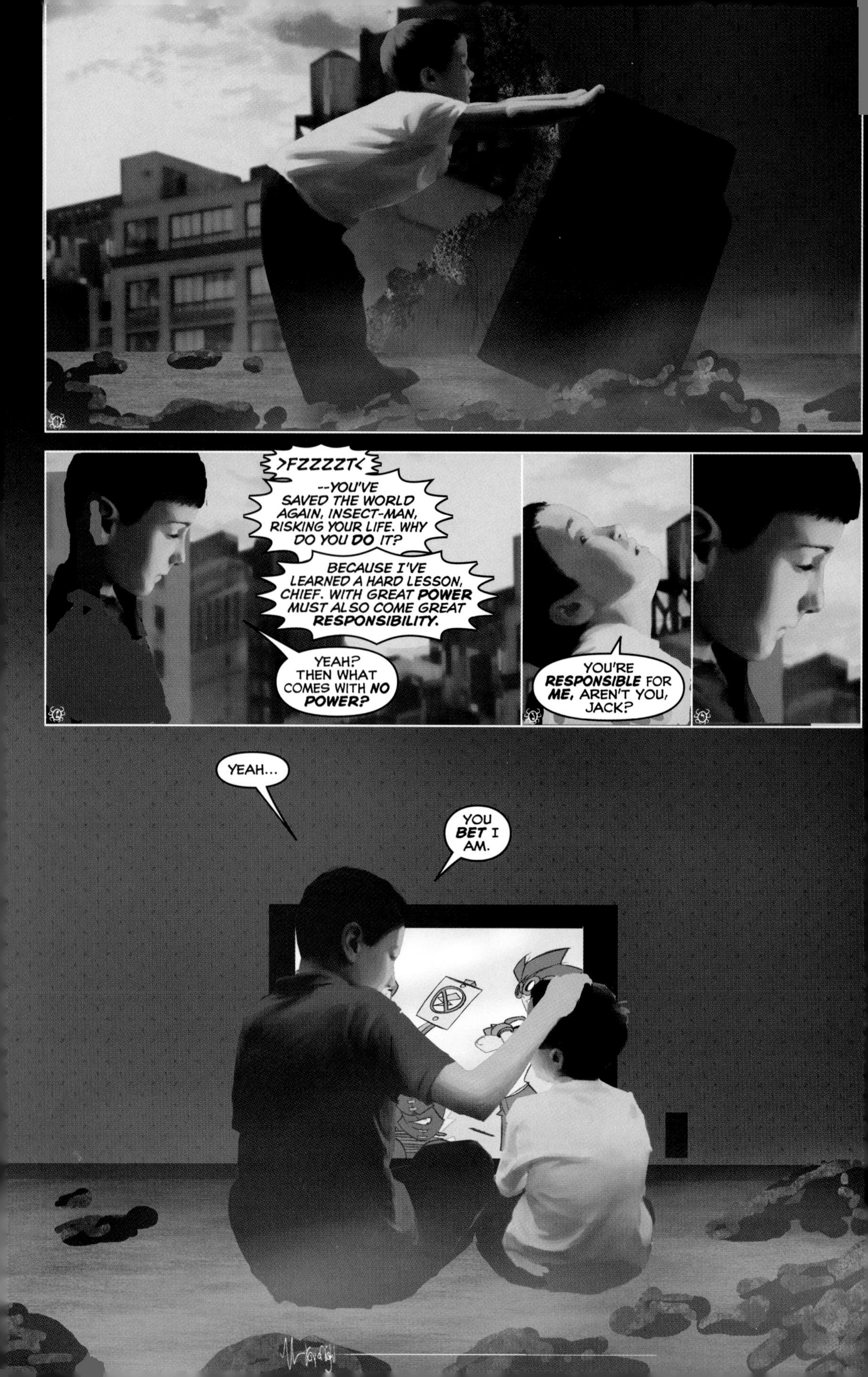

>FZZZZT<
--YOU'VE SAVED THE WORLD AGAIN, INSECT-MAN, RISKING YOUR LIFE. WHY DO YOU DO IT?
BECAUSE I'VE LEARNED A HARD LESSON, CHIEF. WITH GREAT POWER MUST ALSO COME GREAT RESPONSIBILITY.
YEAH? THEN WHAT COMES WITH NO POWER?
YOU'RE RESPONSIBLE FOR ME, AREN'T YOU, JACK?
YEAH...
YOU BET I AM.

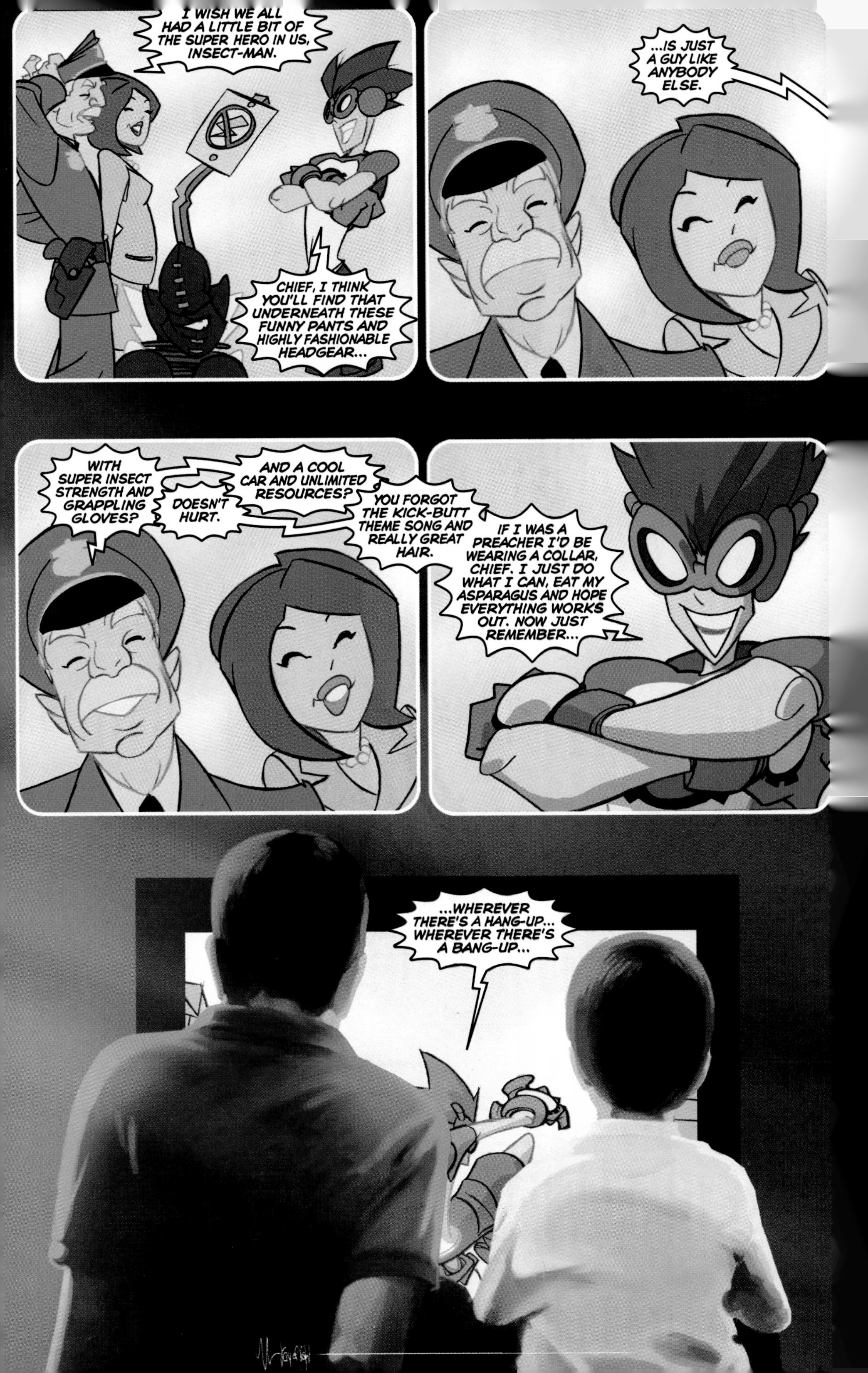
I WISH WE ALL HAD A LITTLE BIT OF THE SUPER HERO IN US, INSECT-MAN.
CHIEF, I THINK YOU'LL FIND THAT UNDERNEATH THESE FUNNY PANTS AND HIGHLY FASHIONABLE HEADGEAR...
...IS JUST A GUY LIKE ANYBODY ELSE.
WITH SUPER INSECT STRENGTH AND GRAPPLING GLOVES?
DOESN'T HURT.
AND A COOL CAR AND UNLIMITED RESOURCES?
YOU FORGOT THE KICK-BUTT THEME SONG AND REALLY GREAT HAIR.
IF I WAS A PREACHER I'D BE WEARING A COLLAR, CHIEF. I JUST DO WHAT I CAN, EAT MY ASPARAGUS AND HOPE EVERYTHING WORKS OUT. NOW JUST REMEMBER...
...WHEREVER THERE'S A HANG-UP... WHEREVER THERE'S A BANG-UP...

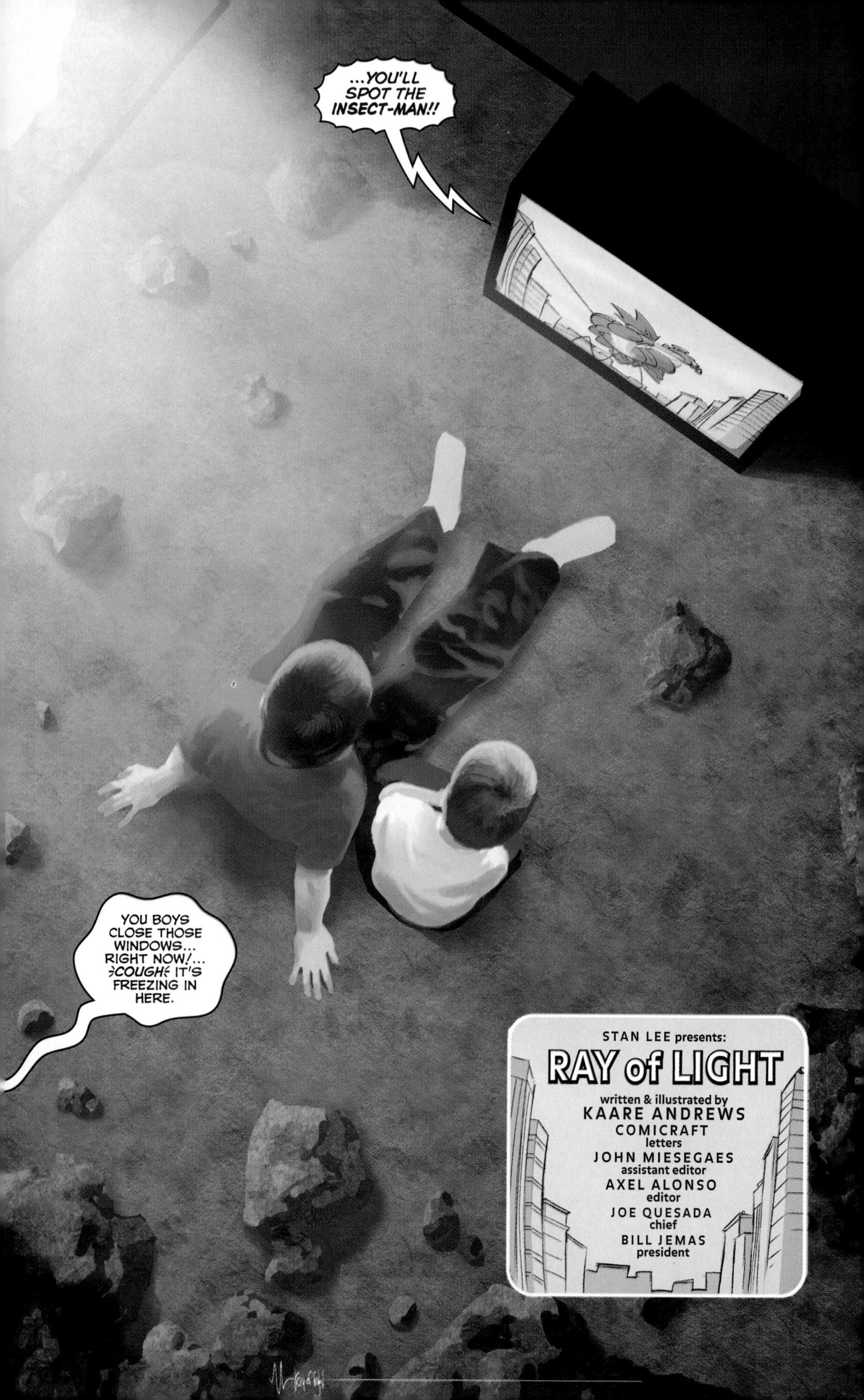

...YOU'LL SPOT THE INSECT-MAN!!
YOU BOYS CLOSE THOSE WINDOWS... RIGHT NOW!... *COUGH* IT'S FREEZING IN HERE.
STAN LEE presents:
RAY of LIGHT
written & illustrated by
KAARE ANDREWS
COMICRAFT
letters
JOHN MIESEGAES
assistant editor
AXEL ALONSO
editor
JOE QUESADA
chief
BILL JEMAS
president

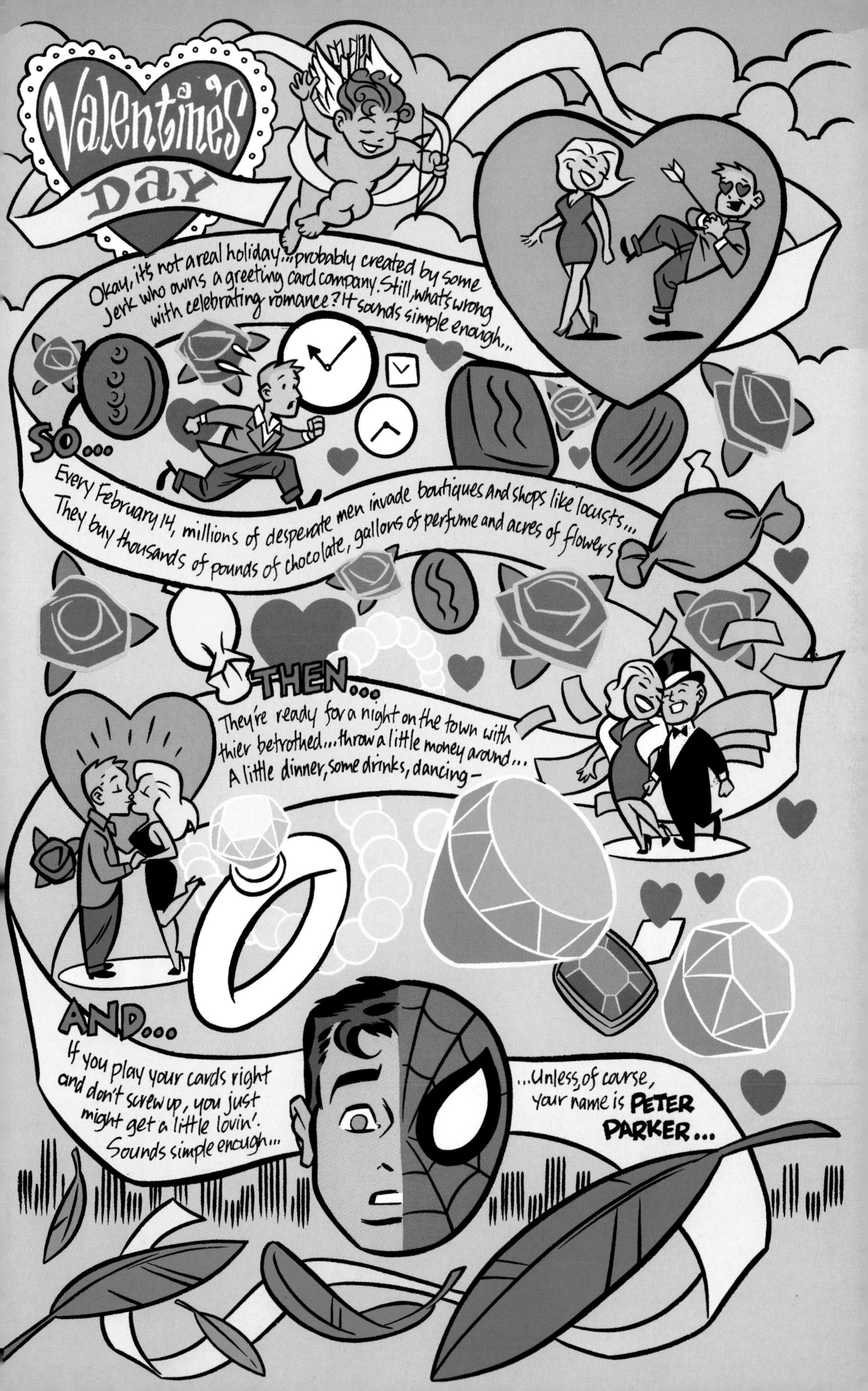
Valentine's Day
Okay, it's not a real holiday...probably created by some Jerk who owns a greeting card company. Still, what's wrong with celebrating romance? It sounds simple enough...
SO...
Every February 14, millions of desperate men invade boutiques and shops like locusts... They buy thousands of pounds of chocolate, gallons of perfume and acres of flowers
THEN...
They're ready for a night on the town with thier betrothed... throw a little money around... A little dinner, some drinks, dancing–
AND...
If you play your cards right and don't screw up, you just might get a little lovin'. Sounds simple enough...
...Unless, of course, your name is PETER PARKER...

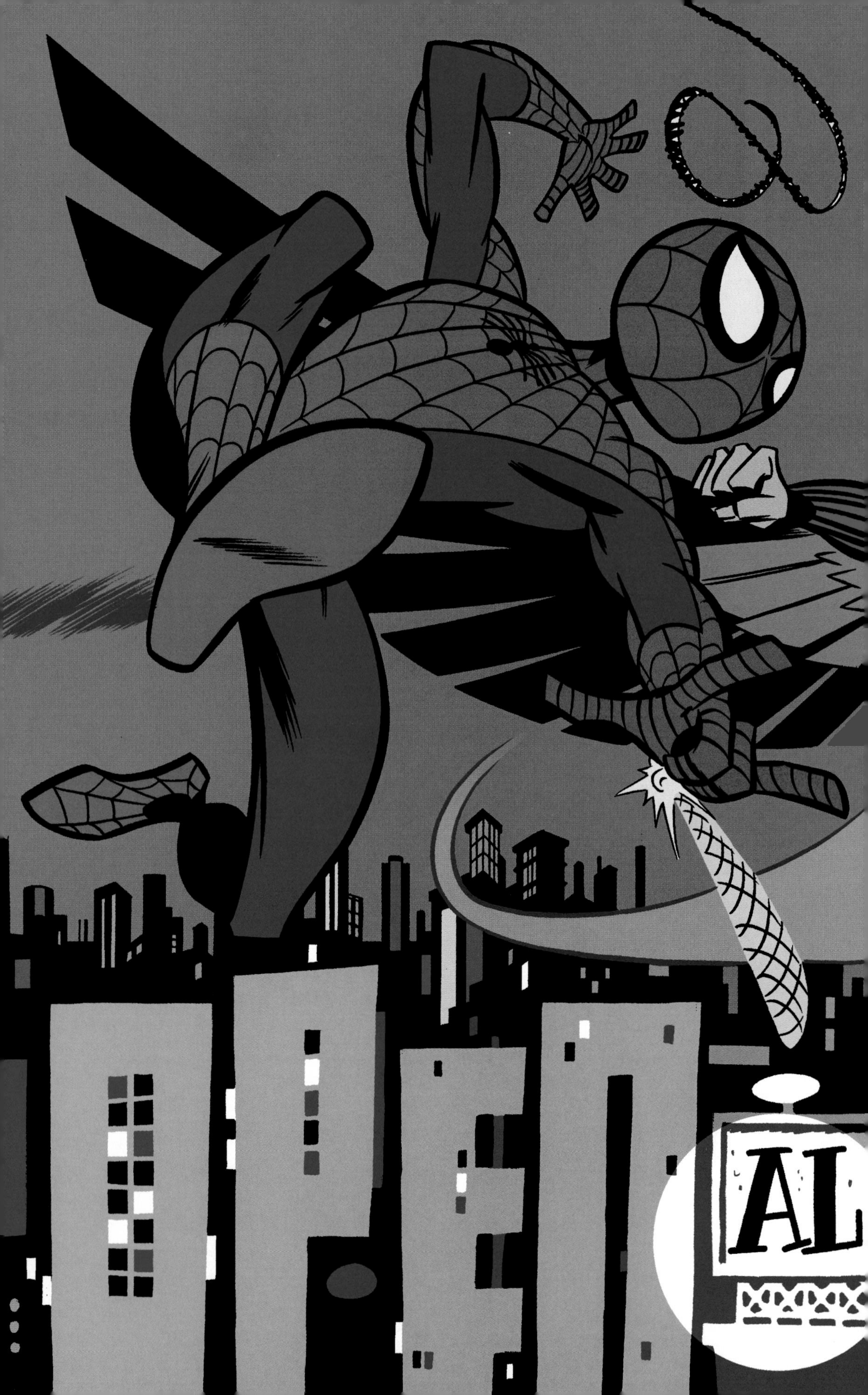
AL

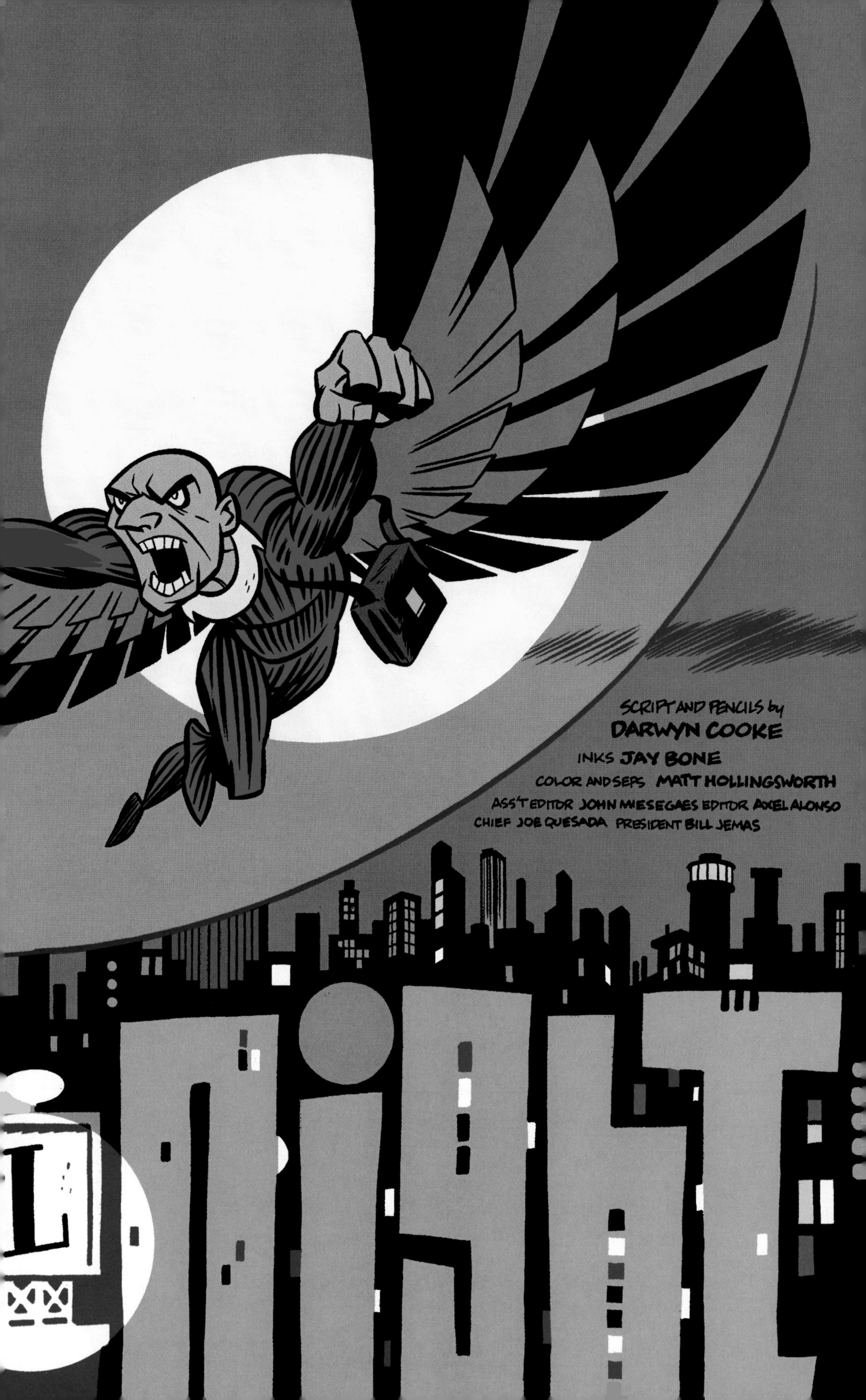
SCRIPT AND PENCILS by
DARWYN COOKE
INKS JAY BONE
COLOR AND SEPS MATT HOLLINGSWORTH
ASS'T EDITOR JOHN MIESEGAES EDITOR AXEL ALONSO
CHIEF JOE QUESADA PRESIDENT BILL JEMAS

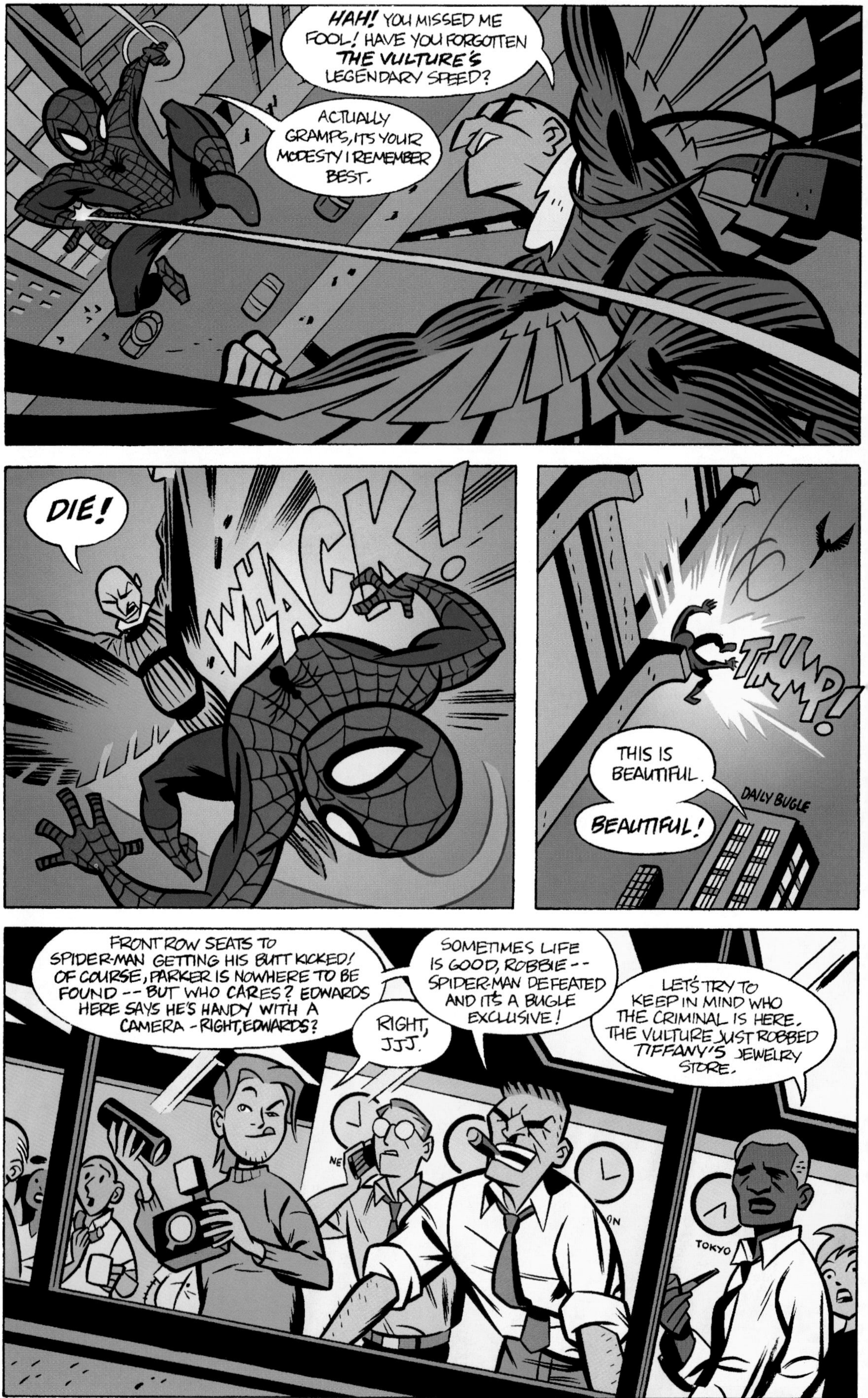
HAH! YOU MISSED ME FOOL! HAVE YOU FORGOTTEN THE VULTURE'S LEGENDARY SPEED?
ACTUALLY GRAMPS, ITS YOUR MODESTY I REMEMBER BEST.
DIE!
WHACK!
THUMP!
THIS IS BEAUTIFUL.
BEAUTIFUL!
DAILY BUGLE
FRONT ROW SEATS TO SPIDER-MAN GETTING HIS BUTT KICKED! OF COURSE, PARKER IS NOWHERE TO BE FOUND -- BUT WHO CARES? EDWARDS HERE SAYS HE'S HANDY WITH A CAMERA - RIGHT, EDWARDS?
RIGHT, JJJ.
SOMETIMES LIFE IS GOOD, ROBBIE -- SPIDER-MAN DEFEATED AND IT'S A BUGLE EXCLUSIVE!
LET'S TRY TO KEEP IN MIND WHO THE CRIMINAL IS HERE. THE VULTURE JUST ROBBED TIFFANY'S JEWELRY STORE.
TOKYO

I DON'T CARE IF HE ROBBED *TIFFANY'S ORPHANAGE*, ROBBIE! LOOK AT THAT OLD FOOL HAMMERING THE *WALL-CRAWLER*!

HE'S CIRCLING FOR THE KILL NOW -- GET READY, EDWARDS... *EDWARDS?* I DON'T HEAR THAT CAMERA CLICKING--

EDWARDS?

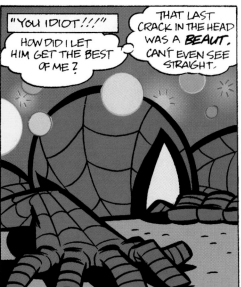
"YOU *IDIOT!!!!*"

HOW DID I LET HIM GET THE BEST OF ME?

THAT LAST CRACK IN THE HEAD WAS A *BEAUT.* CAN'T EVEN SEE STRAIGHT.

HERE HE COMES... HOOBOY, THIS IS BAD.

GOTTA FOCUS... TAKE THE FIGHT TO HIM.

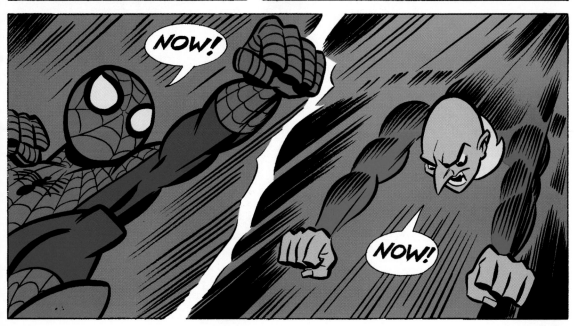
NOW!

NOW!

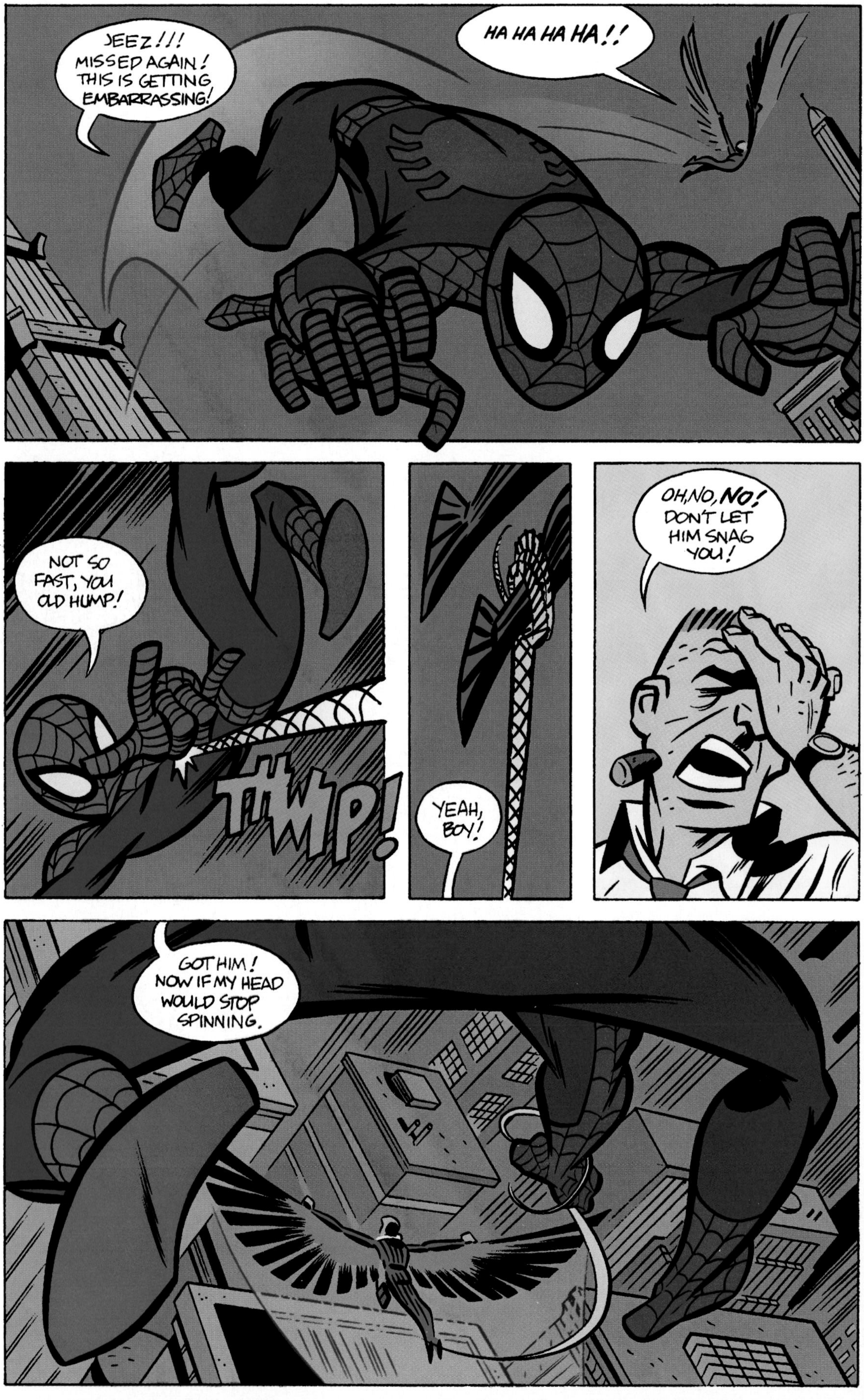
JEEZ!!! MISSED AGAIN! THIS IS GETTING EMBARRASSING!
HA HA HA HA!!
NOT SO FAST, YOU OLD HUMP!
THWP!
YEAH, BOY!
OH, NO, NO! DON'T LET HIM SNAG YOU!
GOT HIM! NOW IF MY HEAD WOULD STOP SPINNING.

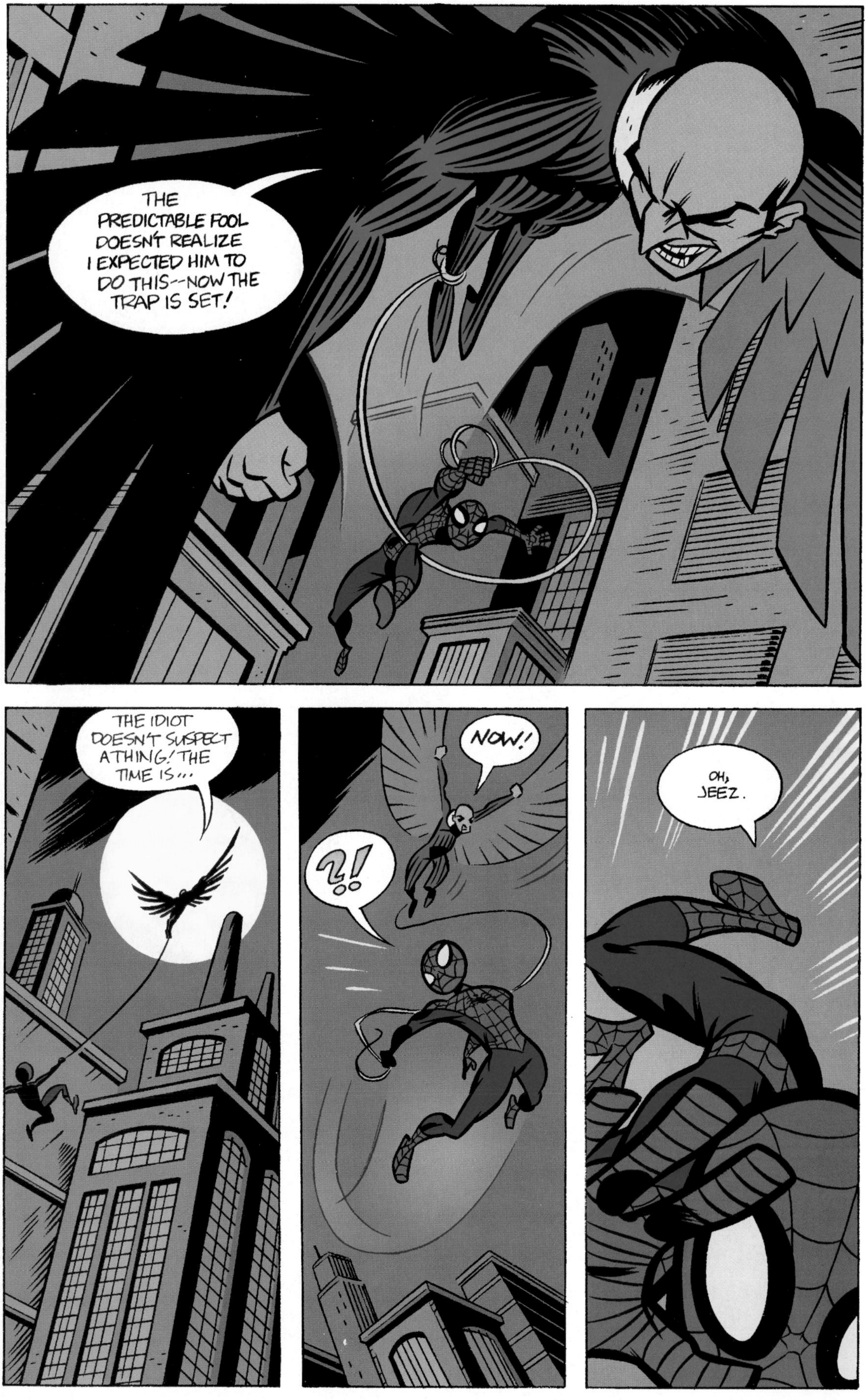
THE PREDICTABLE FOOL DOESN'T REALIZE I EXPECTED HIM TO DO THIS--NOW THE TRAP IS SET!
THE IDIOT DOESN'T SUSPECT A THING! THE TIME IS...
NOW!
?!
OH, JEEZ.

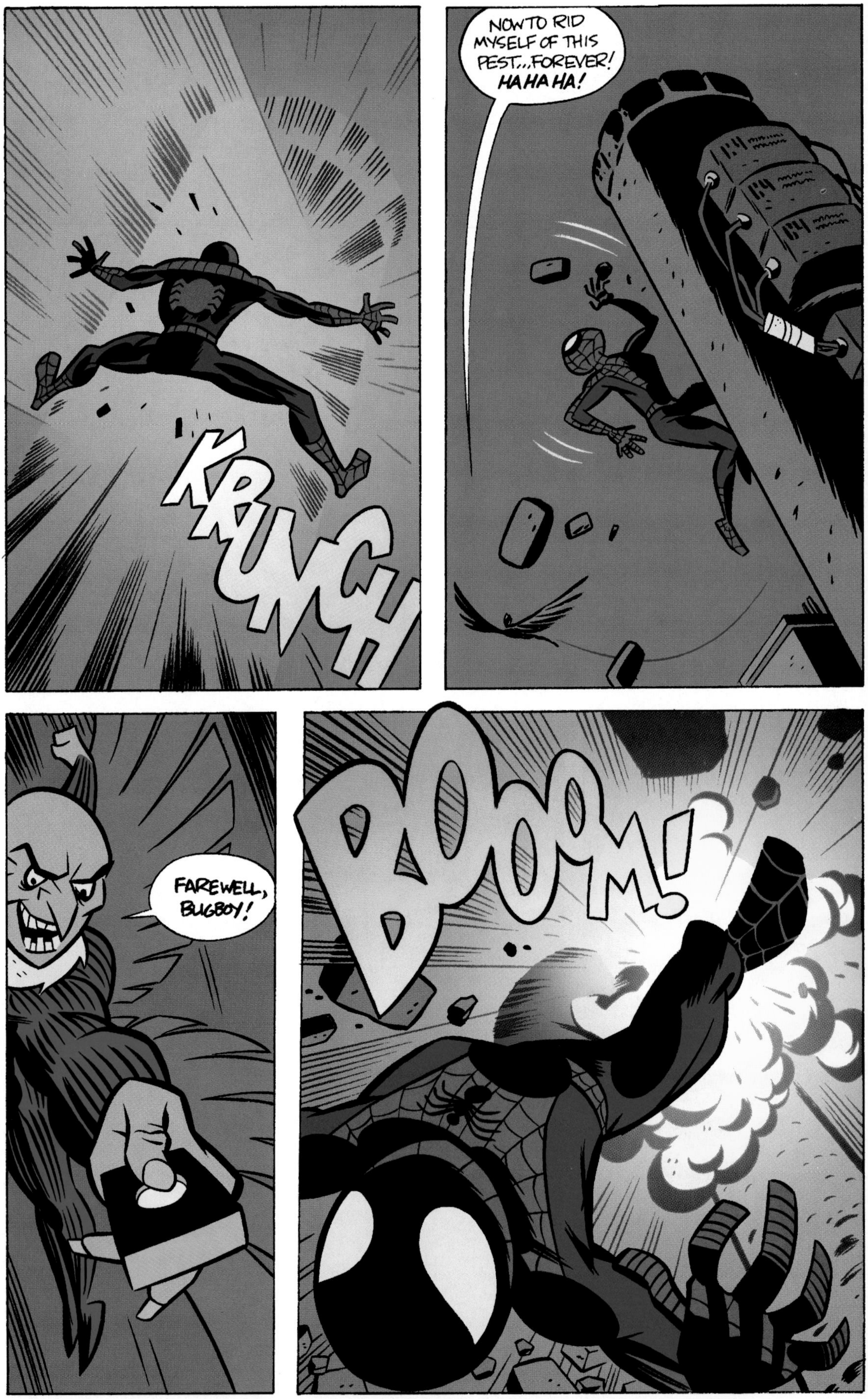
KRUNCH
NOW TO RID MYSELF OF THIS PEST...FOREVER! HA HA HA!
FAREWELL, BUGBOY!
BOOOM!

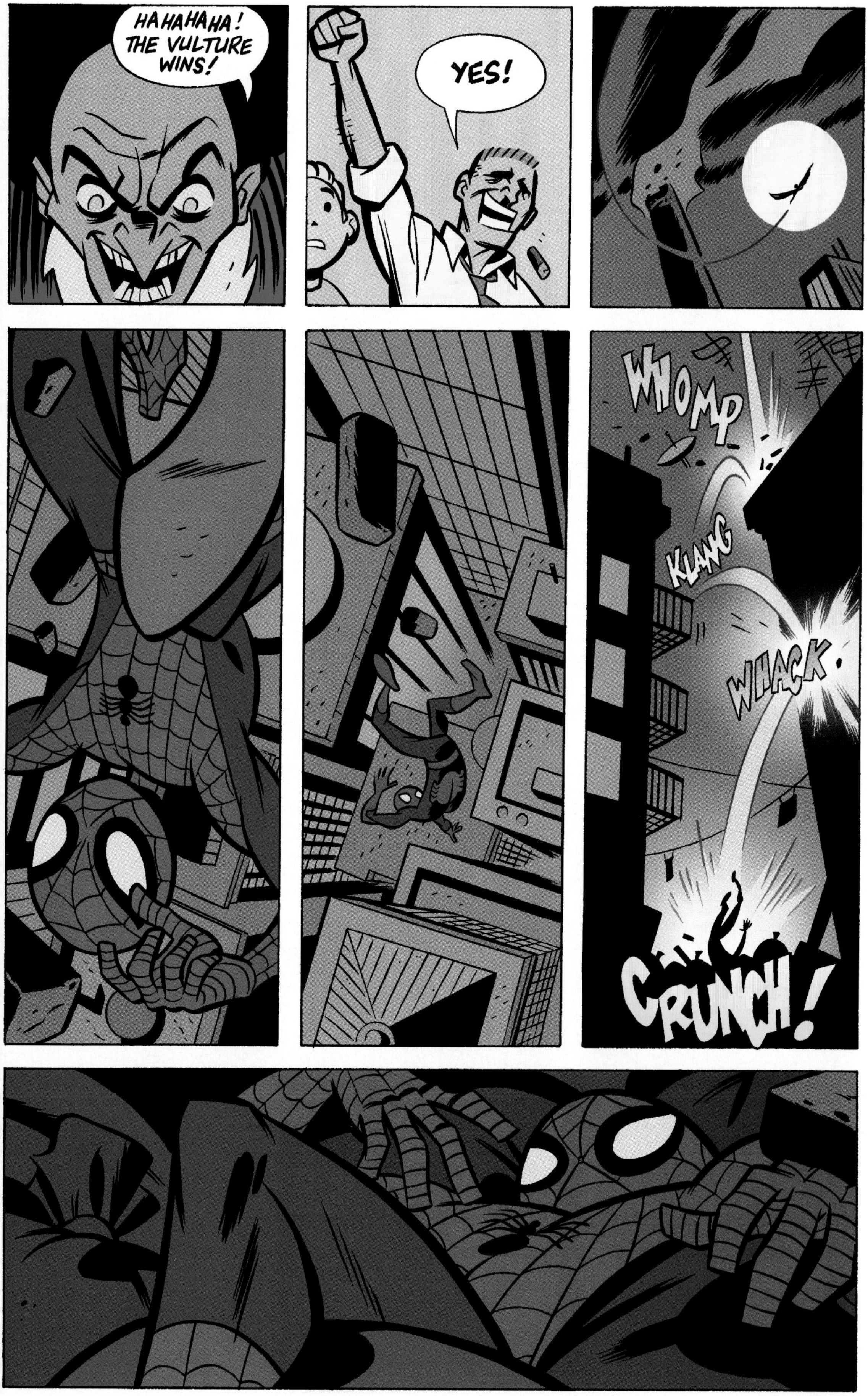
HAHAHAHA! THE VULTURE WINS!
YES!
WHOMP
KLANG
WHACK
CRUNCH!

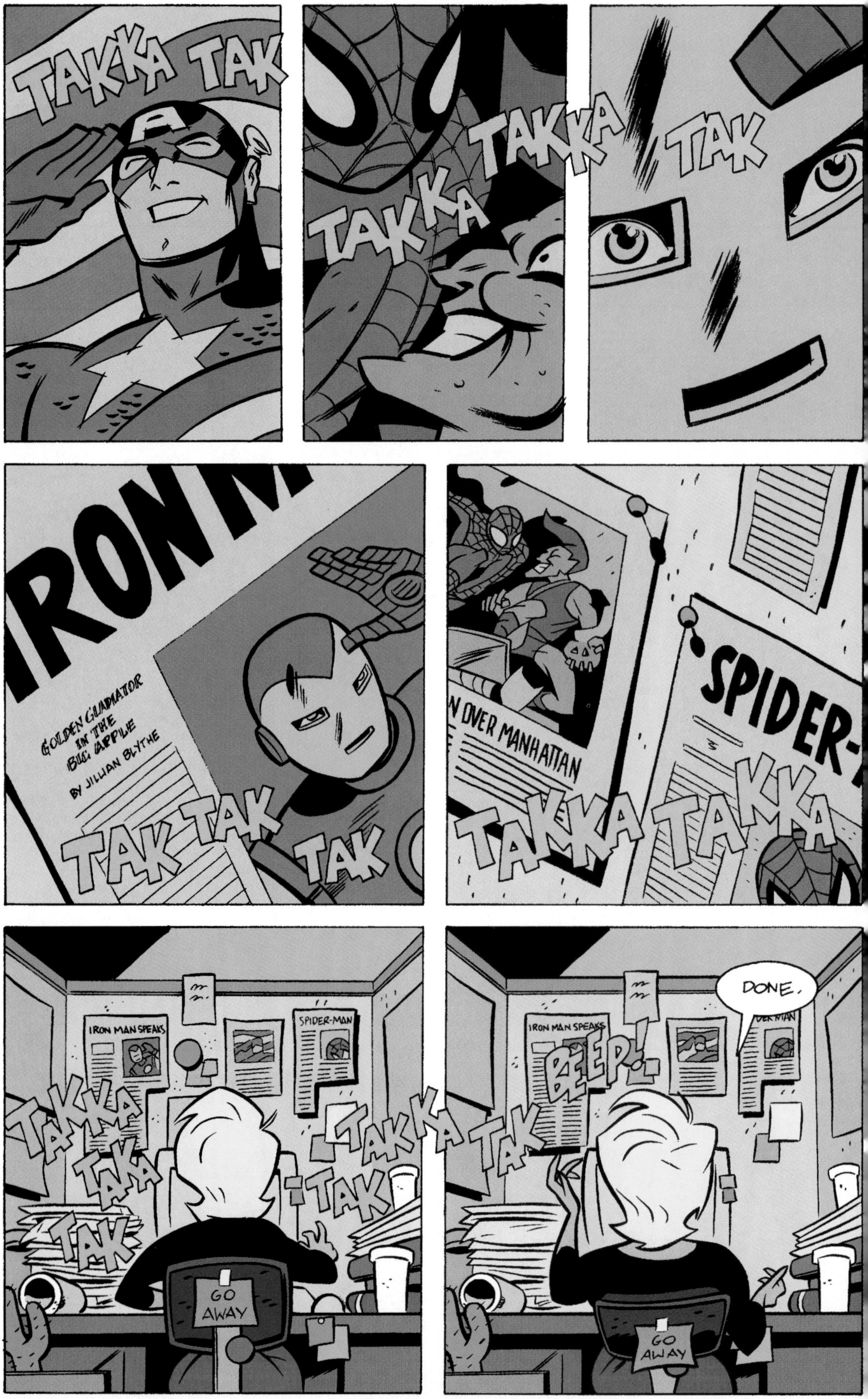
TAKKA TAK
TAKKA TAKKA TAK
IRON M
GOLDEN GLADIATOR IN THE BIG APPLE
BY JILLIAN BLYTHE
TAK TAK TAK
N OVER MANHATTAN
SPIDER-
TAKKA TAKKA
IRON MAN SPEAKS
SPIDER-MAN
TAKKA TAKA TAK
TAK
GO AWAY
TAKKA TAK
BEEP!
IRON MAN SPEAKS
DONE.
GO AWAY

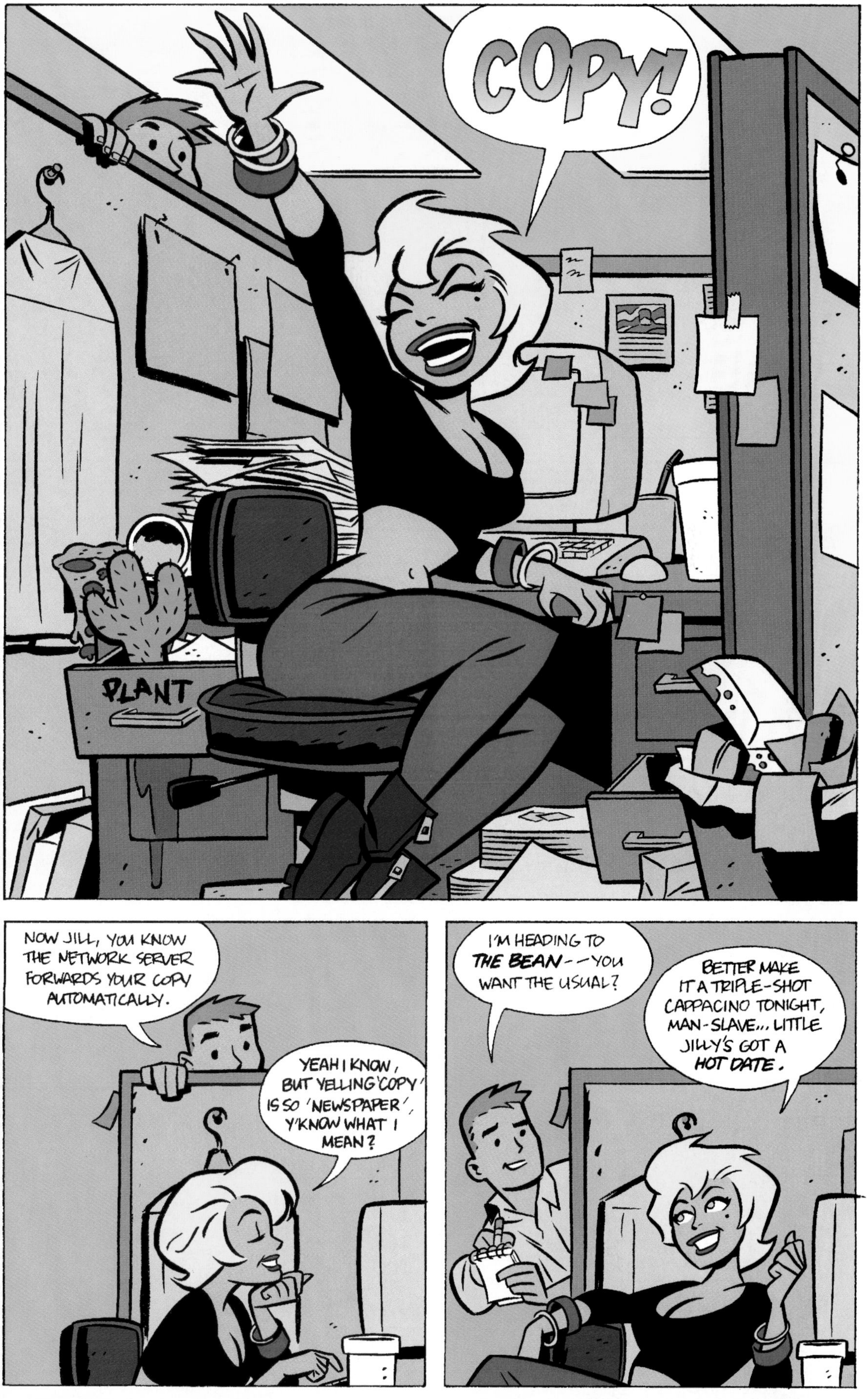
COPY!
NOW JILL, YOU KNOW THE NETWORK SERVER FORWARDS YOUR COPY AUTOMATICALLY.
YEAH I KNOW, BUT YELLING 'COPY' IS SO 'NEWSPAPER', Y'KNOW WHAT I MEAN?
I'M HEADING TO THE BEAN--YOU WANT THE USUAL?
BETTER MAKE IT A TRIPLE-SHOT CAPPACINO TONIGHT, MAN-SLAVE... LITTLE JILLY'S GOT A HOT DATE.
PLANT

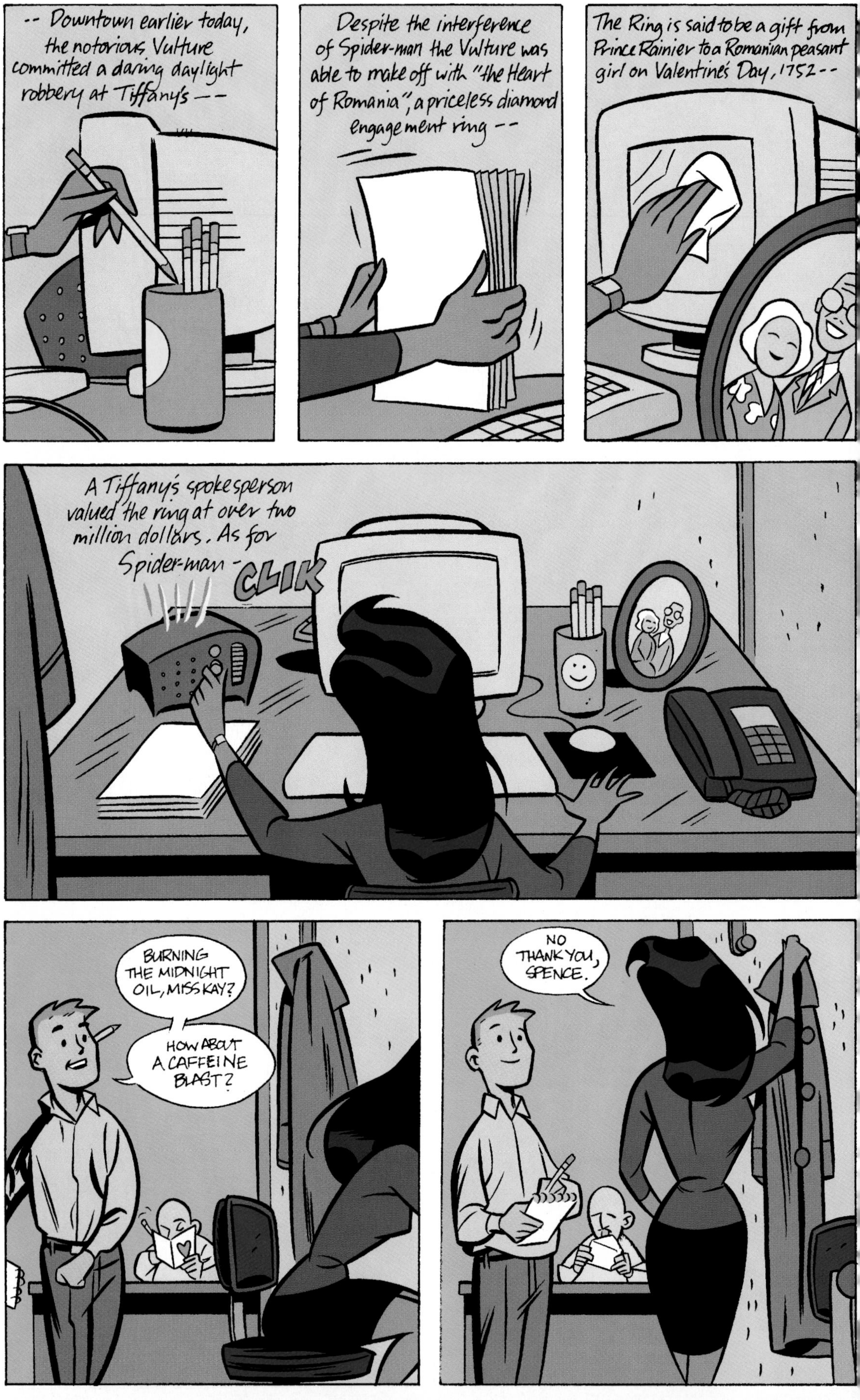
-- Downtown earlier today, the notorious Vulture committed a daring daylight robbery at Tiffany's --
Despite the interference of Spider-man the Vulture was able to make off with "the Heart of Romania", a priceless diamond engagement ring --
The Ring is said to be a gift from Prince Rainier to a Romanian peasant girl on Valentine's Day, 1752 --
A Tiffany's spokesperson valued the ring at over two million dollars. As for Spider-man -
CLIK
BURNING THE MIDNIGHT OIL, MISS KAY?
HOW ABOUT A CAFFEINE BLAST?
NO THANK YOU, SPENCE.

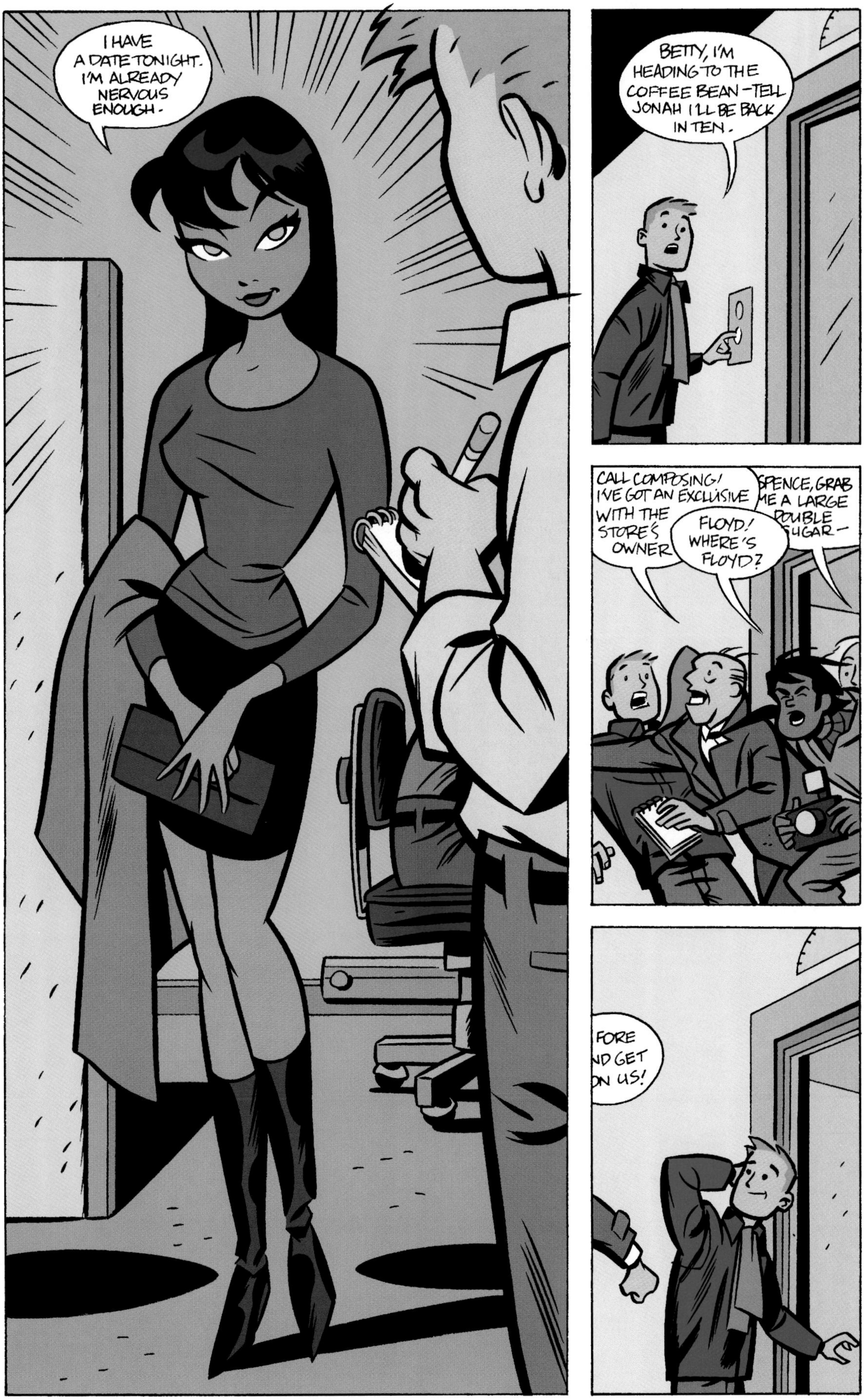
I HAVE A DATE TONIGHT. I'M ALREADY NERVOUS ENOUGH-
BETTY, I'M HEADING TO THE COFFEE BEAN-TELL JONAH I'LL BE BACK IN TEN.
CALL COMPOSING! I'VE GOT AN EXCLUSIVE WITH THE STORE'S OWNER
FLOYD! WHERE'S FLOYD?
SPENCE, GRAB ME A LARGE DOUBLE SUGAR-
FORE ND GET ON US!

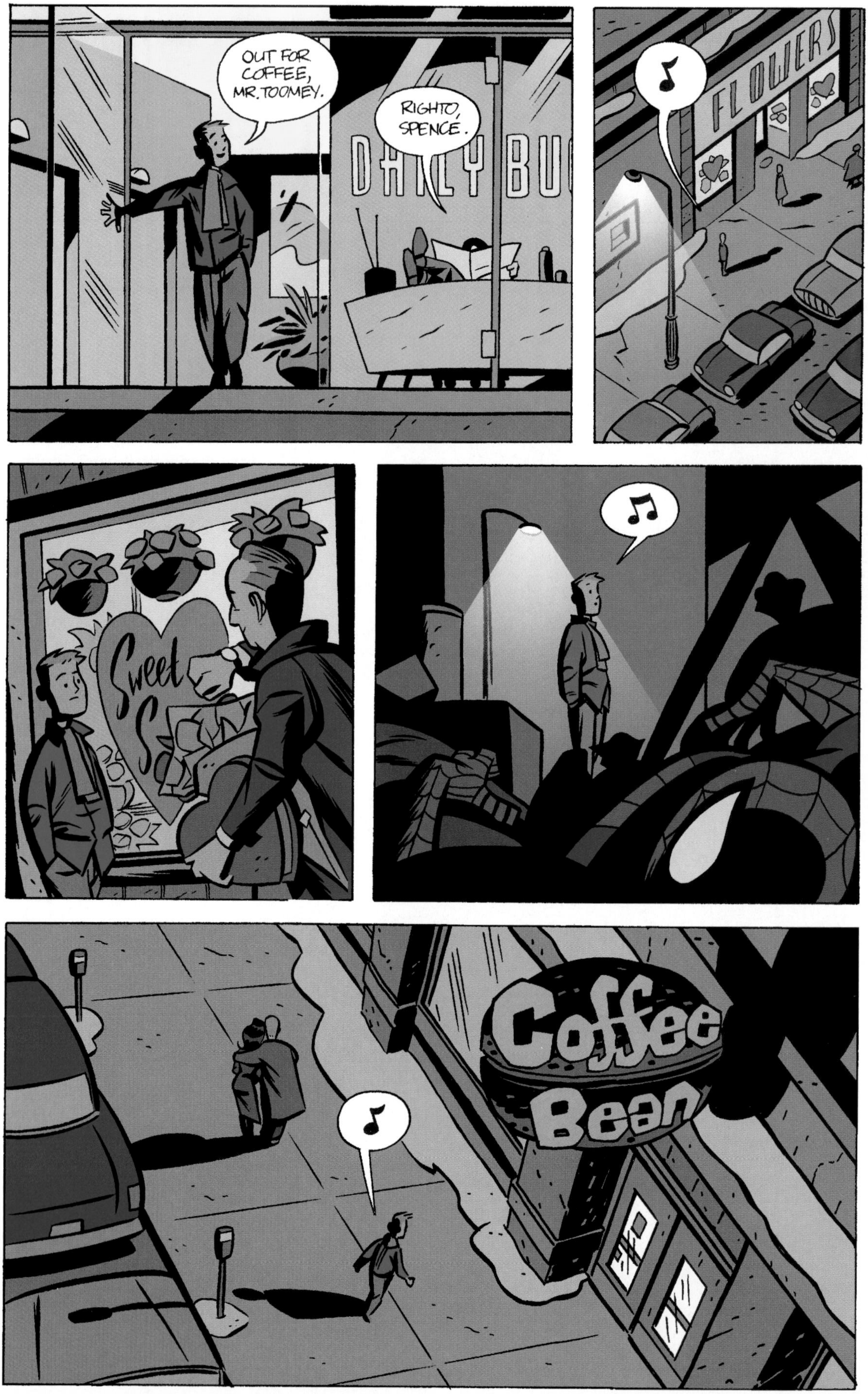
OUT FOR COFFEE, MR. TOOMEY.
RIGHTO, SPENCE.
DAILY BU
FLOWERS
♪
Sweet S
♫
Coffee Bean
♪

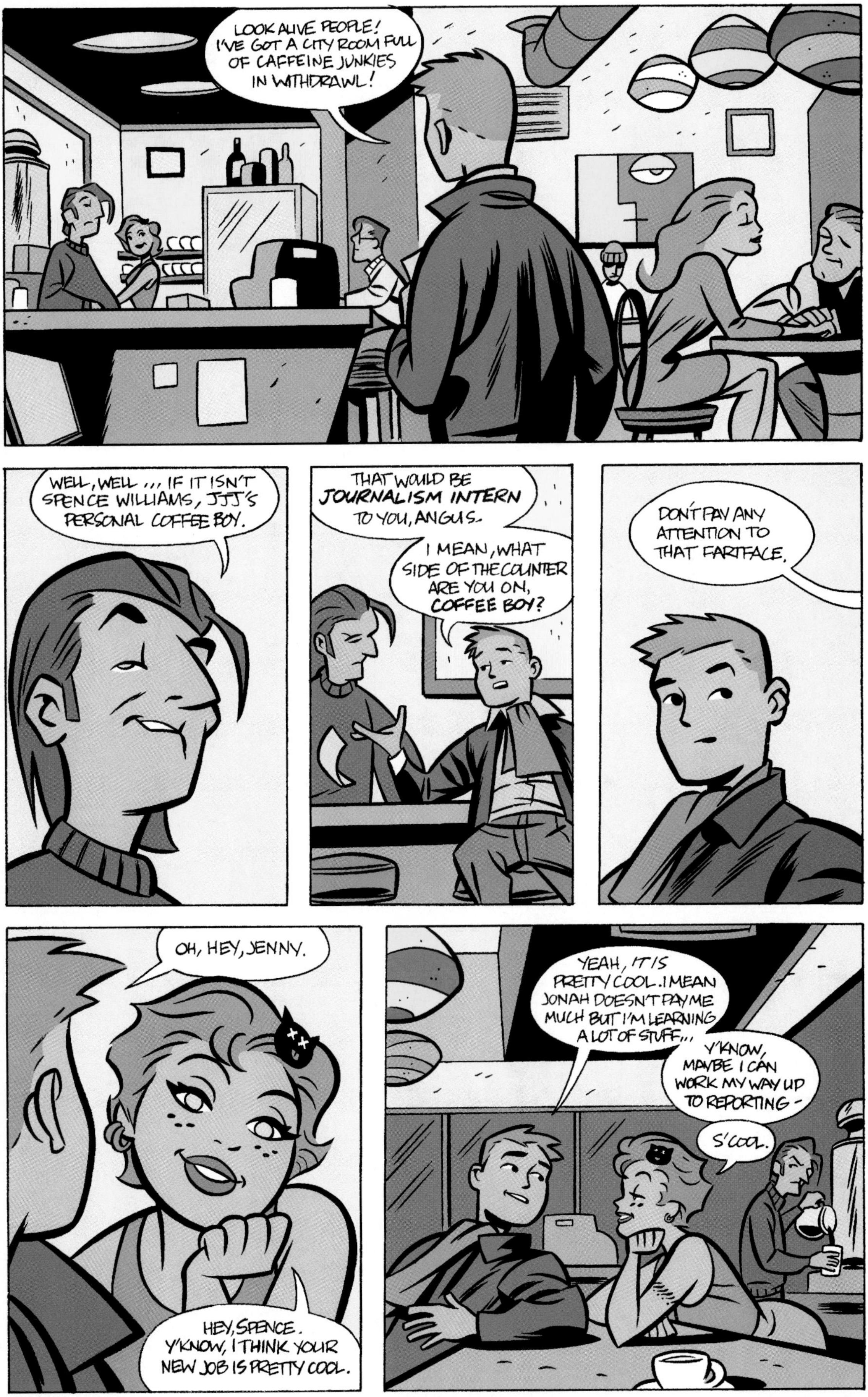
LOOK ALIVE PEOPLE! I'VE GOT A CITY ROOM FULL OF CAFFEINE JUNKIES IN WITHDRAWL!
WELL, WELL ... IF IT ISN'T SPENCE WILLIAMS, JJJ'S PERSONAL COFFEE BOY.
THAT WOULD BE JOURNALISM INTERN TO YOU, ANGUS.
I MEAN, WHAT SIDE OF THE COUNTER ARE YOU ON, COFFEE BOY?
DON'T PAY ANY ATTENTION TO THAT FARTFACE.
OH, HEY, JENNY.
HEY, SPENCE. Y'KNOW, I THINK YOUR NEW JOB IS PRETTY COOL.
YEAH, IT IS PRETTY COOL. I MEAN JONAH DOESN'T PAY ME MUCH BUT I'M LEARNING A LOT OF STUFF...
Y'KNOW, MAYBE I CAN WORK MY WAY UP TO REPORTING -
S'COOL.

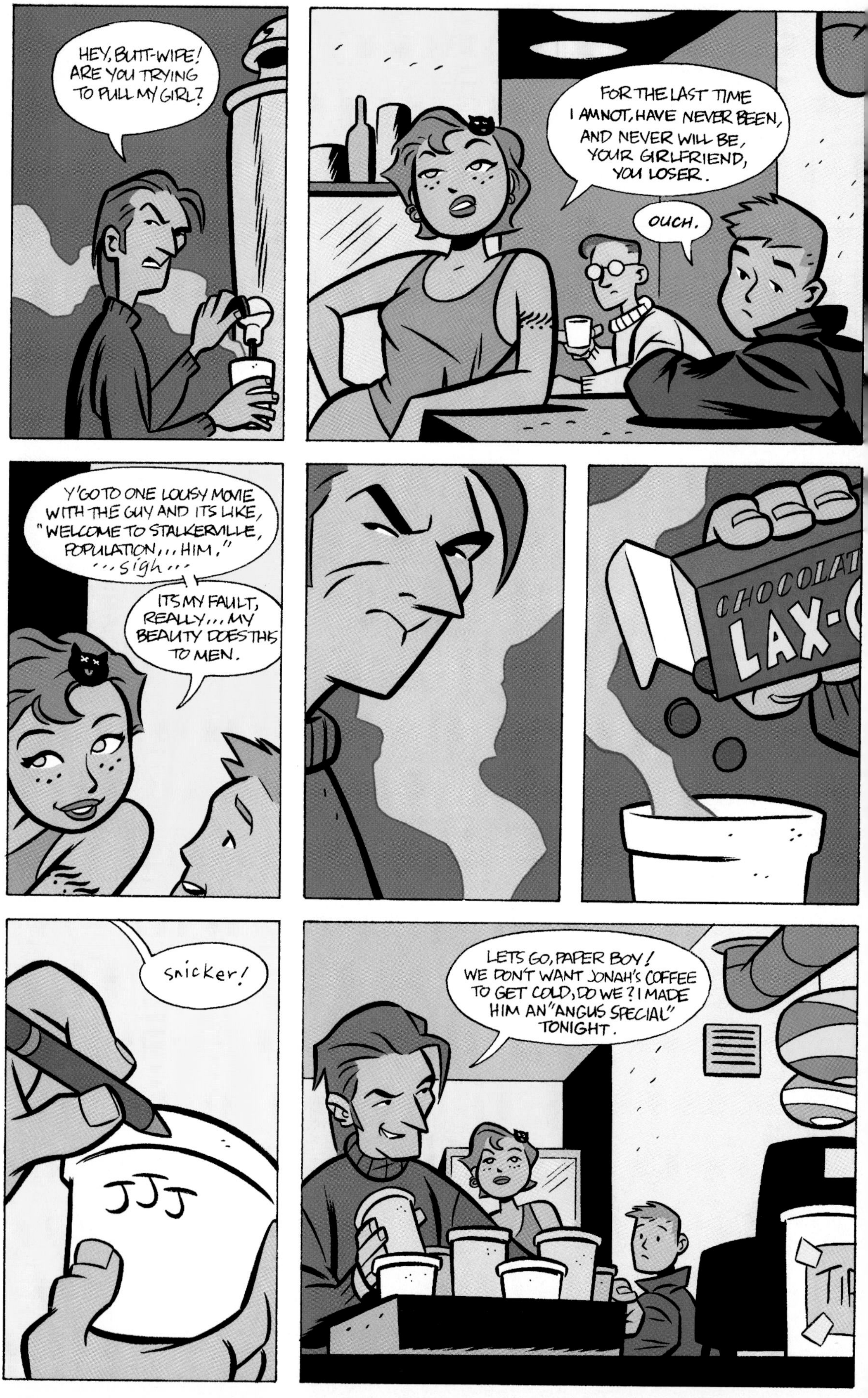
HEY, BUTT-WIPE! ARE YOU TRYING TO PULL MY GIRL?
FOR THE LAST TIME I AM NOT, HAVE NEVER BEEN, AND NEVER WILL BE, YOUR GIRLFRIEND, YOU LOSER.
OUCH.
Y'GO TO ONE LOUSY MOVIE WITH THE GUY AND ITS LIKE, "WELCOME TO STALKERVILLE, POPULATION... HIM." ...sigh...
ITS MY FAULT, REALLY... MY BEAUTY DOES THIS TO MEN.
CHOCOLAT
LAX-
snicker!
JJJ
LETS GO, PAPER BOY! WE DON'T WANT JONAH'S COFFEE TO GET COLD, DO WE? I MADE HIM AN "ANGUS SPECIAL" TONIGHT.
TI

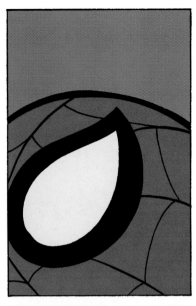

SCHHHK

SCHZIK

NNNF!

YARF!

I'LL GET UP IN A MINUTE, AUNT MAY,, I JUST NEED... ZZZZ...

URF?

HEY, LITTLE GUY!

ARF!

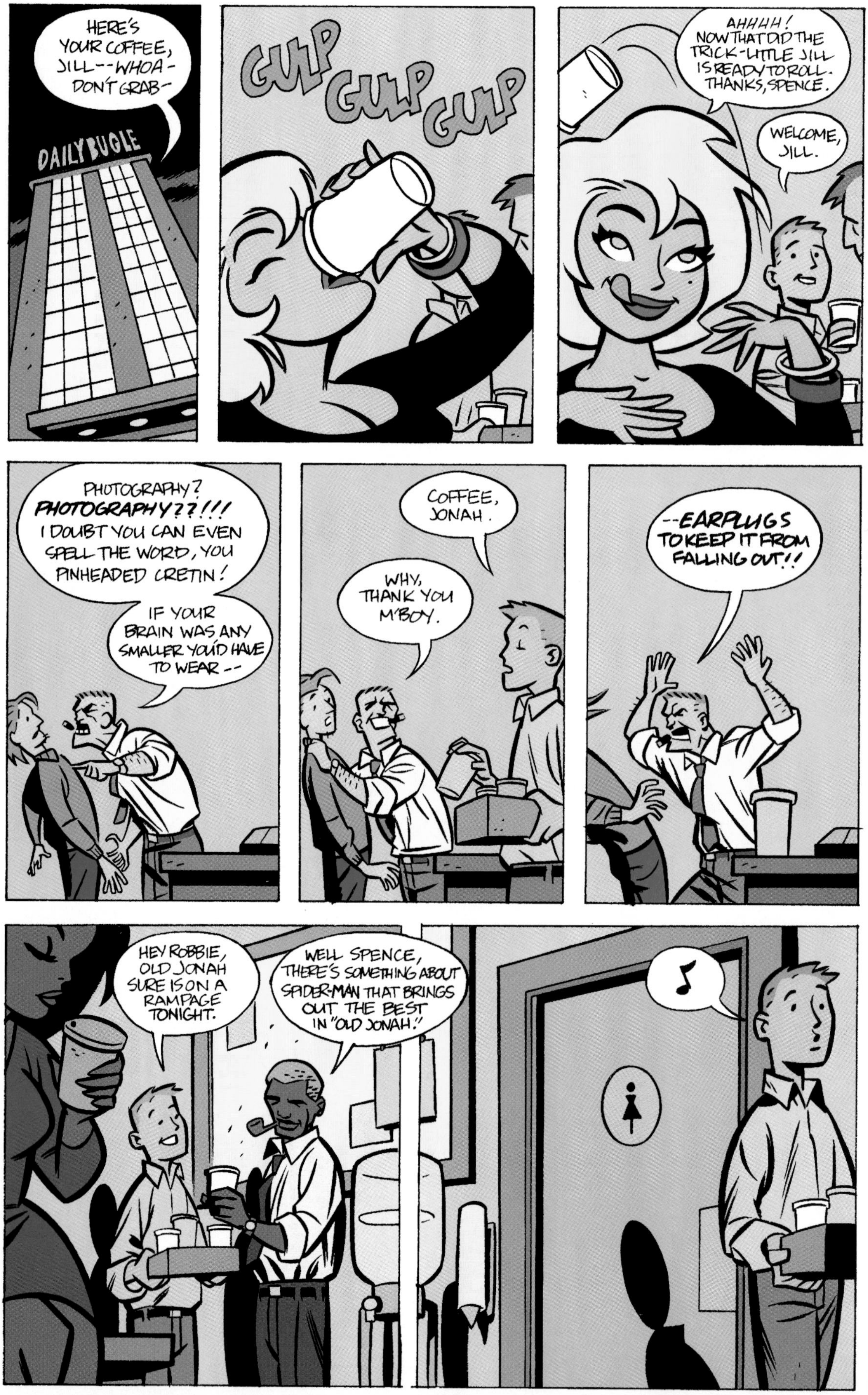
HERE'S YOUR COFFEE, JILL--WHOA-DON'T GRAB-
DAILY BUGLE
GULP GULP GULP
AHHHH! NOW THAT DID THE TRICK-LITTLE JILL IS READY TO ROLL. THANKS, SPENCE.
WELCOME, JILL.
PHOTOGRAPHY? PHOTOGRAPHY??!!! I DOUBT YOU CAN EVEN SPELL THE WORD, YOU PINHEADED CRETIN!
IF YOUR BRAIN WAS ANY SMALLER YOU'D HAVE TO WEAR--
COFFEE, JONAH.
WHY, THANK YOU M'BOY.
--EARPLUGS TO KEEP IT FROM FALLING OUT!!
HEY ROBBIE, OLD JONAH SURE IS ON A RAMPAGE TONIGHT.
WELL SPENCE, THERE'S SOMETHING ABOUT SPIDER-MAN THAT BRINGS OUT THE BEST IN "OLD JONAH."
♪

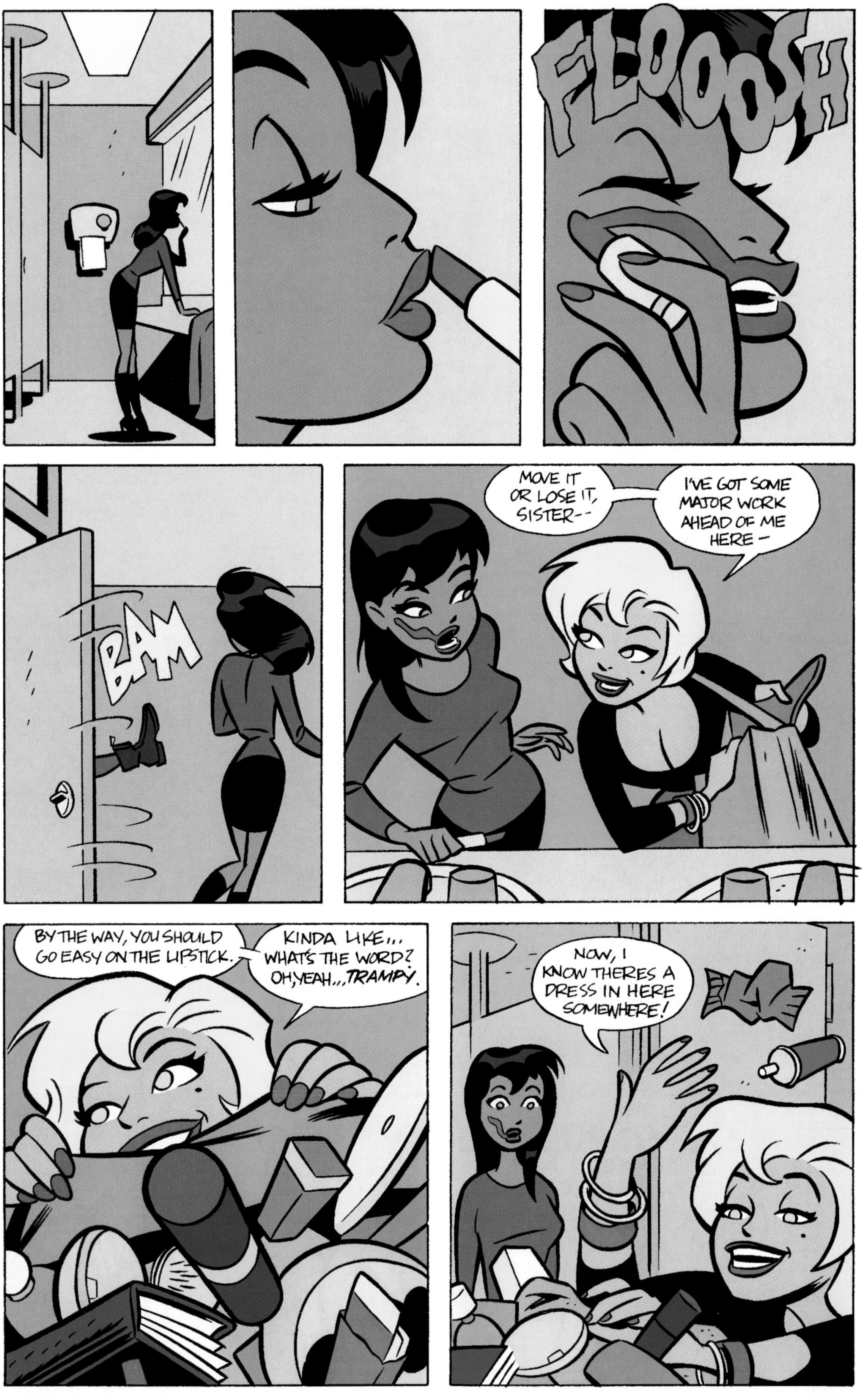
FLOOOSH
BAM
MOVE IT OR LOSE IT, SISTER--
I'VE GOT SOME MAJOR WORK AHEAD OF ME HERE -
BY THE WAY, YOU SHOULD GO EASY ON THE LIPSTICK.
KINDA LIKE... WHAT'S THE WORD? OH, YEAH... TRAMPY.
NOW, I KNOW THERES A DRESS IN HERE SOMEWHERE!

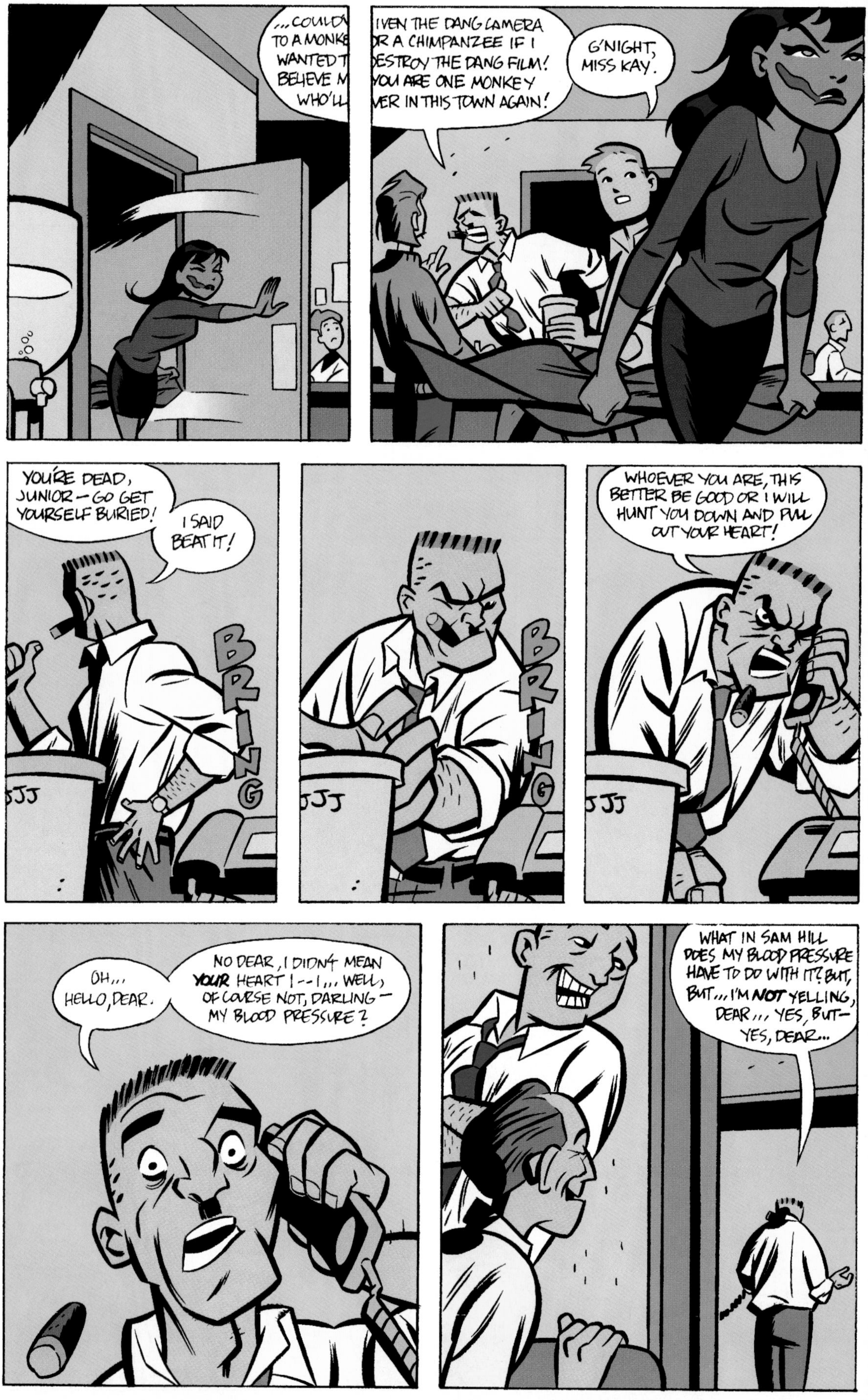
...COULDN'
TO A MONKE
WANTED T
BELIEVE M
WHO'LL
IVEN THE DANG CAMERA
OR A CHIMPANZEE IF I
DESTROY THE DANG FILM!
YOU ARE ONE MONKEY
VER IN THIS TOWN AGAIN!
G'NIGHT, MISS KAY.
YOU'RE DEAD, JUNIOR — GO GET YOURSELF BURIED!
I SAID BEAT IT!
BRING
JJJ
BRING
JJJ
WHOEVER YOU ARE, THIS BETTER BE GOOD OR I WILL HUNT YOU DOWN AND PULL OUT YOUR HEART!
JJJ
OH... HELLO, DEAR.
NO DEAR, I DIDN'T MEAN YOUR HEART! --I... WELL, OF COURSE NOT, DARLING — MY BLOOD PRESSURE?
WHAT IN SAM HILL DOES MY BLOOD PRESSURE HAVE TO DO WITH IT? BUT, BUT... I'M NOT YELLING, DEAR... YES, BUT— YES, DEAR...

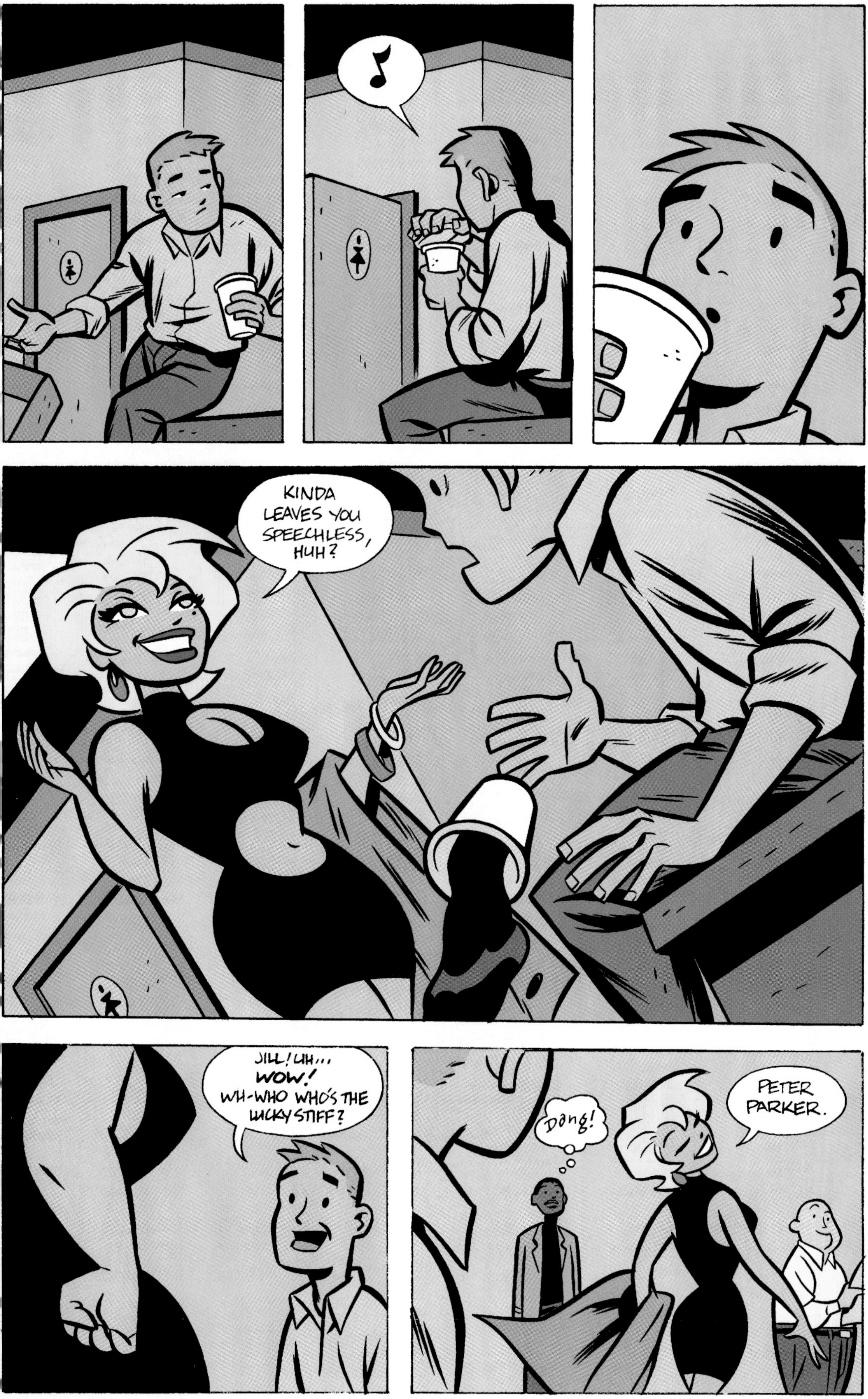
KINDA LEAVES YOU SPEECHLESS, HUH?
JILL! UH... WOW! WH-WHO WHO'S THE LUCKY STIFF?
Dang!
PETER PARKER.

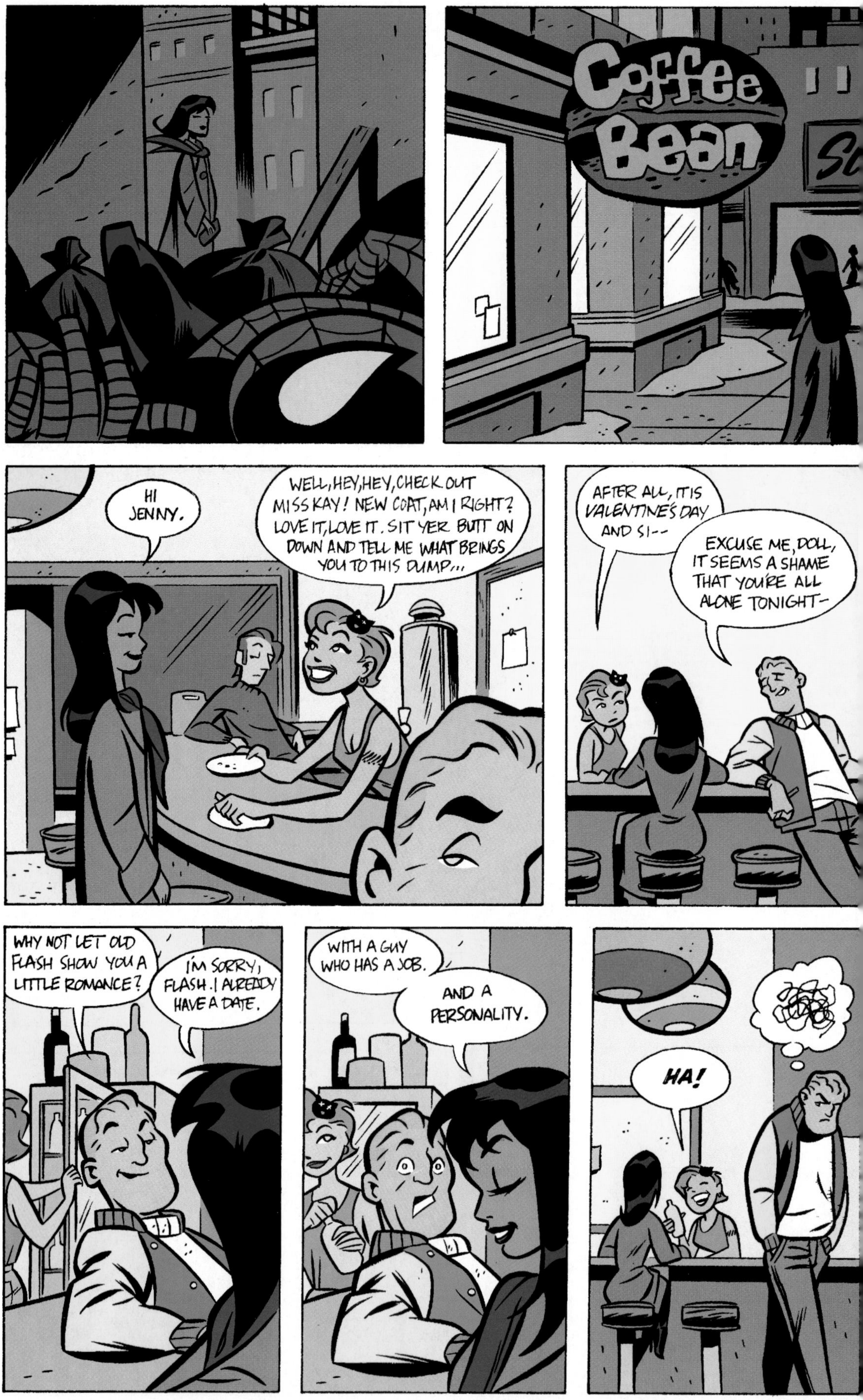
Coffee Bean
HI JENNY.
WELL, HEY, HEY, CHECK OUT MISS KAY! NEW COAT, AM I RIGHT? LOVE IT, LOVE IT. SIT YER BUTT ON DOWN AND TELL ME WHAT BRINGS YOU TO THIS DUMP...
AFTER ALL, IT IS VALENTINE'S DAY AND SI--
EXCUSE ME, DOLL, IT SEEMS A SHAME THAT YOU'RE ALL ALONE TONIGHT-
WHY NOT LET OLD FLASH SHOW YOU A LITTLE ROMANCE?
I'M SORRY, FLASH. I ALREADY HAVE A DATE.
WITH A GUY WHO HAS A JOB.
AND A PERSONALITY.
HA!

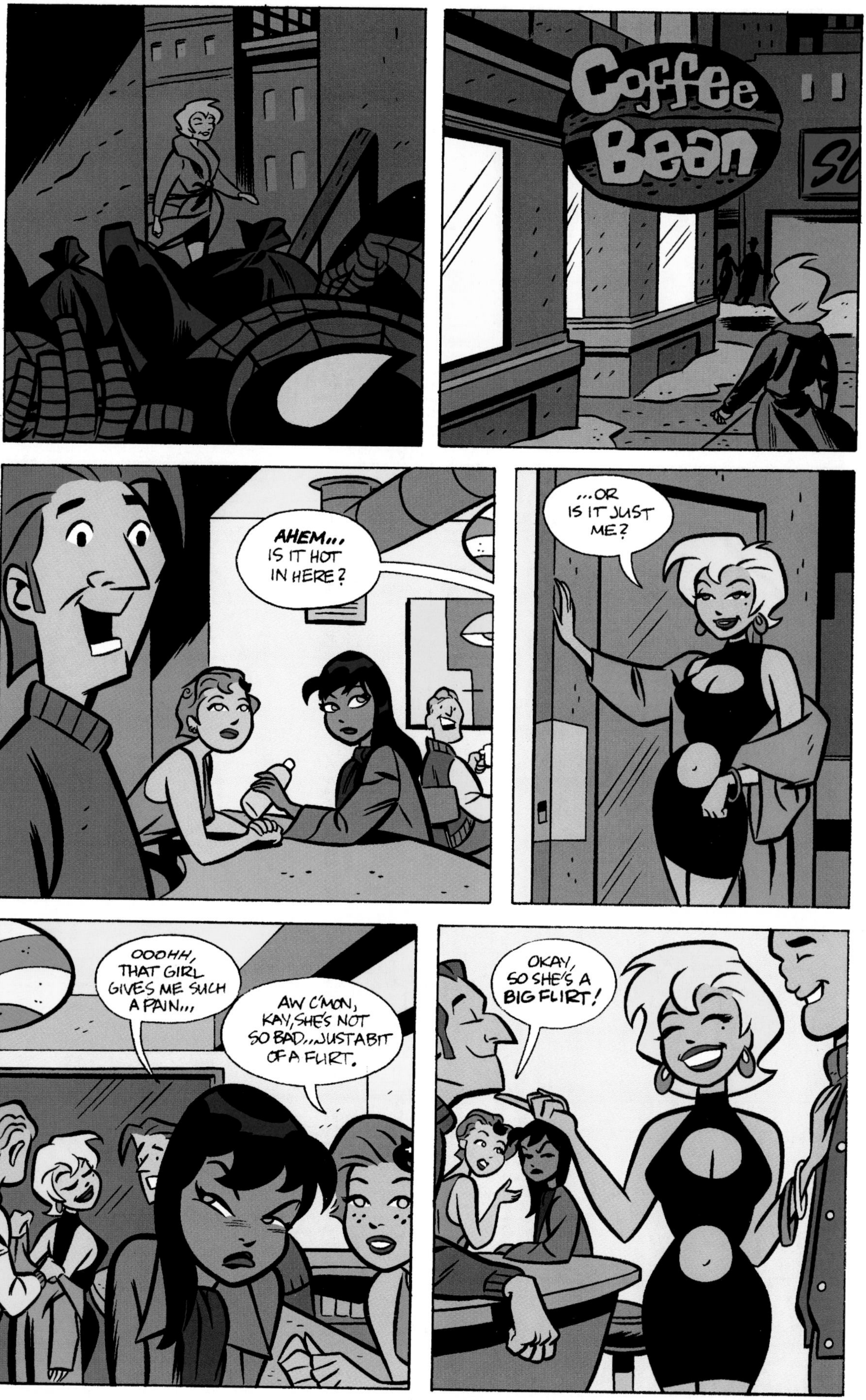
Coffee Bean
AHEM... IS IT HOT IN HERE?
...OR IS IT JUST ME?
OOOHH, THAT GIRL GIVES ME SUCH A PAIN...
AW C'MON, KAY, SHE'S NOT SO BAD... JUST A BIT OF A FLIRT.
OKAY, SO SHE'S A BIG FLIRT!

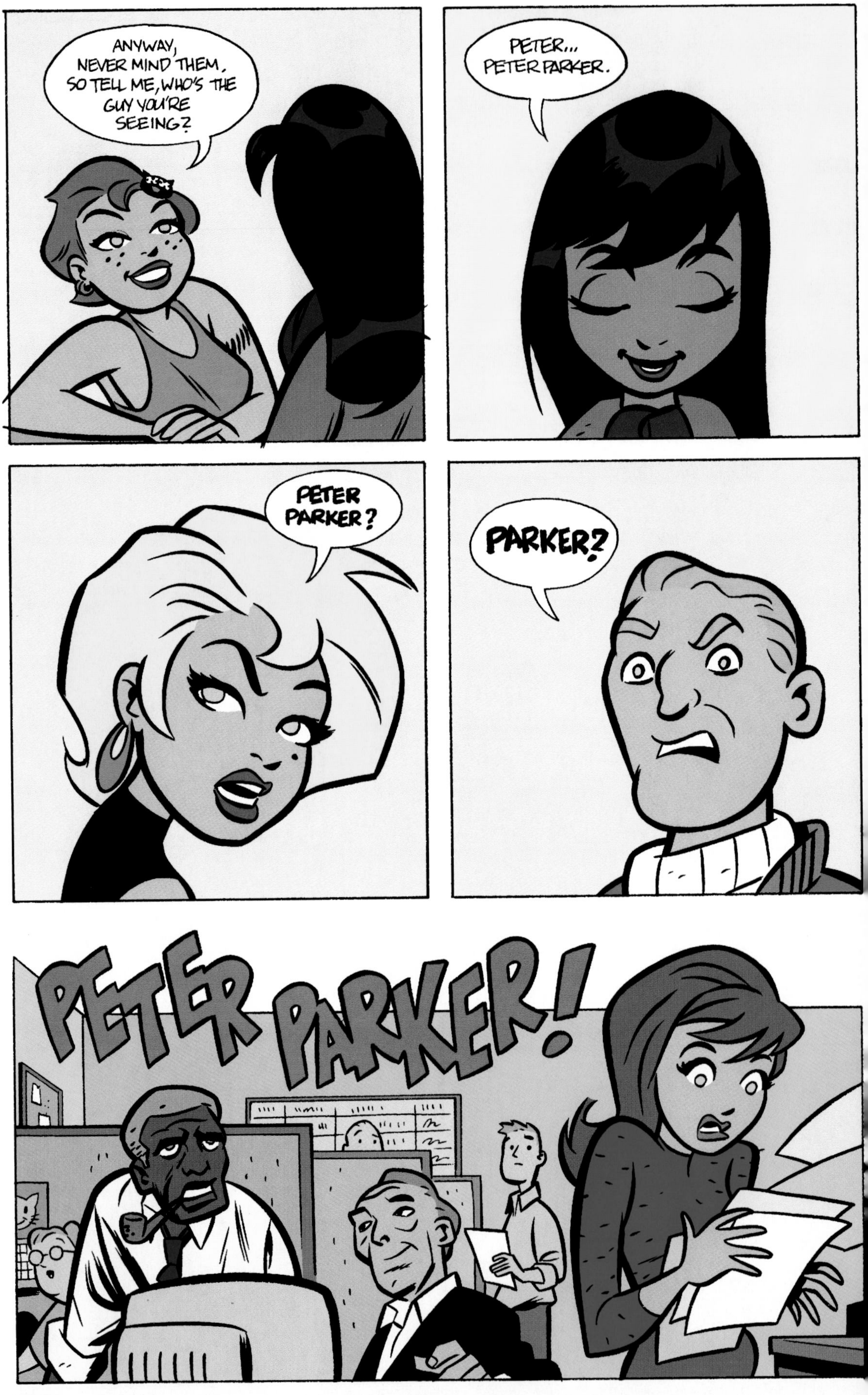
ANYWAY, NEVER MIND THEM, SO TELL ME, WHO'S THE GUY YOU'RE SEEING?
PETER... PETER PARKER.
PETER PARKER?
PARKER?
PETER PARKER!

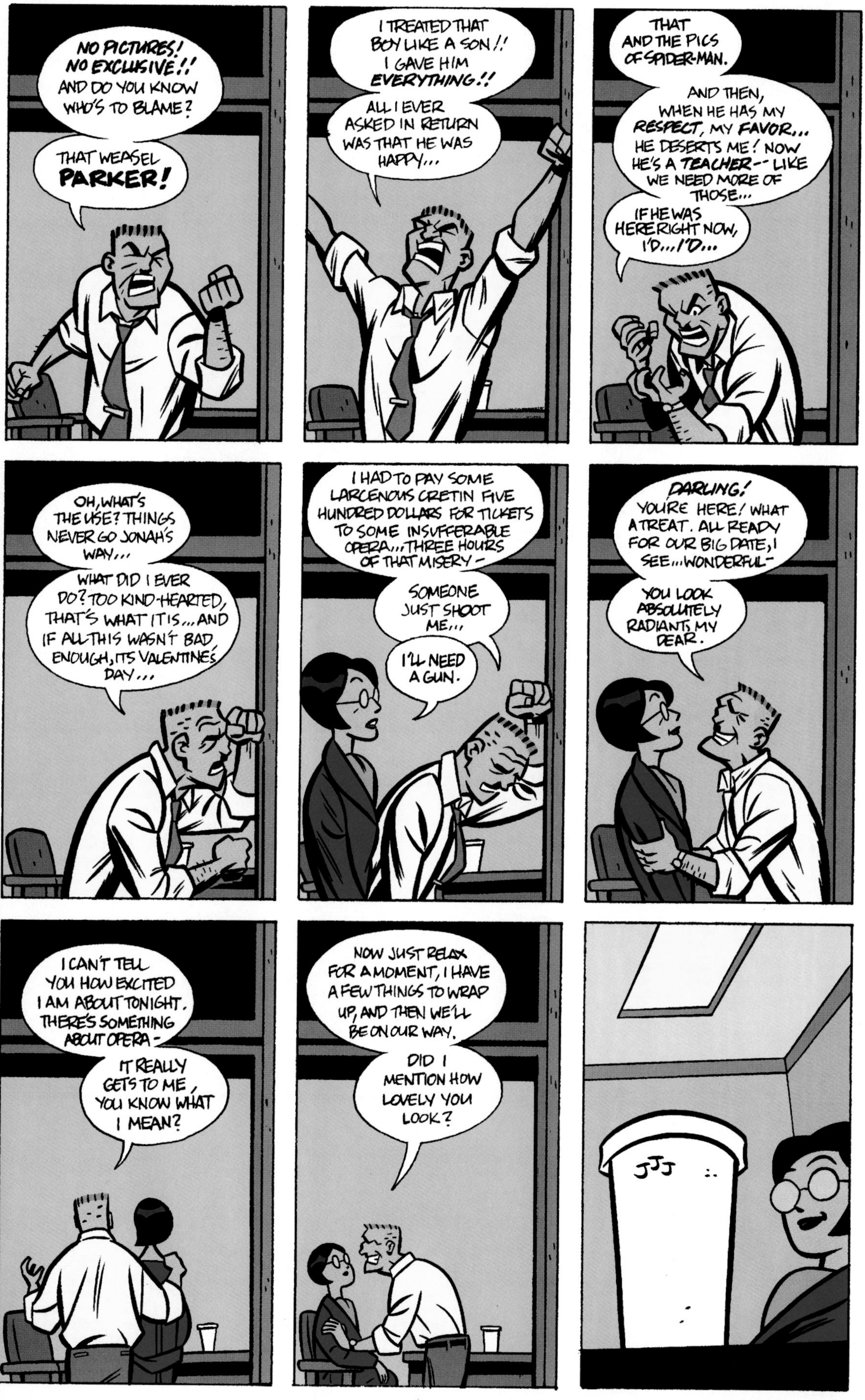
NO PICTURES! NO EXCLUSIVE!! AND DO YOU KNOW WHO'S TO BLAME?
THAT WEASEL PARKER!
I TREATED THAT BOY LIKE A SON!! I GAVE HIM EVERYTHING!!
ALL I EVER ASKED IN RETURN WAS THAT HE WAS HAPPY...
THAT AND THE PICS OF SPIDER-MAN.
AND THEN, WHEN HE HAS MY RESPECT, MY FAVOR... HE DESERTS ME! NOW HE'S A TEACHER-- LIKE WE NEED MORE OF THOSE...
IF HE WAS HERE RIGHT NOW, I'D...I'D...
OH, WHAT'S THE USE? THINGS NEVER GO JONAH'S WAY...
WHAT DID I EVER DO? TOO KIND-HEARTED, THAT'S WHAT IT IS... AND IF ALL THIS WASN'T BAD ENOUGH, ITS VALENTINE'S DAY...
I HAD TO PAY SOME LARCENOUS CRETIN FIVE HUNDRED DOLLARS FOR TICKETS TO SOME INSUFFERABLE OPERA... THREE HOURS OF THAT MISERY-
SOMEONE JUST SHOOT ME...
I'LL NEED A GUN.
DARLING! YOU'RE HERE! WHAT A TREAT. ALL READY FOR OUR BIG DATE, I SEE... WONDERFUL-
YOU LOOK ABSOLUTELY RADIANT, MY DEAR.
I CAN'T TELL YOU HOW EXCITED I AM ABOUT TONIGHT. THERE'S SOMETHING ABOUT OPERA-
IT REALLY GETS TO ME, YOU KNOW WHAT I MEAN?
NOW JUST RELAX FOR A MOMENT, I HAVE A FEW THINGS TO WRAP UP, AND THEN WE'LL BE ON OUR WAY.
DID I MENTION HOW LOVELY YOU LOOK?
JJJ

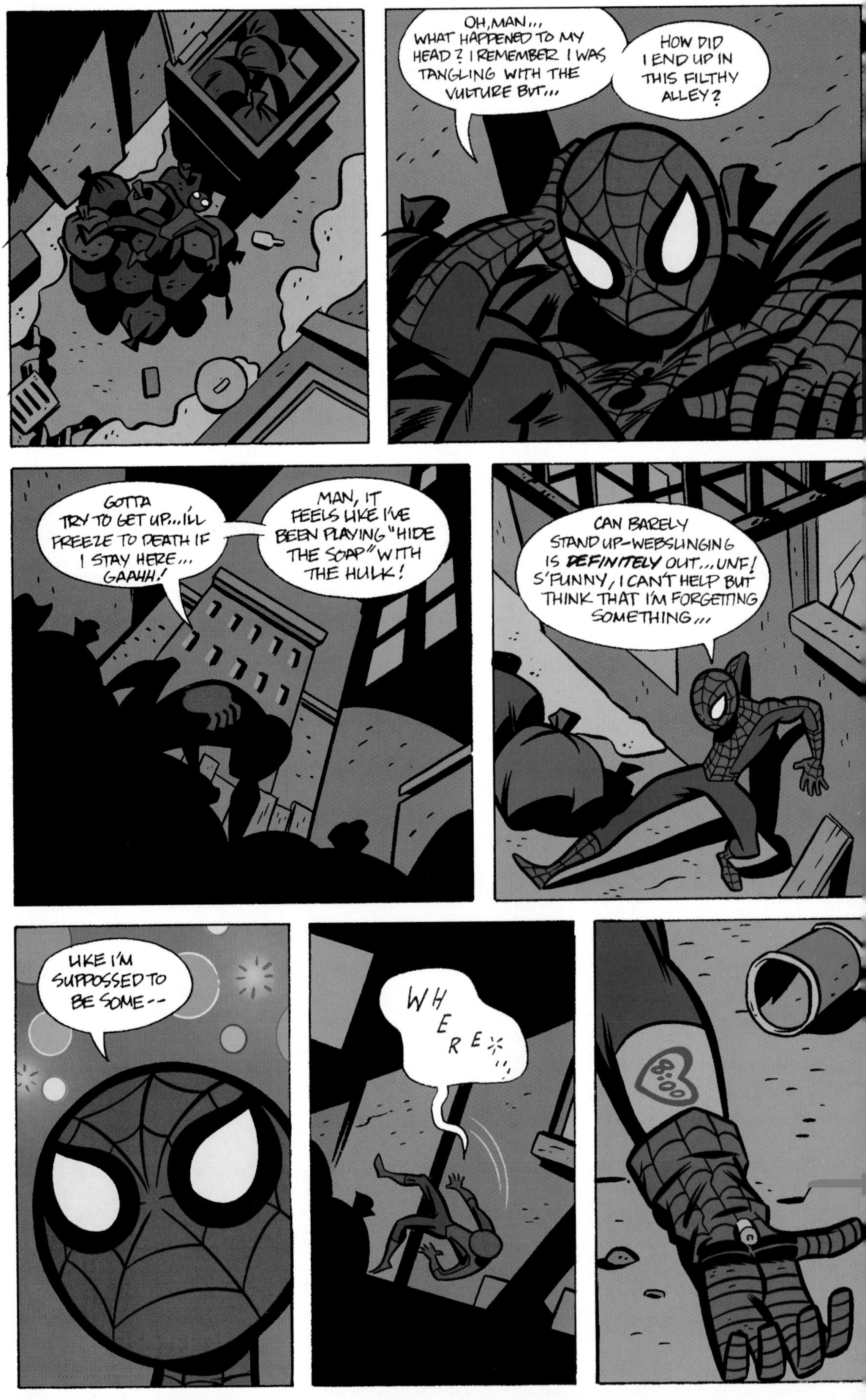
OH, MAN... WHAT HAPPENED TO MY HEAD? I REMEMBER I WAS TANGLING WITH THE VULTURE BUT...
HOW DID I END UP IN THIS FILTHY ALLEY?
GOTTA TRY TO GET UP... I'LL FREEZE TO DEATH IF I STAY HERE... GAAHH!
MAN, IT FEELS LIKE I'VE BEEN PLAYING "HIDE THE SOAP" WITH THE HULK!
CAN BARELY STAND UP--WEBSLINGING IS DEFINITELY OUT... UNF! S'FUNNY, I CAN'T HELP BUT THINK THAT I'M FORGETTING SOMETHING...
LIKE I'M SUPPOSSED TO BE SOME--
WHERE...
8:00

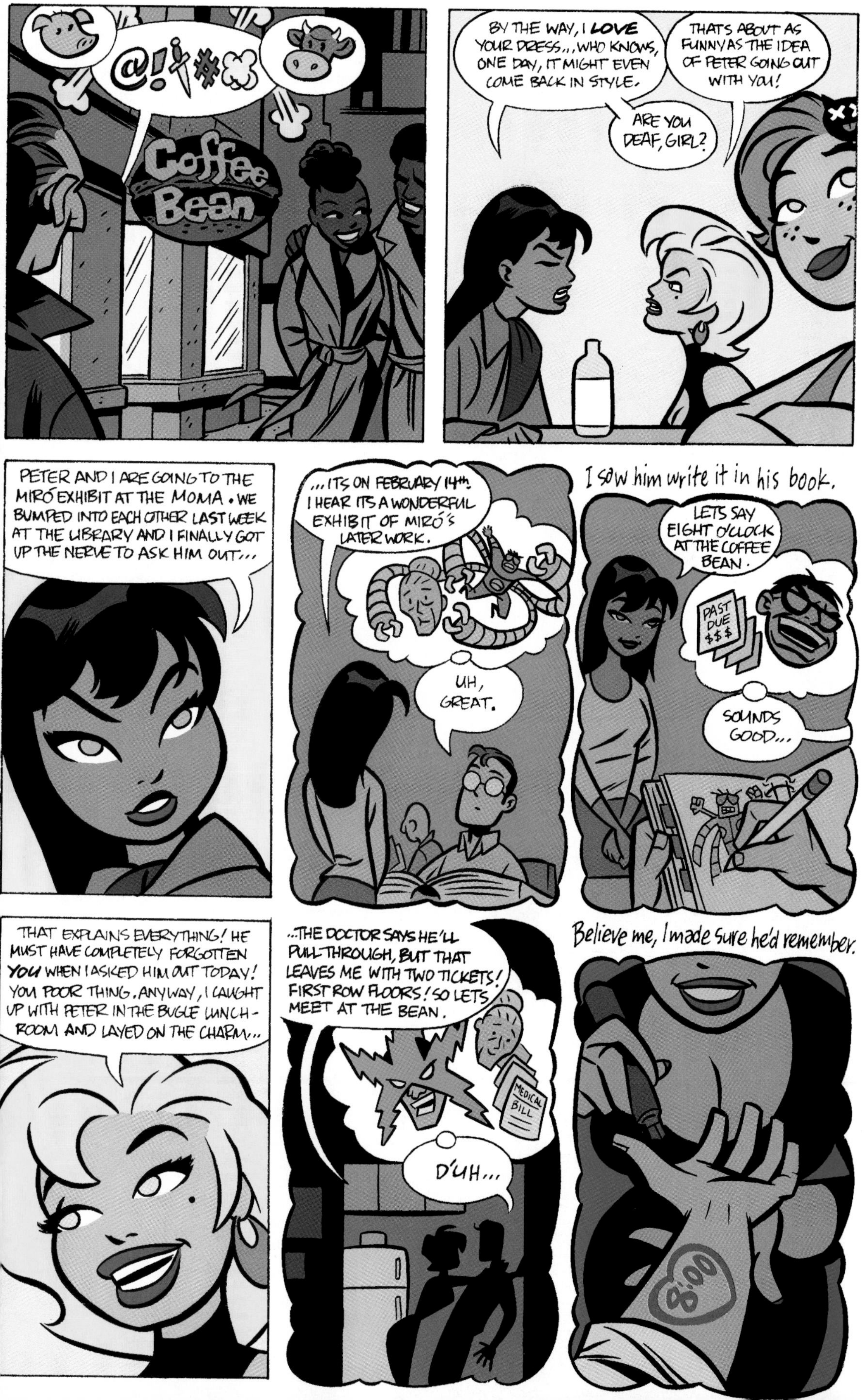
@!#
Coffee Bean
BY THE WAY, I LOVE YOUR DRESS... WHO KNOWS, ONE DAY, IT MIGHT EVEN COME BACK IN STYLE.
THAT'S ABOUT AS FUNNY AS THE IDEA OF PETER GOING OUT WITH YOU!
ARE YOU DEAF, GIRL?
PETER AND I ARE GOING TO THE MIRÓ EXHIBIT AT THE MOMA. WE BUMPED INTO EACH OTHER LAST WEEK AT THE LIBRARY AND I FINALLY GOT UP THE NERVE TO ASK HIM OUT...
...ITS ON FEBRUARY 14th. I HEAR ITS A WONDERFUL EXHIBIT OF MIRÓ'S LATER WORK.
UH, GREAT.
I saw him write it in his book.
LETS SAY EIGHT O'CLOCK AT THE COFFEE BEAN.
PAST DUE $$$
SOUNDS GOOD...
THAT EXPLAINS EVERYTHING! HE MUST HAVE COMPLETELY FORGOTTEN YOU WHEN I ASKED HIM OUT TODAY! YOU POOR THING. ANYWAY, I CAUGHT UP WITH PETER IN THE BUGLE LUNCH-ROOM AND LAYED ON THE CHARM...
...THE DOCTOR SAYS HE'LL PULL THROUGH, BUT THAT LEAVES ME WITH TWO TICKETS! FIRST ROW FLOORS! SO LETS MEET AT THE BEAN.
MEDICAL BILL
D'UH...
Believe me, I made sure he'd remember.
8:00

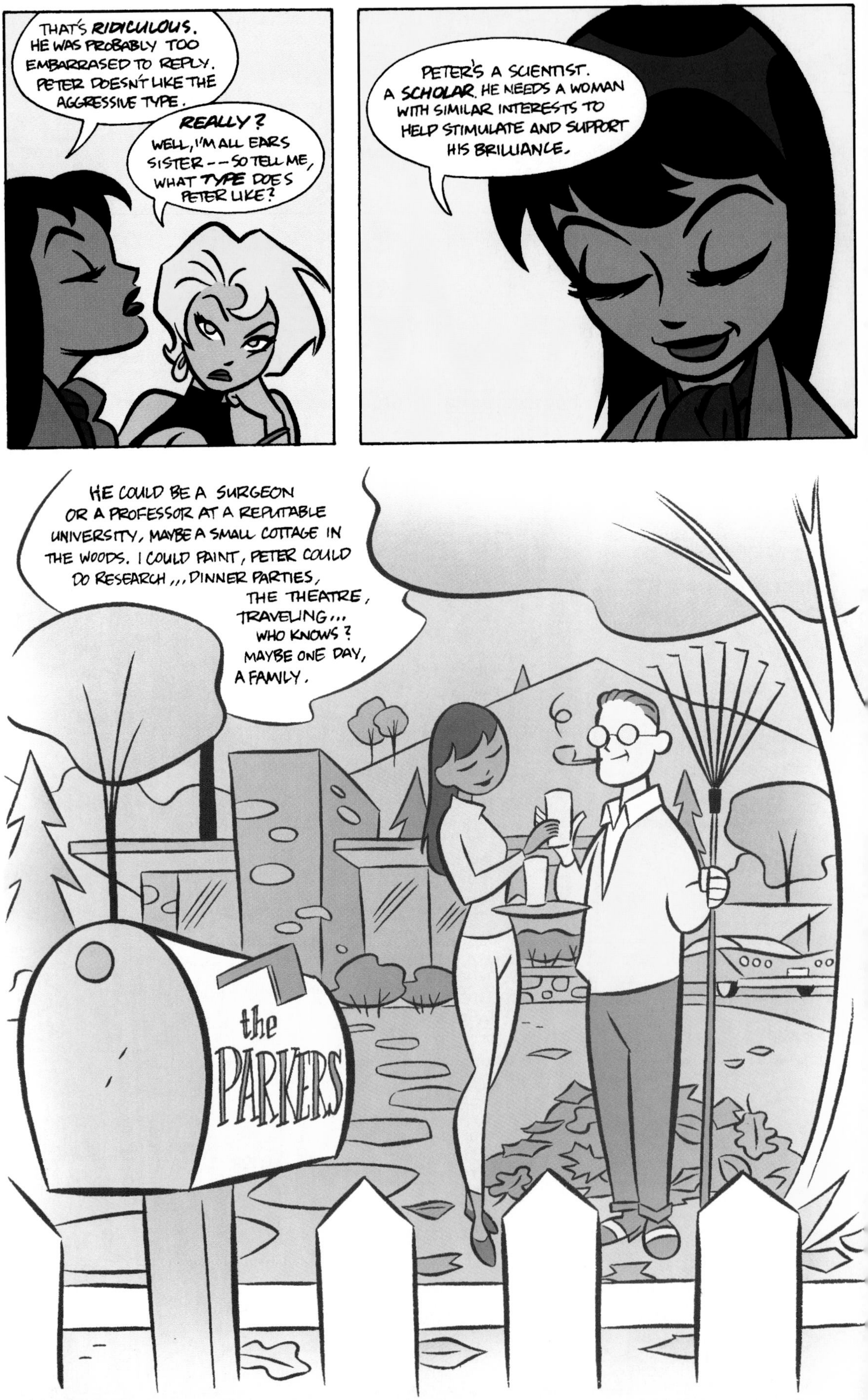
THAT'S RIDICULOUS. HE WAS PROBABLY TOO EMBARRASED TO REPLY. PETER DOESN'T LIKE THE AGGRESSIVE TYPE.
REALLY? WELL, I'M ALL EARS SISTER--SO TELL ME, WHAT TYPE DOES PETER LIKE?
PETER'S A SCIENTIST. A SCHOLAR. HE NEEDS A WOMAN WITH SIMILAR INTERESTS TO HELP STIMULATE AND SUPPORT HIS BRILLIANCE.
HE COULD BE A SURGEON OR A PROFESSOR AT A REPUTABLE UNIVERSITY, MAYBE A SMALL COTTAGE IN THE WOODS. I COULD PAINT, PETER COULD DO RESEARCH,,, DINNER PARTIES, THE THEATRE, TRAVELING... WHO KNOWS? MAYBE ONE DAY, A FAMILY.
the PARKERS

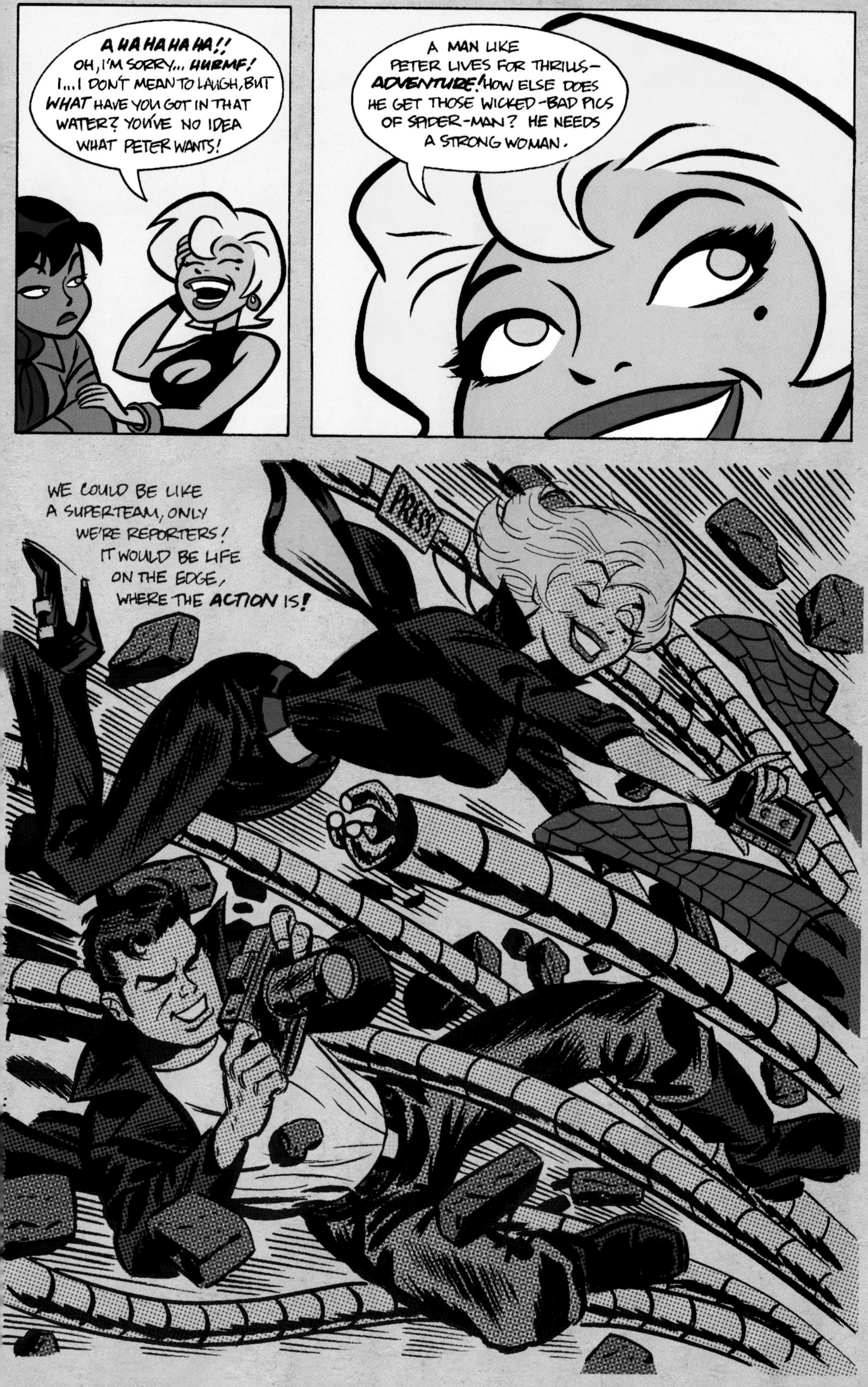
AHAHAHAHA!! OH, I'M SORRY... HURMF! I...I DON'T MEAN TO LAUGH, BUT WHAT HAVE YOU GOT IN THAT WATER? YOU'VE NO IDEA WHAT PETER WANTS!
A MAN LIKE PETER LIVES FOR THRILLS— ADVENTURE! HOW ELSE DOES HE GET THOSE WICKED-BAD PICS OF SPIDER-MAN? HE NEEDS A STRONG WOMAN.
WE COULD BE LIKE A SUPERTEAM, ONLY WE'RE REPORTERS! IT WOULD BE LIFE ON THE EDGE, WHERE THE ACTION IS!
PRESS

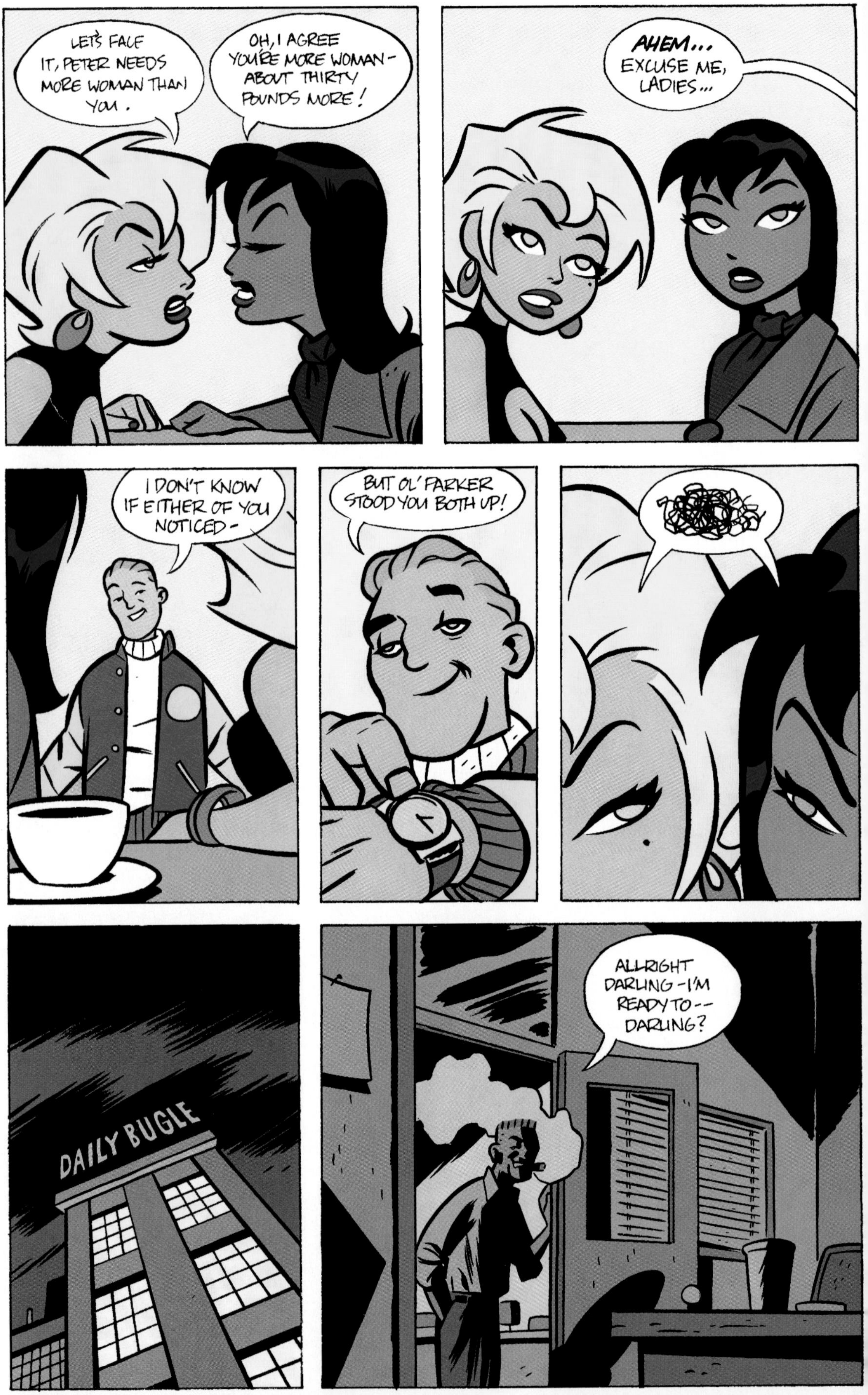
LET'S FACE IT, PETER NEEDS MORE WOMAN THAN YOU.
OH, I AGREE YOU'RE MORE WOMAN - ABOUT THIRTY POUNDS MORE!
AHEM... EXCUSE ME, LADIES...
I DON'T KNOW IF EITHER OF YOU NOTICED -
BUT OL' PARKER STOOD YOU BOTH UP!
DAILY BUGLE
ALLRIGHT DARLING - I'M READY TO -- DARLING?

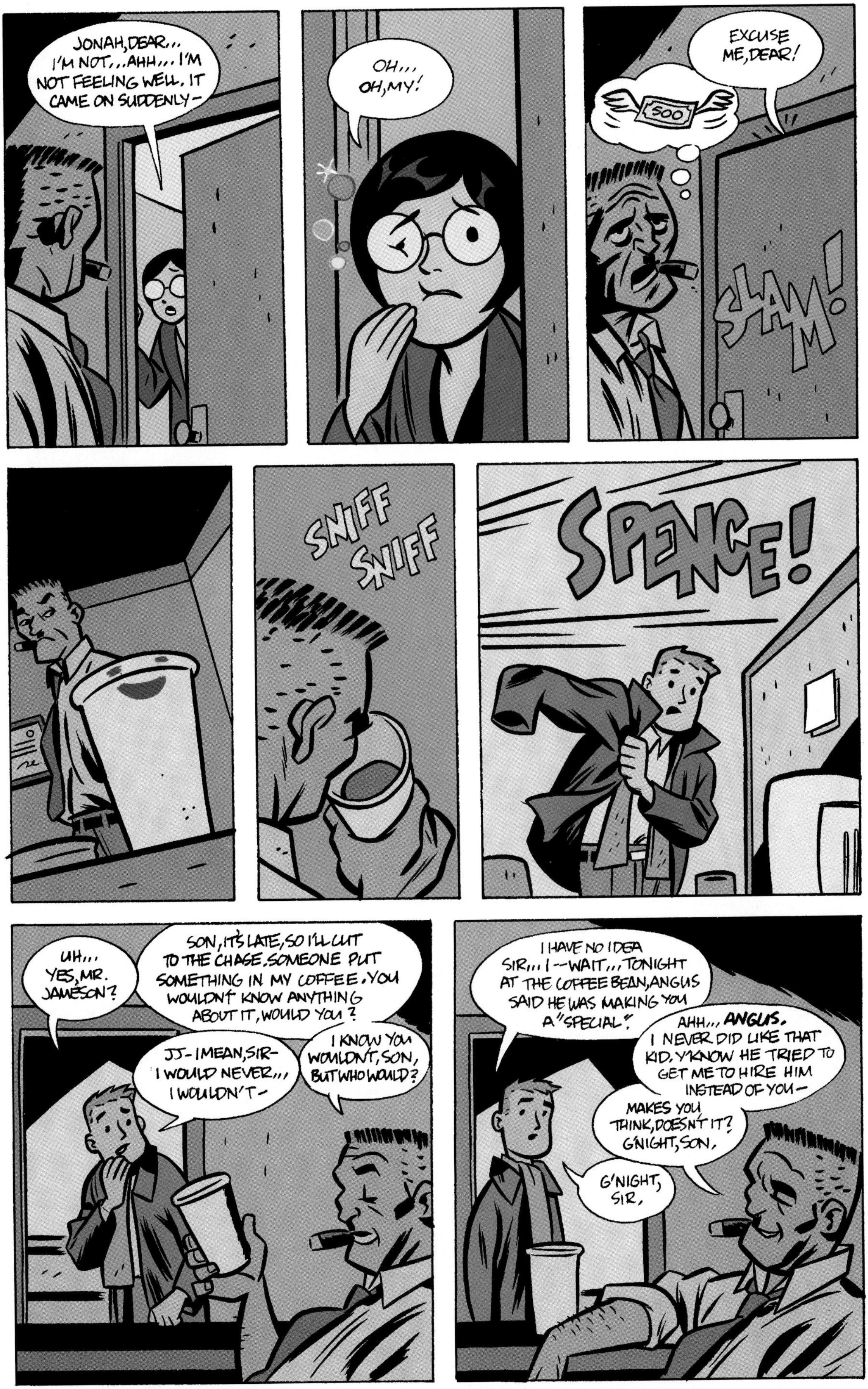

JONAH, DEAR... I'M NOT... AHH... I'M NOT FEELING WELL. IT CAME ON SUDDENLY—
OH... OH, MY!
500
EXCUSE ME, DEAR!
SLAM!
SNIFF SNIFF
SPENCE!
UH... YES, MR. JAMESON?
SON, IT'S LATE, SO I'LL CUT TO THE CHASE. SOMEONE PUT SOMETHING IN MY COFFEE. YOU WOULDN'T KNOW ANYTHING ABOUT IT, WOULD YOU?
JJ- I MEAN, SIR- I WOULD NEVER... I WOULDN'T-
I KNOW YOU WOULDN'T, SON, BUT WHO WOULD?
I HAVE NO IDEA SIR... I --WAIT... TONIGHT AT THE COFFEE BEAN, ANGUS SAID HE WAS MAKING YOU A "SPECIAL."
AHH... ANGUS. I NEVER DID LIKE THAT KID, Y'KNOW HE TRIED TO GET ME TO HIRE HIM INSTEAD OF YOU—
MAKES YOU THINK, DOESN'T IT? G'NIGHT, SON.
G'NIGHT, SIR.

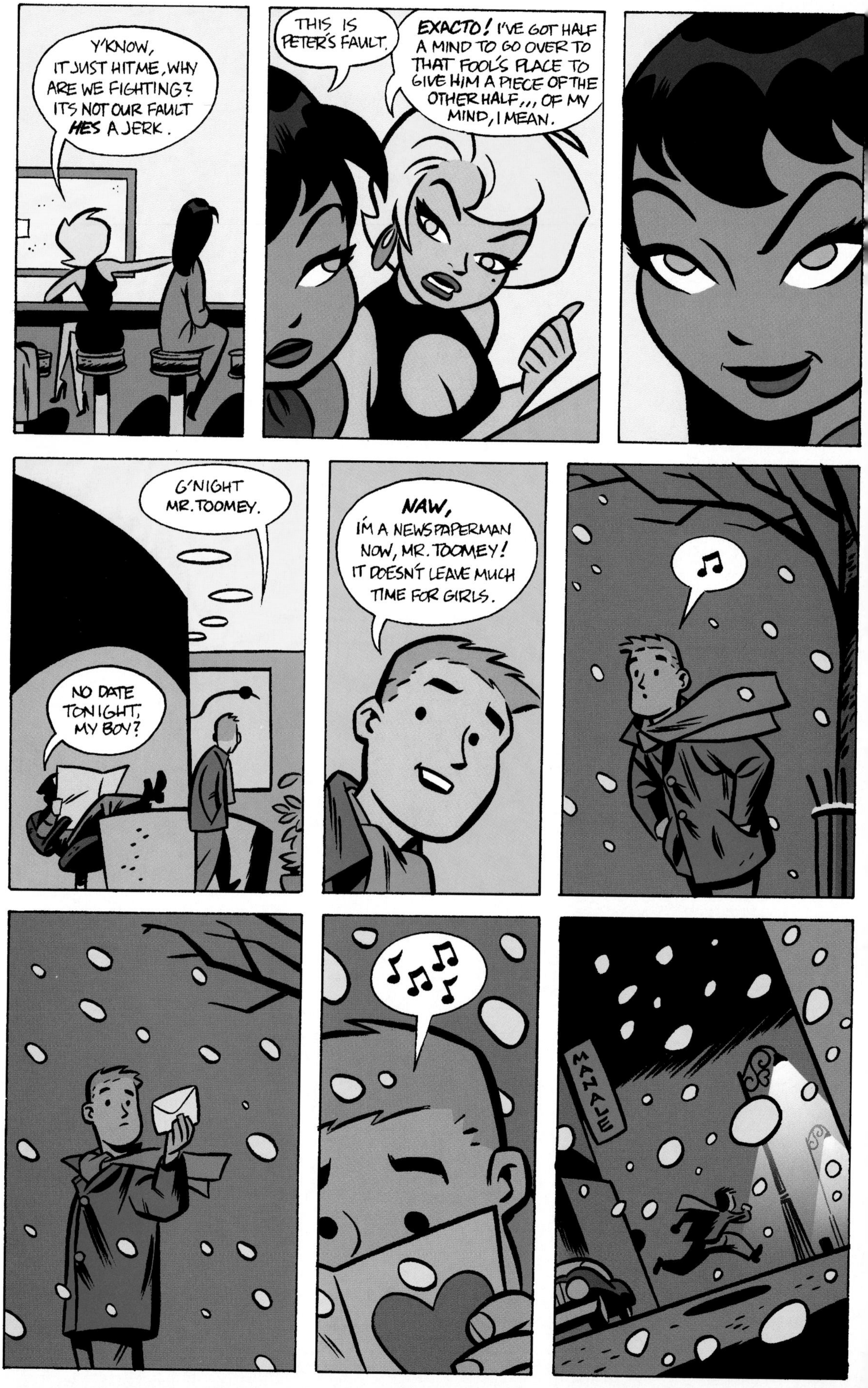
Y'KNOW, IT JUST HIT ME, WHY ARE WE FIGHTING? ITS NOT OUR FAULT HES A JERK.
THIS IS PETER'S FAULT.
EXACTO! I'VE GOT HALF A MIND TO GO OVER TO THAT FOOL'S PLACE TO GIVE HIM A PIECE OF THE OTHER HALF,,, OF MY MIND, I MEAN.
G'NIGHT MR. TOOMEY.
NO DATE TONIGHT, MY BOY?
NAW, I'M A NEWSPAPERMAN NOW, MR. TOOMEY! IT DOESN'T LEAVE MUCH TIME FOR GIRLS.
♫
♫ ♫ ♫ ♪
MANALE

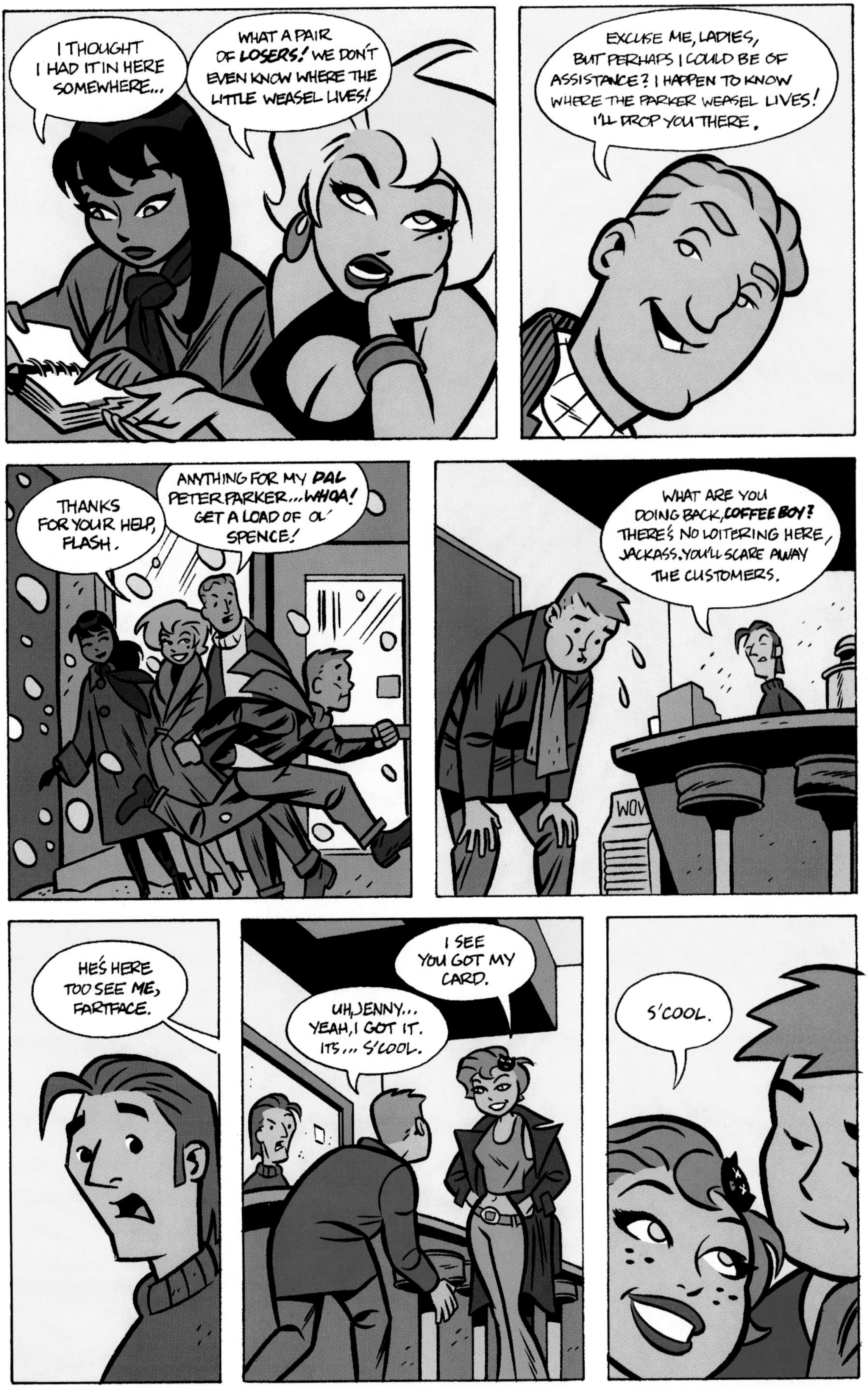
I THOUGHT I HAD IT IN HERE SOMEWHERE...
WHAT A PAIR OF **LOSERS!** WE DON'T EVEN KNOW WHERE THE LITTLE WEASEL LIVES!
EXCUSE ME, LADIES, BUT PERHAPS I COULD BE OF ASSISTANCE? I HAPPEN TO KNOW WHERE THE PARKER WEASEL LIVES! I'LL DROP YOU THERE.
THANKS FOR YOUR HELP, FLASH.
ANYTHING FOR MY **PAL** PETER PARKER... **WHOA!** GET A LOAD OF OL' SPENCE!
WHAT ARE YOU DOING BACK, **COFFEE BOY?** THERE'S NO LOITERING HERE, JACKASS. YOU'LL SCARE AWAY THE CUSTOMERS.
HE'S HERE TOO SEE **ME**, FARTFACE.
I SEE YOU GOT MY CARD.
UH, JENNY... YEAH, I GOT IT. ITS... S'COOL.
S'COOL.

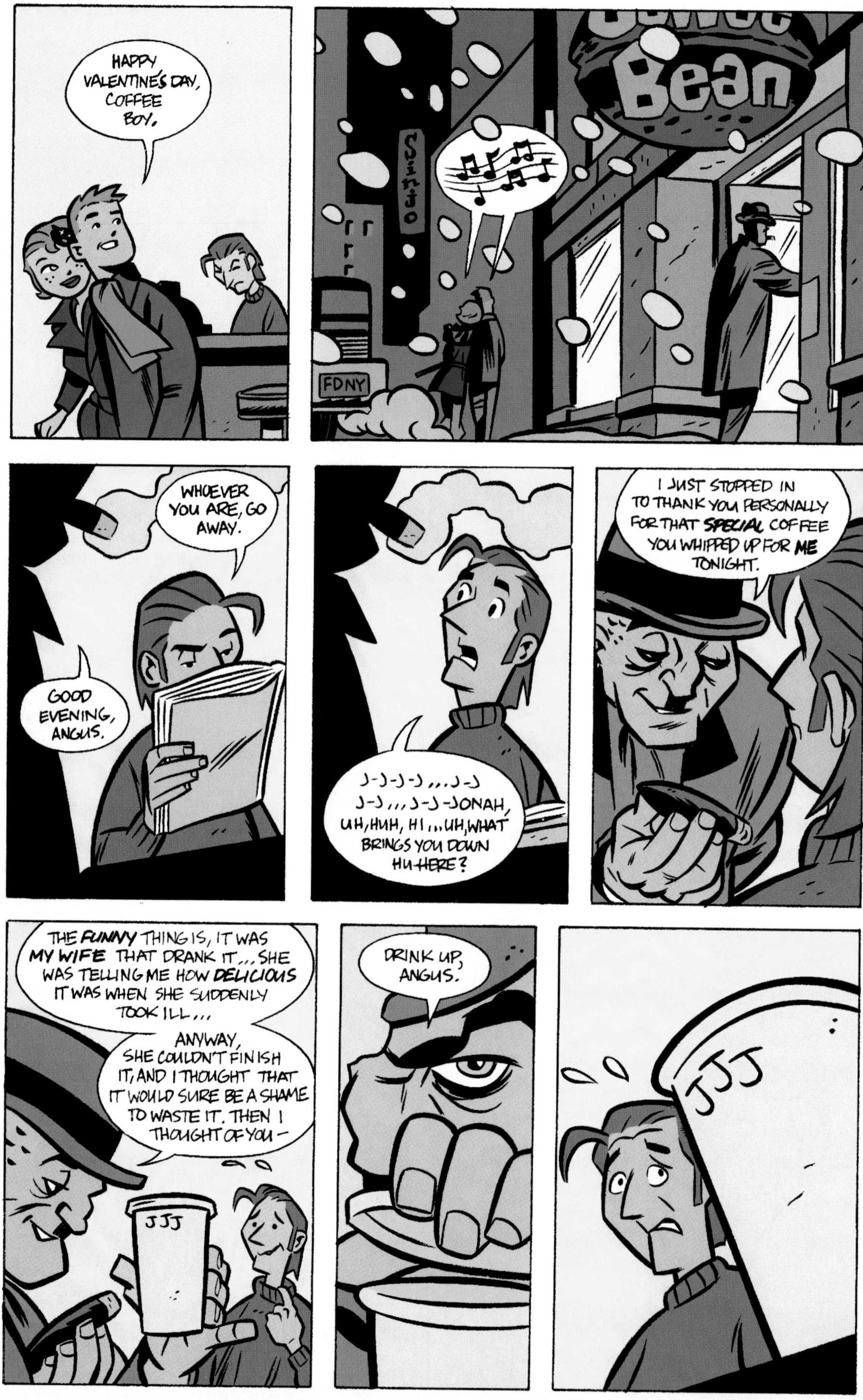
HAPPY VALENTINE'S DAY, COFFEE BOY.
Bean
FDNY
WHOEVER YOU ARE, GO AWAY.
GOOD EVENING, ANGUS.
J-J-J-J,,,.J-J J-J,,,J-J-JONAH, UH, HUH, HI,,,UH, WHAT BRINGS YOU DOWN HU-HERE?
I JUST STOPPED IN TO THANK YOU PERSONALLY FOR THAT SPECIAL COFFEE YOU WHIPPED UP FOR ME TONIGHT.
THE FUNNY THING IS, IT WAS MY WIFE THAT DRANK IT,,, SHE WAS TELLING ME HOW DELICIOUS IT WAS WHEN SHE SUDDENLY TOOK ILL,,,
ANYWAY, SHE COULDN'T FINISH IT, AND I THOUGHT THAT IT WOULD SURE BE A SHAME TO WASTE IT. THEN I THOUGHT OF YOU—
JJJ
DRINK UP, ANGUS.
JJJ

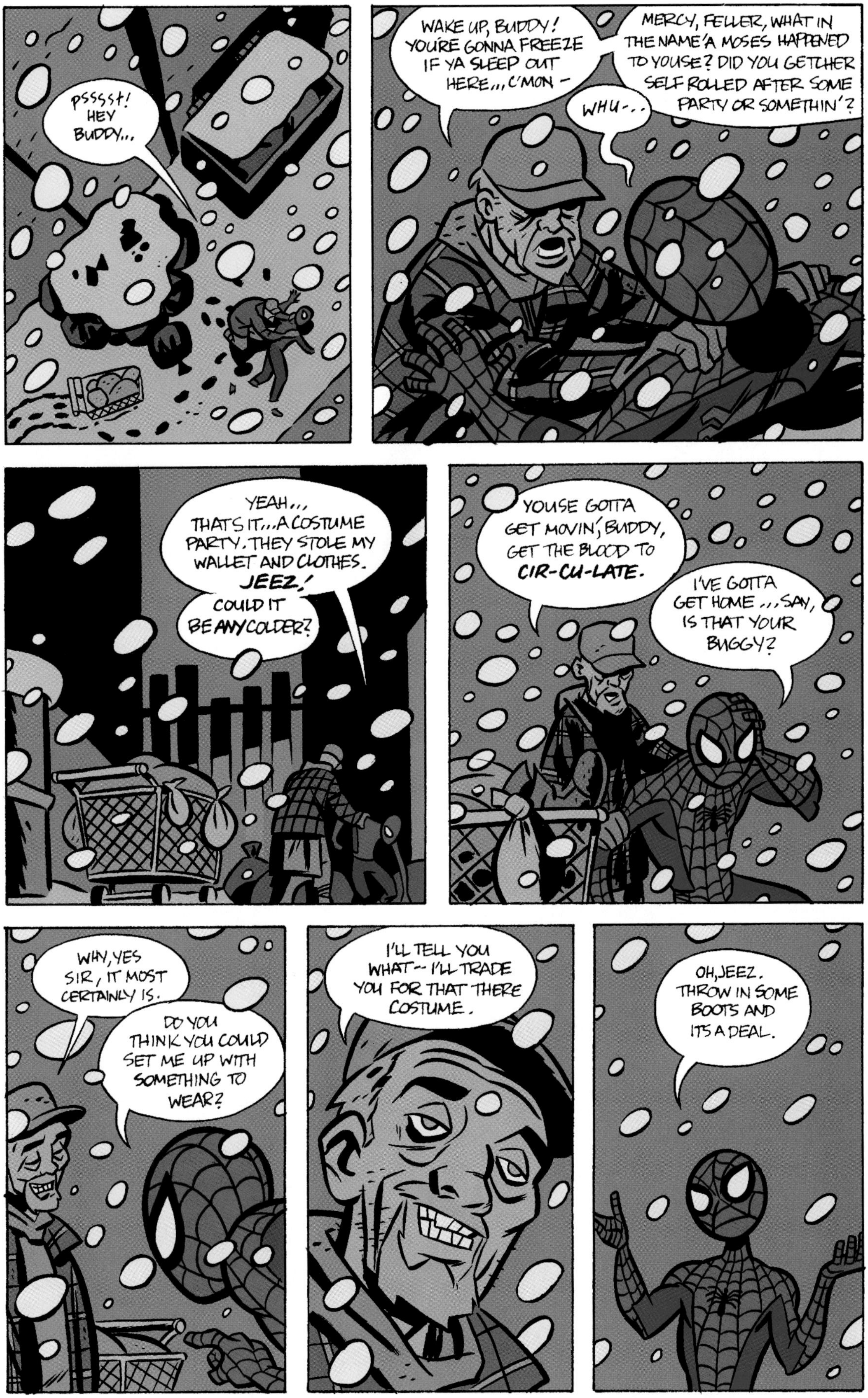
PSSSST! HEY BUDDY...
WAKE UP, BUDDY! YOU'RE GONNA FREEZE IF YA SLEEP OUT HERE... C'MON -
WHU-..
MERCY, FELLER, WHAT IN THE NAME 'A MOSES HAPPENED TO YOUSE? DID YOU GETCHER SELF ROLLED AFTER SOME PARTY OR SOMETHIN'?
YEAH... THAT'S IT...A COSTUME PARTY. THEY STOLE MY WALLET AND CLOTHES. JEEZ!
COULD IT BE ANY COLDER?
YOUSE GOTTA GET MOVIN', BUDDY, GET THE BLOOD TO CIR-CU-LATE.
I'VE GOTTA GET HOME ..., SAY, IS THAT YOUR BUGGY?
WHY, YES SIR, IT MOST CERTAINLY IS.
DO YOU THINK YOU COULD SET ME UP WITH SOMETHING TO WEAR?
I'LL TELL YOU WHAT-- I'LL TRADE YOU FOR THAT THERE COSTUME.
OH, JEEZ. THROW IN SOME BOOTS AND ITS A DEAL.

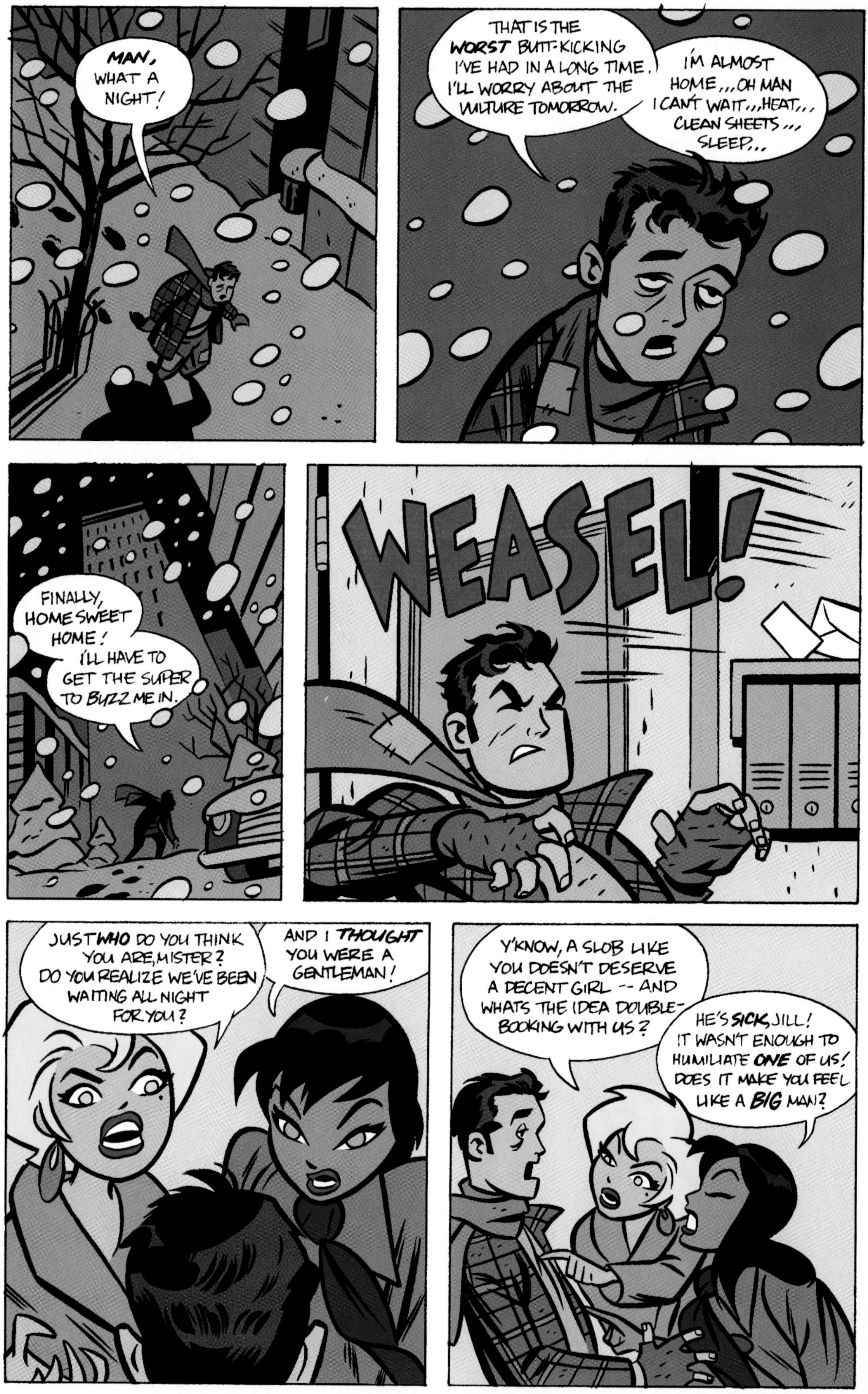
MAN, WHAT A NIGHT!
THAT IS THE WORST BUTT-KICKING I'VE HAD IN A LONG TIME. I'LL WORRY ABOUT THE VULTURE TOMORROW.
I'M ALMOST HOME,,, OH MAN I CAN'T WAIT,,, HEAT,,, CLEAN SHEETS,,, SLEEP,,,
FINALLY, HOME SWEET HOME!
I'LL HAVE TO GET THE SUPER TO BUZZ ME IN.
WEASEL!
JUST WHO DO YOU THINK YOU ARE, MISTER? DO YOU REALIZE WE'VE BEEN WAITING ALL NIGHT FOR YOU?
AND I THOUGHT YOU WERE A GENTLEMAN!
Y'KNOW, A SLOB LIKE YOU DOESN'T DESERVE A DECENT GIRL -- AND WHATS THE IDEA DOUBLE-BOOKING WITH US?
HE'S SICK, JILL! IT WASN'T ENOUGH TO HUMILIATE ONE OF US! DOES IT MAKE YOU FEEL LIKE A BIG MAN?

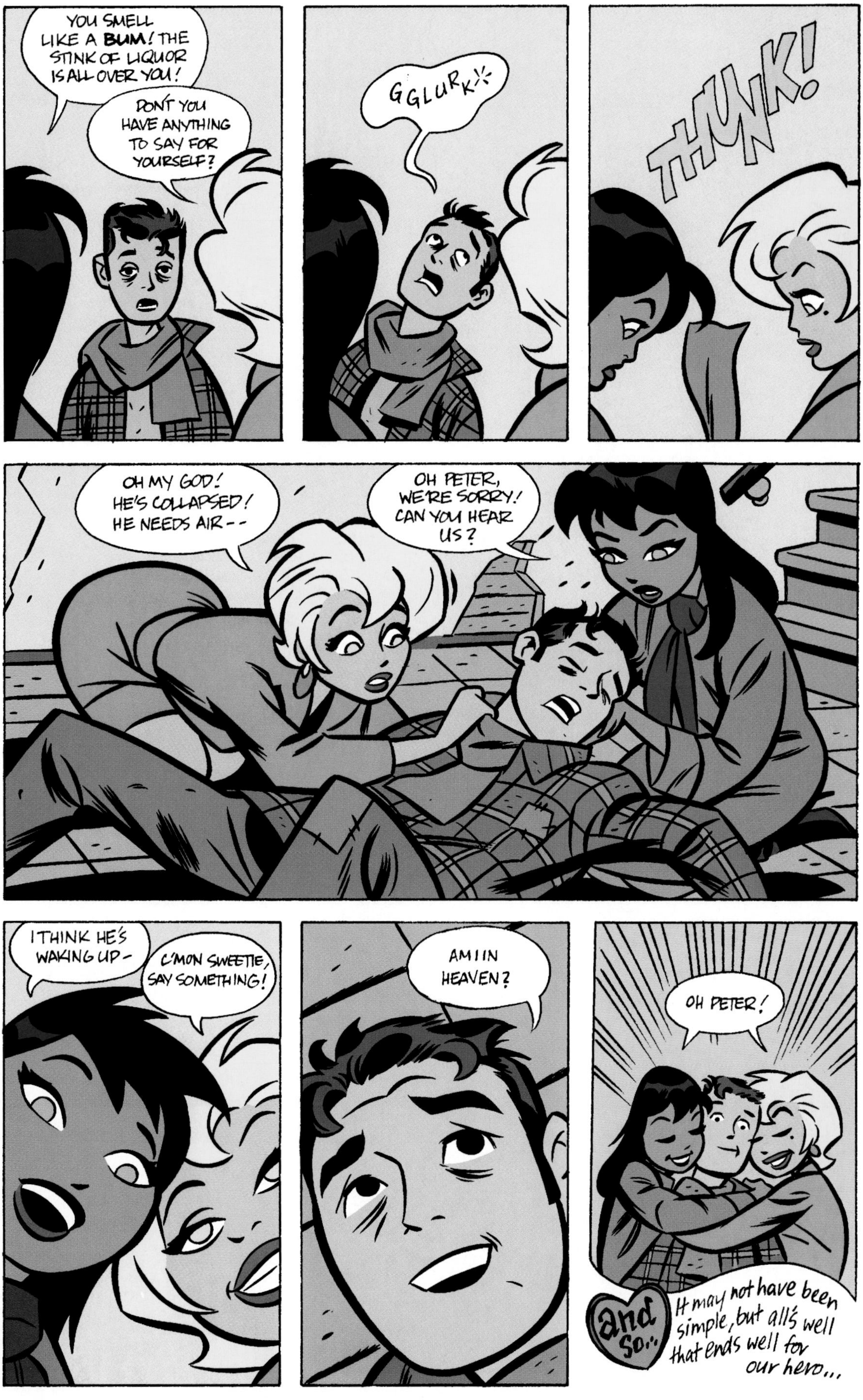
YOU SMELL LIKE A **BUM**! THE STINK OF LIQUOR IS ALL OVER YOU!
DON'T YOU HAVE ANYTHING TO SAY FOR YOURSELF?
GGLURK
THUNK!
OH MY GOD! HE'S COLLAPSED! HE NEEDS AIR--
OH PETER, WE'RE SORRY! CAN YOU HEAR US?
I THINK HE'S WAKING UP-
C'MON SWEETIE, SAY SOMETHING!
AM I IN HEAVEN?
OH PETER!
and so..
It may not have been simple, but all's well that ends well for our hero...

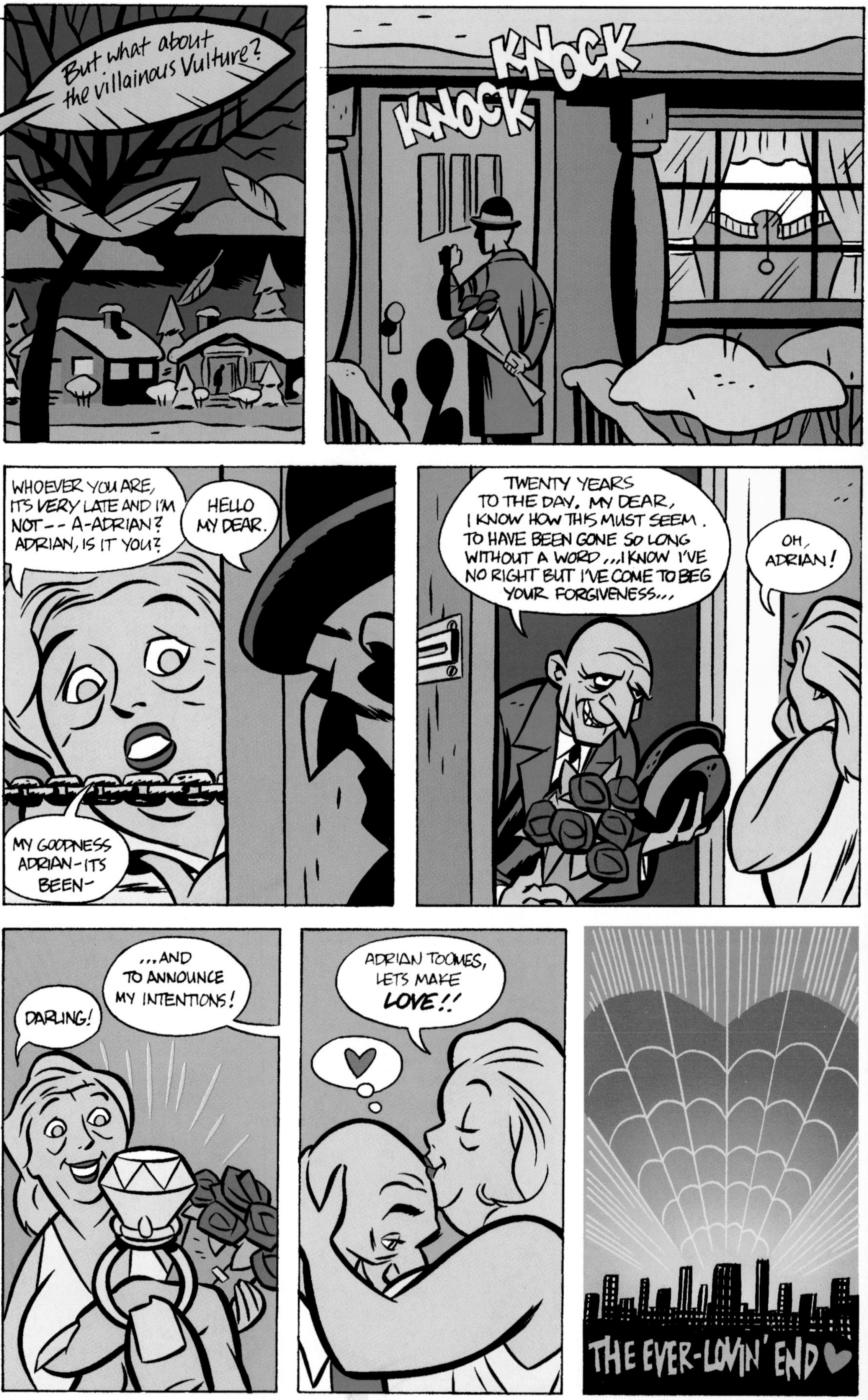
But what about the villainous Vulture?
KNOCK KNOCK
WHOEVER YOU ARE, ITS VERY LATE AND I'M NOT -- A-ADRIAN? ADRIAN, IS IT YOU?
HELLO MY DEAR.
MY GOODNESS ADRIAN - ITS BEEN-
TWENTY YEARS TO THE DAY, MY DEAR, I KNOW HOW THIS MUST SEEM. TO HAVE BEEN GONE SO LONG WITHOUT A WORD ... I KNOW I'VE NO RIGHT BUT I'VE COME TO BEG YOUR FORGIVENESS...
OH, ADRIAN!
...AND TO ANNOUNCE MY INTENTIONS!
DARLING!
ADRIAN TOOMES, LETS MAKE LOVE!!
THE EVER-LOVIN' END